THE FINAL PANDEMIC

THE FINAL PANDEMIC

An Antidote To Medical Tyranny

DR MARK BAILEY &
DR SAMANTHA BAILEY

Foreword by Prof. Tim Noakes

The Final Pandemic: An Antidote To Medical Tyranny
First published in 2024
New Zealand

Paperback ISBN: 978-0-473-70199-4
Hardcover ISBN: 978-0-473-70200-7
Ebook ISBN: 978-0-473-70201-4
Kindle ISBN: 978-0-473-70202-1

Cover design by Samantha Bailey: Masked and clad in a biohazard suit, Big Pharma and vested interests clutch temperature-reading guns in both hands. The plasticine figure has blurred 'feet of clay' and the computer-generated imagined "virus" appears monstrously large; an illusory beachball created and inflated by circular reasoning.

First Edition

Disclaimer

The information contained herein should NOT be used as a substitute for the advice of an appropriately qualified health care provider. The information and content provided here are for informational purposes only. In the event you use any of the information in this book for yourself or your dependents, you assume full responsibility for your actions.

The medical establishment has become a major threat to health...
Medicine is about to become a prime target for political action that aims at an inversion of industrial society.

— Ivan Illich, *Medical Nemesis*, 1975.

antidote (n.) *"remedy counteracting poison," early 15c.*
(c. 1400 as antidotum)

— Online Etymology Dictionary.

Contents

Acknowledgements

Dr M.C.J. McGrath can only be described as a rare gem of an editor whose grammatical prowess is matched by an understanding of medical science, including the sometimes arcane virology publications. We are indebted to him for the numerous helpful suggestions and work in getting the manuscript ready for publication.

Aleksander Bachorski has been one of our most dedicated and generous supporters. We were honored when he volunteered to act as the "civilian" reviewer for our manuscript, helping to ensure that the medical jargon was kept to a minimum.

This book is dedicated to the memory of Eleni Papadopulos-Eleopulos (1936-2022). Eleni's HIV/AIDS work dating over four decades from the 1980s has been inspirational and Sam's phone call with her a few months before she died will always be treasured.

Foreword by Prof. Tim Noakes

"Moral courage is a rarer commodity than bravery in battle or great intelligence. Yet it is the one essential, vital quality for those who seek to change a world that yields most painfully to change."

— Robert Kennedy Snr., 1966.[1]

The book you are holding has been written by two of the most morally courageous physicians on our planet. Why so?

Because they are truth seekers whose conscience does not allow them to remain silent about that which they believe to be untrue, regardless of any unwelcome consequences their principled stance has and will have for their social lives and professional careers. For what they conceive to be the great untruth is nothing less than the most important global medical event of the past 100 years, perhaps ever – the COVID-19 pandemic caused by the SARS-CoV-2 virus.

The narrative untruth with which they disagree runs something like this: Beginning in January 2020 the world's most trusted news agencies began to inform the world that a deadly novel virus – SARS-CoV-2 – was on the loose, certain to kill millions across the globe in just a few months. But that was not all. Later we were warned that this virus was just the first of many yet to come. To be followed in 2025 by the even more scary sounding-Severe Epidemic Enterovirus Respiratory Syndrome (SEERS) - according to one simulated pandemic preparedness exercise.[2]

These deadly viruses, we are told, exist, hidden, in animal reservoirs across the globe, any of which can ignite a global pandemic at any moment, simply by infecting a single human with whom any might come into contact (see Ch. 2 - *Scapegoats for Disease*). Not currently explained though, is why this novel form of disease transmission has surfaced only quite recently, given that our immediate human ancestors have lived in close proximity with these potential animal hosts for centuries.

Once the virus escapes from inside the cells of an animal host, transferring itself into the susceptible organs of that first human contact – now known as 'Patient Zero' – it begins to multiply, rapidly producing millions of identical copies of itself. Unwittingly, but very rapidly, Patient Zero then transfers the virus to all humans with whom he or she is in contact. Conveyed by international air travel and abetted by its very high infectivity, the virus then rapidly circles the globe, igniting a global catastrophe of biblical proportions.

Faced with this inevitability, the responsibility of all governments concerned about their peoples' health, is immediately to protect every individual on the planet "for the greater good" since, "no one is safe until all are safe".

Thus the need for an immediate, carefully co-ordinated, uniform global response that includes restricting everyone's movements to only those that are absolutely essential; wearing face masks in public; and the development of "safe and effective" vaccines that protect against illness whilst blocking any further spread of the virus. In this way the pandemic is brought under control, quickly, safely and effectively, with a minimum loss of life and without imposing an intolerable financial burden on anyone.

But what if all this narrative is just a contrived fiction?

That is a question with which the authors of this book have been grappling for some time.[3, 4, 5, 6] Here they present a concise summary of the most compelling evidence that their search for truth has uncovered.

In this exhaustively researched and carefully documented book they throughly eviscerate that official narrative, not least by exposing a series of basic, indeed elementary, scientific "errors" without which the narrative has no foundation. They also explain how this fake narrative was sold to the world by the compliant and incentivized mainstream media aided by a subservient and well-rewarded medical profession.

> ***The First Error:*** *The method used by virologists to detect the presence of a virus is indirect, unscientific and essentially unproven, not least because it fails to incorporate appropriate experimental controls (as is required in all scientific experimentation).*

The official pandemic narrative requires the presence of a pathogenic virus able to transfer itself without difficulty, first from its host animal to Patient Zero and then from Patient Zero to the rest of humanity. For without a virus there can be no viral pandemic.

The challenge for all those who study viruses, is that unlike other alleged infectious agents claimed to cause human disease including bacteria, fungi, protozoa, and helminths (worms), viruses are tiny, very shy creatures that dislike being seen and are reluctant to replicate in laboratories in the presence of prying humans. So scientists have had to invent a complicated process to identify their presence.

In this process they developed what is considered the gold standard test but which is based on a circular logic that becomes infinitely self-fulfilling (see Figure 1).

The circular logic begins with the virologist's certainty that the sample taken from an ill patient must contain a virus so that any other possible causes of the illness can be ignored. The patient's sample is then mixed

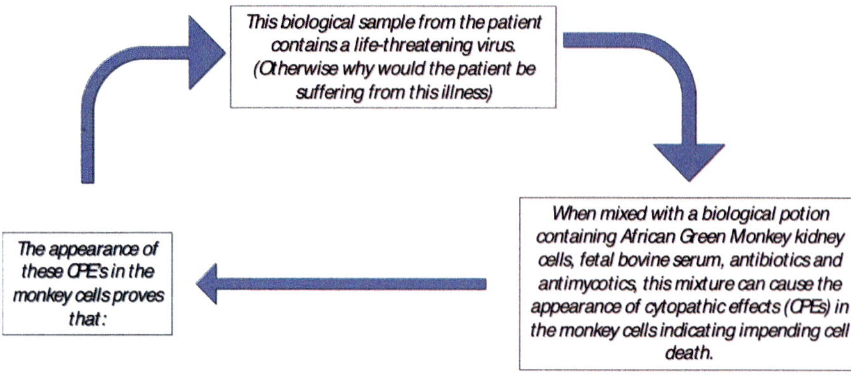

Figure 1. The gold standard test used by virologists to detect the presence of a virus in a biological sample is based on a circular logic that is infinitely self-fulfilling. In addition, this experimental "proof" of viral presence is not scientifically valid because it lacks an essential control experiment in which ***the effects of the proposed virus is tested alone*** *without any added material derived from the patient's sample. This control is essential to prove that CPEs develop* ***only*** *in the presence of a purported virus.*

with a solution containing a multitude of cells and chemicals. If, after a few days the kidney cells show histological evidence of cell death (cytopathic effects - CPEs), it is concluded that a cytopathic virus, present in the patient's sample, is the cause.

But this is not how proper science is conducted.

For this false experimental method cannot exclude the alternative explanation that something other than an unseen virus caused the observed CPEs. This possibility can only be excluded with an experimental control in which the biological potion contains everything but the patient's alleged viruses. If this control experiment does not produce CPEs, then it is reasonable to conclude that a cytopathic agent was present in the patient's sample (although it would still not be definitive evidence that this was the cause of the patient's presentation).

The authors are not the first to criticize the absence of the experimental control; it is clearly described by Dr Stefan Lanka who argues that in the original description of this experimental method, "no control experiments were performed to exclude the possibility that it was the deprivation of nutrients as well as the antibiotics which led to the cytopathic effects."[7] Indeed those who described this novel method noted that many cells also died without being treated with the "infectious" sample. To hide this inconvenient finding, they conveniently concluded that this effect must have been due to the presence of unknown viruses or other factors in the biological potion. This logic is also counter-scientific since it assumes that the outcome of the experiment is already known even before the experiment begins.

But the criticism does not end there. For the authors ask the seemingly obvious question: Since COVID-19 is a human respiratory disease, not a monkey kidney disease, why is it necessary to use monkey kidney cells to detect a viral presence? Especially when kidney cells, "are designed to process mostly sterile blood, not deal with respiratory secretions and all kinds of inhaled particles" (see Ch. 4 - *How to Create 'Virus Genomes'*). The probable answer is that the use of any other cell lines fails to produce the CPEs that are so readily observed when monkey kidney cells are used. Thus other cell lines are unable to "detect" a viral presence with the same certainty as the monkey kidney cells.

The authors wonder why these scientists were not more interested in developing methods to provide direct proof of viral presence.

But there is a simple experiment to document the true precision of this gold standard CPE test.[8] Perform "blinded" tests in certified laboratories by supplying the experts with patient samples without providing any prior information of what the expected results might be. The most important test would be one from a healthy patient in whom there is no likelihood that a life-threatening virus is present. If the experts return a positive viral test, the story ends. If not, the virologists would still need to demonstrate that their *in vitro* (laboratory) cell culture experiments correspond to *in vivo* (living organism) reality. This would include the true physical isolation of the alleged virus particles and subsequent clinical experiments to establish their capacity to *cause* disease.

> ***The Second Error:*** *The method for detecting the genome of the virus does not require that the sample to be tested comes from an isolated (i.e. purified) virus. Instead it is a computer-generated "best guess" genome pieced together from millions of different genetic sequences present in a biological potion.*

Once the presence of CPEs in an initial test has "proven" the presence of an infectious virus in the tested patient, the next step is to isolate a virus particle and extract its genetic structure. But here too there is a significant problem. For the biological potion in which the virus is supposedly "isolated" contains a mass of genetic information and only a tiny section will have come from any alleged virus. To overcome this problem, the scientists came up with another unique solution.

Their solution (see Ch. 4 - *How to Create 'Virus Genomes'*) involves the use of specific computer software to re-splice all the genetic material present in the biological potion to produce a product that has the *appearance* of an isolated viral genome. This process is itself dependent on the existence of a library of viral genomes, all produced by exactly the same methods.

But even if this method does indeed identify a real viral genome, this identification can never prove that: (a) the identified virus is the cause of the patient's (especially Patient Zero's) illness or that, (b) the virus so identified is contagious and transferable and has the capacity to generate the pandemic. As it stands, it has not yet been possible to isolate, purify and describe the complete viral genome from virus particles isolated from a living patient infected with a rapidly-replicating, life-threatening virus. See for example the surprising outcome of the unsuccessful attempts to isolate the measles virus, described in the section *Don't Worry if the Germ Even Exists* (Ch. 3). The authors have indeed, as they say, "opened the door into the world of 'viral genomes' and how they are created, without any proof that the genetic material comes from a virus".

> ***The Third Error:*** *The pandemic was not a viral pandemic. It was a testing pandemic driven by the false interpretation of Polymerase Chain Reaction (PCR) tests which have little or no relevance to the practice of clinical medicine.*

Clinical medicine of the kind that the authors and I were taught in our medical training is based on an historic approach in which the medical diagnosis is made only when the following steps are properly and judiciously enacted:

1. The medical practitioner takes an extensive medical history from the ill patient.
2. The medical practitioner performs a relevant medical examination of the ill patient.
3. On the basis of 1 and 2, the medical practitioner draws up a differential diagnosis of all the conditions that could possibly be causing the patient's ill health.
4. The medical practitioner requests whichever special investigations like blood tests and imaging techniques that will help eliminate all but one of the conditions considered in the differential diagnosis.
5. The medical practitioner draws up a treatment protocol based on the most probable diagnosis.

Day 7 5th of January, 2020

The World Health Organization (WHO) announces they have identified 44 cases of atypical pneumonia of unknown aetiology (APOUA) in a specific population of 8 million people in China.

Day 9 7th of January, 2020

The WHO announces that the APOUA is caused by a novel SARS-like virus.

Day 12 10th of January, 2020

The firm manufacturing the first COVID-19 PCR tests [Olfert Landt's TIB Molbiol[13]] starts shipping them.[14, 15] The first "viral genome" for SARS-CoV-2 is published.[16]

Day 14 12th of January, 2020*[17]

The WHO accepts Professor Christian Drosten's PCR testing protocol as, "the gold standard for testing for this new disease".

Day 23 21st of January, 2020

The Drosten/Landt PCR testing protocol is submitted for review to an international scientific publication.

Day 25 23rd of January, 2020

The paper describing the Drosten/Landt PCR testing protocol is accepted for publication and is published within 27 hours in a journal of which Drosten is an editor.[18]

Day 26. 24th of January, 2020

A paper describing the clinical features of COVID-19 is published by Chinese scientists in *The Lancet*.[19]

Day 32 30th of January, 2020

The first letter describing asymptomatic transmission of COVID-19 is published in *The New England Journal of Medicine*.[20]

One might perhaps conclude that requiring just 32 days to identify and fully describe a novel infectious disease including the genome of the causative agent, whilst also discovering that it can be transmitted by persons without any symptoms of illness, is perhaps just too good to be true.

A Final Word

I began the foreword with a quote from Robert Kennedy Snr's Ripples of Hope speech delivered at my Alma Mater in June 1966. The speech includes another quote relevant to this book, its authors and our modern predicament:

> *Each time a man stands up for an ideal, or acts to improve the lot of others, or strikes out against injustice, he sends forth a tiny ripple of hope, and crossing each other from a million different centers of energy and daring those ripples build a current which can sweep down the mightiest walls of oppression and resistance.*[21]

This book is not the first to expose the false science behind the popular virus and vaccination narratives in general, or those that have sustained the COVID-19 pandemic in particular; but it may just be one of the very best.

Our collective hope must be that when those who read this book truly understand what is the truth and how we have been willfully misled, with catastrophic consequences, their ripples of frustration will coalesce into a giant current sweeping all before it, igniting a global demand for answers from those in government, in politics, in medicine and in science, indeed, from all who are ultimately accountable for their part in the dishonesty of what has happened.

And that this new knowledge will ensure that we, the public, never, ever allow something similar to be repeated.

Prof. Timothy D. Noakes OMS, MB ChB, MD, DSc, PhD (hc),
FACSM, (hc) FFSEM(UK), (hc) FFSEM(Ire)

Prologue

"A public that can no longer distinguish between truth and fiction is left to interpret reality through illusion. Random facts or obscure bits of data and trivia are used either to bolster illusion and give it credibility, or discarded if they interfere with the message...

"This is the real danger of pseudo-events and pseudo-events are far more pernicious than stereotypes. They do not explain reality, as stereotypes attempt to, but replace reality. Pseudo-events redefine reality by the parameters set by their creators. These creators, who make massive profits selling illusions, have a vested interest in maintaining the power structures they control...

"The words, images, stories, and phrases used to describe the world in pseudo-events have no relation to what is happening around us. The advances of technology and science, rather than obliterating the world of myth, have enhanced its power to deceive."

— Chris Hedges, *Empire of Illusion,* 2009.

Introduction

Humanity is under assault from "pandemics" but not for the reasons that the mainstream sources portray. This book examines the claims regarding alleged "contagious" disease outbreaks such as COVID-19 to shed more light on what they are, or perhaps more importantly, what they are not. The *belief* that germs from the natural environment (or a laboratory) are attacking us has led most of the population to go along with lockdowns, civil rights restrictions, unprecedented peacetime censorship and more vaccines. However, when the foundational science is exposed and it is understood how the cases are created, no "pandemic" looks the same ever again.

In line with our other content we dissect multiple aspects of what has been put forward as scientific evidence for germ theory,[*22] alleged "viruses," diagnostic tests, and "treatments" whether they be drugs or vaccines. It is all too often a world of mythology with carefully constructed narratives designed to benefit the medico-pharmaceutical industry and other vested interests. Unfortunately, it pulls the public into a belief system that is not only counterproductive to health but frequently life shortening and sometimes deadly. We have endeavored to illustrate this with famous case examples to demonstrate how the media promotes deception with fear-inducing sensationalized headlines that are often bereft of scientific evidence. Just as important is how the illusions are maintained and we share our own experiences of what happens when doctors speak out against the prevailing narrative. *The Final Pandemic* is a title that announces that the concept of contagious and death-dealing 'germs' is finished. Hopefully this helps people realize that there is no need to participate in these man-made "crises" ever again.

The idea for this book arose from Professor Timothy Noakes, the esteemed sports scientist, author and physician who we are proud to call our friend. Sam first interviewed Tim in mid-2021 where they talked about science and censorship, corruption of the food and medical industries and, of course, COVID-19.[23] Tim had already realized that the COVID narrative was nonsense and could see that the draconian responses were unnecessary and causing great harm to people around the world. However, the notion that SARS-CoV-2 did not even exist as claimed was a new idea to him, one that took the problematic "pandemic" to a whole new level of concern. Unlike most doctors who refused to even look at the material presented against the virus model, Tim's interest was piqued and a copy of *Virus Mania* was soon on its way to his mail box in Cape Town, South Africa. Perhaps his own established record of questioning establishment dogma in his pursuit of scientific integrity allowed him to journey into unknown territory once again.

After reading *Virus Mania* Tim was convinced that the evidence for contagious disease-causing particles known as 'viruses' was indeed questionable. He became a virus sceptic and joined us as a welcome signatory to the "Settling the Virus Debate" Statement in July 2022.[24] Tim's feedback on *Virus Mania* was very positive but he reflected that at more than 400 pages and over 1400 references the size of the book alone could be intimidating, more akin to a reference tome. He pointed out that this was not a criticism but potentially meant that people who would benefit from this information might be missing out. What he suggested was a book about half the size and written in a punchy format with straightforward language. And so the work on *The Final Pandemic* began...

The book can be read from start to finish but has also been arranged into subchapters that can be read as "bite-sized" stand-alone pieces. In other words, a book that is suitable for the coffee table or a night time read. Material concerning medical science and virology can be difficult to read even for doctors and scientists when it is outside their usual area. We have strived to make the language as simple as possible without compromising the underlying scientific principles. For those wanting to take a deeper dive, they can explore the many scientific papers that are referenced or read our more technical publications such as *A Farewell to Virology (Expert Edition)*, Mark's formal refutation of the virus model.[25] And those who have been following our work for years can rest assured that this book is packed with all new material.

In writing about "pandemics" we are well aware that they need to be considered within a wider global context. In 2021, Mark and co-author Dr John Bevan-Smith wrote in *The COVID-19 Fraud & War on Humanity*, "this assault on humanity relies on a Trojan horse to deliver the fraud into our minds and bodies, making possible the fulfillment of the globalist agenda of a population control grid with the apparent ultimate aim of controlling populations in every way possible."[26] As John Titus also said in 2021, "the bankers don't care about any sort of scientific event, they don't care about your health, they do care however about 24/7 fear porn and news coverage because it can drive behavior and that's exactly what they're after."[27] So although the present book focusses on the misplaced beliefs regarding so-called contagious germs, we hope the reader will appreciate how this fostered belief is used to manipulate the public in areas extending far beyond the medico-pharmaceutical industry.

Finally, this book is not about what makes people ill. Its primary purpose is to address the misplaced beliefs regarding the concepts of contagion*[28] and infectious disease pandemics. The cause of illness and tips on how to be well is dealt with in our other publications including *Terrain Therapy*.[29]

Dr Samantha A. H. Bailey MB ChB
Dr Mark J. Bailey MB ChB, PGDipMSM, MHealSc
North Canterbury, New Zealand, February 2024.

Chapter 1 - Creating A Pandemic

"The medical cartel...They have no problem whatever in creating diseases and disease panic, spread through the media and legislated by various puppet agencies. I will show you how they systematically created a disease panic, using their powers in the media and the Federal Drugs Administration to provide mass panic, followed by their own brand of 'cure' and vaccine...The brain washed aspect of society then runs for these cures. State health departments are offered more cash in 'federal aid' if they comply with appropriate law making campaigns to support the medical cartels' lies."

— William Trebing D.C., 2006.[30]

"However, in the very next sentence they announce to the world that, 'this virus strain was designated as WH-Human 1 coronavirus (WHCV)'. We need to pause at this point as it is where the fraudulent virus, soon to be renamed SARS-CoV-2, was invented out of thin air. A virus that the WHO claims, with no evidential support whatsoever, is the causative agent of COVID-19...It is this invention that is responsible for the whole bag of destructive tricks imposed on the world following the announcement of the pandemic by the WHO on the 11th of March 2020."

— Dr Mark Bailey, 2022.[31]

Allopathic Medicine Invents Diseases

The term 'allopathic medicine' sits uncomfortably with the powers that control the medical system. For example, the online public encyclopedia *Wikipedia* deceptively states, "allopathic medicine, or allopathy, is an archaic and derogatory label originally used by 19th-century homeopaths to describe heroic medicine, the precursor of modern evidence-based medicine."[32] The Merriam-Webster dictionary has been assisting in this public deception involving a gross departure of the definition from its original meaning. This is clearly evident in how the dictionary's entry for 'allopathy' has changed in recent years:

> ***May 2022:*** *"a system of medical practice that aims to combat disease by use of remedies (as drugs or surgery) producing effects different from or incompatible with those produced by the disease being treated.*[33]
>
> ***November 2022:*** *"a system of medical practice that emphasizes diagnosing and treating disease and the use of conventional, evidence-based therapeutic measures (such as drugs or surgery).*[34]

As well as trying to distract the public from its very nature, allopathic medicine has a long history of manipulating disease classification to suit its purposes. Of particular relevance to the themes of this book was the invention of 'germ theory' *syndromes* in the 1970s. A syndrome is a loose collection of symptoms, often with obscure or unknown causes. Sometimes syndromes are presented to the public but for one reason or another they do not "take" and are relegated to the archives of history. One such example was the attempt to create a newly proposed syndrome based on a range of highly diverse gastrointestinal symptoms.[35] The claim was that only gay men were affected and on that basis the "new" syndrome was called 'gay bowel syndrome'.[36] This preposterous diagnosis showed how the targeting of a particular population group could be used for the purposes of inventing new diagnoses out of thin air and then marketing novel and unnecessary treatments.

Unfortunately, many of these invented syndromes (and diseases) do "take" and the world can then be turned upside down. Indeed, this epidemiological approach has also been used to construct phony "evidence" around the concept of *contagion*. The repeated failures to demonstrate disease transmission by "germs" through natural routes in real-life experiments should have ended the notion of "infectious" diseases long ago. However, this condemning scientific evidence has been largely ignored while pseudoscience (and marketing) is used to keep the concept of contagion alive.

As this book will explore and reveal, allopathy is a system where 'illness' may or may not have symptoms and where 'disease' may or may not come with any actual dis-ease. As mentioned earlier, allopathy changes disease definitions to manipulate alleged case numbers for its own purposes. These disease models are welcomed by the vested interests that have traditionally capitalized from being allied with germ theory, such as the pharmaceutical and biotechnology industries. In essence, fictional diseases are created by and for the medico-pharmaceutical industry to garner very real profits, all the while having nothing to do with improving health.[*37] As philosopher Ivan Illich warned in his book *Medical Nemesis* published in 1975, the process could be called, "the medicalization of life".[38]

In recent decades the target population has widened and apparently we are now *all* at risk of new contagious diseases. Additionally we are being recurrently told to expect them to come at us in increasing numbers in the future. While the mass media and Big Tech marketing campaigns may have convinced the majority of the population to buy into such fear narratives there is a stunning absence of scientific evidence to back up these claims. What is presented as 'the science' can in general be ignored as it does not consist of any findings that arise from the scientific method. On the 28th of November, 2021, Dr Anthony Fauci's claim to "represent science"[39] explicitly summed up the state of affairs: science was being *re*-presented as something else. Dr Fauci was director of the National Institute of Allergy and Infectious Diseases (NIAID) from 1984 to 2022. He has been a key player in promoting "pandemics" for four decades. With apparent prescience, this career bureaucrat said in 2017 that, "there is 'no doubt' Donald J. Trump will be confronted with a surprise infectious disease outbreak during his presidency."[40] Sure enough, and right on time, the world was delivered the "surprise" with COVID-19.

COVID-19: The Bait-and-Switch

In late 2019 and early 2020, the internet was awash with images and videos purportedly depicting people dropping dead in the streets of Chinese cities. Some of the casualties appeared to be middle-aged or younger and it was inferred that a new disease (later to be named 'COVID-19') could strike dead almost anyone in the population. The mainstream "coverage" was typically presented with a great deal of morbid hype and a corresponding paucity of facts. For example, in late January 2020, *The Guardian* published a story headlined, "A man lies dead in the street: the image that captures the Wuhan coronavirus crisis."[41] It portrayed the following situation in Wuhan:

> *It is an image that captures the chilling reality of the coronavirus outbreak in the Chinese city of Wuhan: a grey-haired man wearing a face mask lies dead on the pavement, a plastic shopping bag in one hand, as police and medical staff in full protective suits and masks prepare to take him away... Journalists from Agence France-Presse saw the body on Thursday morning, not long before a vehicle arrived carrying emergency workers. AFP could not determine how the man, who appeared to be aged in his 60s, had died...AFP contacted police and local health officials afterwards but could not get details on his case.*

In other words, almost nothing was known about the man regarding his underlying health conditions and why he had collapsed on the street. Such

'These days, many have died,' says bystander as image shows workers in protective suits and masks taking body away

Coronavirus - latest updates

The Guardian, *31st of January, 2020: "Emergency staff in protective suits check the body of a man who collapsed and died in the street in Wuhan on Thursday." Despite the paucity of information surrounding the odd image of the perfectly supine figure wearing a mask, the article inferred that he had been struck down by a contagious virus.*

details were obviously not required by the media outlets to infer that it was due to, "the Wuhan coronavirus crisis". The words and images were clearly aimed at instilling fear in the readers without any genuine scientific investigation or explanation.

This type of report was at complete odds with experience in other parts of the world. In almost every other country, there were no reports of people unusually dropping dead in the street in 2020. Additionally, on the 13th of May, 2020, Dr John Ioannidis submitted his paper on the infection fatality rate (IFR) of COVID-19 for the *Bulletin of the World Health Organization* (WHO).[42] (The WHO did not publish it online until the 14th of October that year.) He reported that not only was the IFR low, but it could be, "substantially lower than the 0.23%," he calculated in his analysis. Furthermore, he reported that the deaths *attributed* to COVID-19 were mostly in the elderly, with an IFR of 0.05% in people younger than 70 years. Even on their own (unjustified) terms, the "novel" disease was nothing like the deadly scenario fraudulently depicted in the early news coverage. In reality it was remarkably similar to influenza that suspiciously "disappeared" in some countries just as COVID cases went up.[43] However, hysteria was ignited and there was a widespread belief that COVID-19 was a deadly and contagious disease that could kill almost anyone. This belief undoubtedly helped feed mass compliance with lock downs, face masks, vaccine acceptance, and a dystopian surrender of civil rights.

Another aspect of the bait-and-switch was the attachment of the 'SARS' moniker to the supposed virus to produce the ominous sounding 'SARS-CoV-2'. Up until 2002, "coronaviruses" were considered relatively harmless by the virologists. In fact, over many decades there were thousands of human volunteers lining up for the chance to be exposed to these "germs" in the holiday park setting of The Common Cold Unit.[44] Neither the doctors running the unit nor their human guinea pigs would have thought for a second that anyone was putting themselves in danger. The unit quietly closed in 1990 but then just over a decade later the conceived "coronaviruses" were reclassified as deadly killers with the onset of the alleged SARS epidemic in 2002. 'SARS' means severe acute respiratory syndrome and as stated on the *Wikipedia* entry:

> *SARS was a relatively rare disease; at the end of the epidemic in June 2003, the incidence was 8,469 cases with a case fatality rate (CFR) of 11%. No cases of SARS-CoV-1* [the purported "virus"] *have been reported worldwide since 2004...The only symptom common to all patients appears to be a fever above 38°C (100°F). SARS often leads to shortness*

> *of breath and pneumonia, which may be direct viral pneumonia or secondary bacterial pneumonia...For a case to be considered probable, a chest X-ray must be indicative for atypical pneumonia or acute respiratory distress syndrome.*[45]

Here we have a classic example of allopathic medicine inventing a new disease. How could it be considered a specific disease entity when, "the only symptom common to all patients appears to be a fever above 38°C (100°F)"? Fever is a highly non-specific symptom even within allopathic medicine. Outside the allopathic paradigm it is simply considered to be part of a healing crisis and is used by the body to enhance elimination processes after a wide variety of illnesses.[46] SARS was purported to be a respiratory illness but how was a respiratory illness with fever supposed to be differentiated from influenza or pneumonia for example? For a large part of the duration of the alleged SARS outbreak there were no laboratory tests available. In fact, the WHO announced on the 23rd of April, 2003, that, "at present, no validated specific diagnostic test exists for detection of SARS coronavirus or antibodies."[47]

Later, a Polymerase Chain Reaction (PCR) kit was made available, even though the PCR is unable to diagnose such illnesses - as will be explained in chapter 4. Therefore, even on their own terms, they had no confirmatory investigations for the newly-invented condition SARS. Moreover, with PCR and other tests being some years away from mass production and distribution, only a very modest number of SARS cases would ever end-up being clinically diagnosed. Perhaps the other reason that doctors did not 'find' many cases of SARS in the early 2000s, despite having relatively free rein to arbitrarily declare such cases, was due to the necessary requirement to assess the patient's symptoms as 'severe' and 'acute'. At that stage at least, those words still carried some well-defined meaning and health professionals were disinclined to throw them around casually.

TIME *magazine covers on the 5th of May, 2003: United States and Europe editions (left) and Asia edition (right). All of the themes of SARS would be rebooted in 2020 with COVID-19 including deadly "virus," face masks, China, and fear campaigns. Sound science was conspicuously lacking both times, what was different was that COVID-19 had a much bigger marketing campaign and was promoted in social media streams everywhere, not just in paid news magazines.*

Fast forward to 2020 when it was announced that there was a new disease called 'COVID-19', short for "Coronavirus disease 2019" that was caused by SARS-CoV-2, the public was presented with another imagined deadly disease. After all, the new virus was said to be related to SARS-CoV-1. Naturally this caused and fed panic in 2020, for the 2002-2004 SARS "epidemic" had an official case fatality rate of 11%. Once again the damage was done and COVID-19 was forever linked to the feared condition of SARS. The public were tricked into believing in an invisible threat and were primed for the impending lockdowns. (See also, "Why was SARS-2 (COVID-19) Bigger than SARS-1?" in chapter 4 of this book.)

Meaningless Cases

To see how preposterous the "diagnosis" of COVID-19 was, one had to look no further than the WHO's own case definition - one that was eventually embraced by most countries around the world. This was formalized on the 7th of August, 2020, when they published a document titled, "WHO COVID-19: Case Definitions," which can still be accessed on archive.org.[48] The sections for a "suspected case" and a "probable case" included clinical and epidemiological features as well as chest imaging findings such as X-rays. However, this could all be conveniently ignored because a "confirmed" case was declared by the WHO to be, "a person with laboratory confirmation of COVID-19 infection, **irrespective of clinical signs and symptoms.**" (authors' emphasis)

When it comes to diagnostics within the allopathic medical paradigm, circular reasoning is often evident to some degree. However, the WHO's case definition took this trick in logical thinking to a whole new level. In "Lesson 1: Introduction to Epidemiology" the Centers for Disease Control and Prevention (CDC) state that:

> *A case definition is a set of standard criteria for classifying whether a person has a particular disease, syndrome, or other health condition...A case definition consists of clinical criteria and, sometimes, limitations on time, place, and person. The clinical criteria usually include confirmatory laboratory tests, if available, or combinations of symptoms (subjective complaints), signs (objective physical findings), and other findings.*[49]

In a broader sense a 'case' can simply be a, "set of criteria used in making a decision as to whether an individual has a disease or health event of interest."[50] The WHO had no evidence of a specific disease so utilized an 'event of interest' that could apparently be diagnosed, "irrespective of clinical signs and symptoms." In other words, it was disconnected from the concept of disease. What was asserted instead was a claim that the result of a biochemical reaction in a laboratory 'test' constituted a case of disease. Initially this was via Christian Drosten's RT-PCR protocol and later through the rapid antigen (or 'lateral flow') tests that were also based on biochemical reactions. In reality these tests are chemical processes that can be "positive" when minute amounts of target molecules are present in a sample. They are not capable of determining the origin of the molecules and in this application, cannot inform us about the health of the individual. (There are useful lateral flow tests, for example the well-known urine pregnancy tests. Such tests have been independently validated for their accuracy to correspond to an actual pregnancy, and the origin and effects of the detected hormone/protein have been scientifically established.)

When Drosten et al. published "Detection of 2019 novel coronavirus (2019-nCoV) by real-time RT-PCR" in the *Eurosurveillance* journal in January 2020[51] there was no evidence presented for any "virus" or a novel disease that would later be called 'COVID-19'. Their paper simply described a protocol for the detection of short genetic sequences *already declared* to have come from a virus. The sequences they selected were based upon a handful of computer simulation results that teams in China had uploaded onto the genetic database cloud. (See chapter 4 for an explanation of these pseudoscientific practices.) What was of further interest was the bizarre rapidity with which the Drosten et al. paper was published. Their article was submitted on the 21st of January, accepted on the 22nd of January and published on the 23rd of January. Such a turnaround is unheard of in the world of medical journals and by all accounts *Eurosurveillance* did not even attempt to create a facade that a formal peer review process had been undertaken.

On the 19th of March, 2020, the WHO published a document titled "Laboratory testing for coronavirus disease (COVID-19) in suspected human cases".[52] Release of this publication heralded the WHO's apparent enthusiasm to fast track the production of COVID-19 cases around the world. Suspiciously however, the first "Diagnostic detection of 2019-nCoV by real-time RT-PCR" documents appeared on the WHO website on the 13th and then the 17th of January, 2020[53] - more than a week before Christian Drosten's paper was published in *Eurosurveillance* on the 23rd of January. The WHO were certainly eager to seize upon the preliminary PCR protocol, especially considering this was almost two months before they even declared COVID-19 to be a "pandemic".[54]

Enter "Patient Zero"

One of the key aspects in the portrayal of legitimacy of an alleged pandemic is a so-called 'patient zero' - that is the person documented as the first known case of an infectious disease (sometimes called an 'index case'). This book will demonstrate that the entire premise of a patient zero is fictitious due to the lack of scientific evidence that diseases are contagious - that is, spread by alleged infectious germs. In particular, chapter 4 expands on the spurious practices with regard to how "cases" are created. COVID-19 cases were preposterous as there was no requirement for the person to be symptomatic, unwell, or even be at risk of becoming unwell in any way. They simply had to have a certain manufactured test result that was thoroughly disconnected from the reality of a specific disease. Regardless of an individual's circumstances, the pandemic model that the WHO and their acolytes wanted people around the world to accept was, "you are infected and need to follow our instructions."

Not to be denied their COVID patient zero, the media have portrayed a specter of mystery over who the invented case may have been. For example, on the 24th of February, 2020, the *BBC* published an article on their website with the title, "Who is 'patient zero' in the coronavirus outbreak?". It read:

> *As the cases of coronavirus increase in China and around the world, the hunt is on to identify "patient zero". But can singling out one person as causing an outbreak do more harm than good? Chinese authorities and experts are at odds about the origin of the ongoing coronavirus outbreak. More specifically, who is "patient zero" for the outbreak. Also known as an index case, patient zero is a term used to describe the first human infected by a viral or bacterial disease in an outbreak. Advances in genetic analysis now make it possible to trace back the lineage of a virus through those it has infected. Combined with epidemiological studies, scientists can pinpoint individuals who may have been the first people to start spreading the disease and so trigger the outbreak. Identifying who these people are can help address crucial questions about how, when and why it started. These can then help to prevent more people from getting infected now or in future outbreaks. Do we know who patient zero is in the Covid-19 coronavirus outbreak that started in China? The short answer is – no.*[55]

In other words, even on their own terms they could not decide if identifying a patient zero was a good idea or not - but in any event, the "hunt" proceeded apace. And despite "advances" in the technology available to pinpoint the alleged instigator of the pandemic - they turned up a blank. This style of mainstream media article was prolific during the COVID-19 era: assuring the audience that the ordained science 'experts' were hard at work for humanity, while playing everything both ways to leave the reader in a state of confusion. Typically, a few paragraphs later the *BBC* article stated that:

> *However, a study, by Chinese researchers published in the Lancet medical journal, claimed the first person to be*

> *diagnosed with Covid-19, was on 1 December 2019 (a lot of* [sic] *earlier) and that person had "no contact" with the Huanan Seafood Wholesale Market. Wu Wenjuan, a senior doctor at Wuhan's Jinyintan Hospital and one of the authors of the study, told the BBC Chinese Service that the patient was an elderly man who suffered from Alzheimer's disease.*[56]

It would seem that the alleged patient zero was clearly identified by the Chinese researchers and one can only speculate that the *BBC* was inferring that China cannot be trusted on such matters? In any case, the aim of the article was not to provide the public with any useful or accurate information but to convince them that a dangerous pandemic was afoot and even the alleged experts were struggling to get a handle on things. While many things needed to be questioned and investigated, apparently the existence of a deadly "pathogen" that was said to be causing a new fearful disease was an established given and not something that the public needed to know anything further about.

Perhaps the most famous patient zero of all time was Gaëten Dugas.[57] Dugas, a gay Canadian flight attendant, was part of a 1984 CDC study called "Cluster of Cases of the Acquired Immune Deficiency Syndrome - Patients Linked by Sexual Contact."[58]

The study was based on interviews of men diagnosed with AIDS who were asked to recall their sexual partners during the five-year period before they became ill. The study design was not capable of testing a hypothesis but the authors unjustifiably concluded that, "the finding of a cluster of AIDS patients linked by sexual contact is consistent with the hypothesis that AIDS is caused by an infectious agent." The developing mythology spread widely in 1987 when Randy Shilts published his best-selling book *And the Band Played On*.[59] Shilts wrote that, "whether Gaëtan Dugas actually was the person who brought AIDS to North America remains a question of

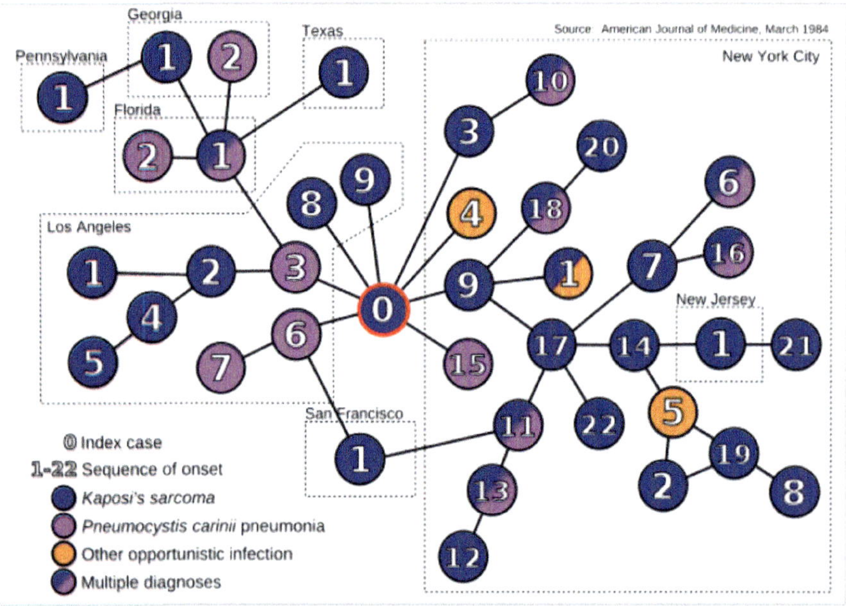

The CDC's 1984 study "Cluster of Cases of the Acquired Immune Deficiency Syndrome - Patients Linked by Sexual Contact": 'Patient 0' in the center is Gaëten Dugas with his links to reported sexual contacts. The investigators cast their net extremely widely: "Homosexual men with AIDS who could be linked by sexual contact were considered to belong to a cluster of AIDS patients if the sexual exposure occurred within five years of the onset of illness." Source: *American Journal of Medicine*, March 1984.

debate and is ultimately unanswerable... there's no doubt that Gaëtan played a key role in spreading the new virus from one end of the United States to the other." *National Review* then embellished the fictional story even more stating that, "[Dugas] picked up the disease in Europe through sexual contact with Africans. Traveling on his airline-employee privileges, he spread it here from coast to coast."[60]

Ironically, Dugas was later "cleared" of introducing the claimed 'human immunodeficiency virus' (HIV) to the United States and the story has been replaced by other equally fictional narratives. However, the damage was done and an invented "contagion" was firmly implanted into the minds of the public. It had been given a face in the form of the handsome and athletic Dugas, who was imagined to be spreading it around with the greatest of ease. Never mind the fact that the majority of men in the CDC study were very heavy users of body-destroying inhaled nitrites ("poppers") and were engaged in other unhealthy lifestyle practices before they became ill. The general public were at no risk of developing AIDS illnesses such as Kaposi's sarcoma because there was nothing of this nature to be "caught". However, the 1980s was arguably the decade when a perceived threat of contagion resurged: if someone like Gaëten Dugas could spread death around, then who else did we need "protection" from?

Clustering and "Asymptomatic Transmission"

The Gaëten Dugas affair was an example of the practice of 'clustering', a technique that can be used, or at least interpreted inappropriately, to claim that an infectious agent is spreading around. English physician John Snow (1813-1858) is considered to be one of the founders of modern epidemiology for his development of cluster analysis. During the often cited Broad Street cholera outbreak in London in 1854, Snow collected data on death rates related to two water suppliers that were drawing their water from the heavily contaminated Thames River:

> *Cowsheds, slaughter houses and grease-boiling dens lined the streets and contributed animal droppings, rotting fluids and other contaminants to the primitive Soho sewer system. Many cellars had cesspools underneath their floorboards, which formed from the sewers and filth seeping in from the outside. Since the cesspools were overrunning, the London government decided to dump the waste into the River Thames, contaminating the water supply.*[61]

While Snow's analysis was correct in concluding that it was contaminated water from the Broad Street pump making people sick, the modern day story that it was an infection (from the bacterium *Vibrio cholerae*) is not. There is no scientific evidence that the ingestion of the bacteria by itself will make anyone sick. However, the ingestion of fecal material, decomposing biological tissue, and other toxins can certainly make people sick. So the cluster of cases had nothing to do with bacterial "infection" and everything to do with the common factor of drinking filthy waste-containing River Thames water. It is not evidence for germ theory at work as has been widely celebrated. As documented in *Virus Mania*, the medical establishment has long struggled to appreciate that clusters of illness do not mean infection and contagion:

> *Every cold, every seasonal influenza, every hepatitis disease, or whatever other syndrome has become an inexhaustible source for epidemic hunters armed with their clustering methods to declare ever new epidemics that pose threats to the world...Just how ineffective clustering is in finding epidemics becomes evident, moreover, if we look more closely at cases where clustering has been used as a tool to sniff out (allegedly impending) epidemics. This happened with the search for the causes of scurvy, beriberi and pellagra at the beginning of the 20th century. But, as illustrated, it proved groundless to assume that these are infectious diseases with epidemic potential.*[62]

Clustering remains one of the favored types of indirect evidence for the disease-inventors and germ theorists. The danger is that its misuse results in completely incorrect conclusions about why people get sick. Unsurprisingly, the "mistakes" of cluster analysis continued in the COVID-19 era. For example, a key study published in *The Lancet* in April 2020 claimed to have linked groups of COVID-19 cases in two churches and a family gathering in Singapore.[63] But one only has to look at their definition of a "confirmed case" (which was a PCR test) to see how absurd it was. There was no evidence of any "transmission" as they claimed and no controls in place at all (it was not blinded and the researchers did not apply their "test" on anyone outside the groups) so it could not be said to follow the scientific method. The mere detection of genetic sequences cannot provide evidence of a "virus," transmission of an infectious agent or the existence of an alleged infectious disease.

The problem of drawing faulty conclusions from the clustering technique has been apparent since it was first introduced. However, in modern times the epidemiologists have become even more cavalier with the wholesale acceptance of laboratory tests that do not even relate to illness. It is the perfect recipe for creating meaningless "cases" and a tool for the invention of new "epidemics". The COVID-19 cases were concocted with PCR and antigen tests on a grand scale. When people started noticing that many of the so-called cases had no symptoms, the term 'asymptomatic transmission' was subsequently promulgated by governments and the media.[64] Once this kind of nonsense was smuggled and carved into the public's mindset then it paved the way for further buzz words such as 'superspreader', said to an individual who has a "super" propensity to pass on a disease to a large number of others. While this has never been demonstrated in practice, the epidemiologists can once again create their superspreaders with phony tests and clustering. They literally create an "outbreak" that has no existence in nature.

'Typhoid Mary' - The Original "Superspreader" Story

Perhaps the most famous story of all time regarding claimed superspreaders is that of Mary Mallon (1869-1938), more commonly known as 'Typhoid Mary'. The history books state that the Irish-born American cook is believed to have "infected" between 51 and 122 people with typhoid fever as she moved between households in the New York City area in the early 1900s. *Wikipedia* states that she, "was the first person in the United States identified as an asymptomatic carrier of the pathogenic bacteria *Salmonella typhi*."[65] Here on full display is the contradiction of germ theory where its proponents have no problem with the fact that there is no relationship between the presence of the "germ" and sickness in the person. The sanitation engineer George Soper helped apprehend Mary Mallon in 1907 and wrote about her appearance in the *Bulletin of the New York Academy of Medicine* in 1939:

> *I first saw Mary Mallon thirty-two years ago, that is, in 1907. She was then about forty years of age and at the height of her physical and mental faculties. She was five feet six inches tall, a blond with clear blue eyes, a healthy color and a somewhat determined mouth and jaw. Mary had a good figure and might have been called athletic had she not been a little too heavy... As a matter of fact, I did not need the specimens in order to prove that Mary was a focus of typhoid germs. My epidemiological evidence had proved that. Laboriously I had worked out every one of the seven outbreaks and I was positive that Mary had produced them all.*[66]

However, Soper never produced any evidence that the typhoid "germs," in particular the bacteria known as *Salmonella typhi,* caused typhoid fever. Neither has any one else in history. A study published in the journal *Clinical infectious diseases* in 2014[67] claimed to cause typhoid fever in some of the human volunteers who swallowed the bacteria but there were a number of monumental scientific deficiencies:

1. Typhoid fever is supposed to be a serious life-threatening condition that has been described as follows: "High fever gradually develops, with delirium. A rash appears on the trunk. The sites where the bacilli multiplied become inflamed and may ulcerate, leading to intestinal

bleeding or peritonitis. Patients become exhausted and emaciated; up to 25% die if not treated."[68] In the 2014 study it was reported that of the 40 volunteers who swallowed the bacteria: "Challenge was well tolerated; no participants required hospital admission, intravenous antibiotics, or fluids." That does not sound like typhoid fever.

2. The majority of the participants did not develop any fever at all and to increase the "attack rates" to above 50% the researchers had to lower the bar and use "alternative diagnostic criteria."
3. It was not at all apparent that the large amount of concentrated bacteria that were swallowed would ever be swallowed in such amounts in natural settings. (See note regarding,"the dose makes the poison."*[69])
4. There was no control arm in the study. There should have been a comparable group of volunteers who were given the same broth with the bacteria removed +/- a comparable group given "non pathogenic" bacteria to see what symptoms and signs they developed.
5. The study was not blinded so both the volunteers and the researchers would have expected a certain result from swallowing bacteria said to be potentially fatal and a, "major global health problem."[70] (This is known as the *nocebo effect*: "With a nocebo effect, if test subjects believe there may be side effects, they often experience them."[71])

Points 1-3 alone raise serious doubts about the hypothesis that *Salmonella typhi* is the cause of typhoid fever. Points 4 and 5 completely disqualified the study from adhering to the scientific method, meaning that by its own design it was not suitable to even test a hypothesis. So their claims fell flat and it has never been established that the bacteria are to blame. Unfortunately, since the time of George Soper it has not been felt necessary to obtain the missing evidence - everyone simply assumes that the germ "fact" must have been established in an experimental study.

Of course, that still leaves the question of why cases of typhoid fever often appeared in households where Mary Mallon was working? That question may never be answered because we only have a few commentaries such as that of George Soper and almost no verifiable scientific data. It is certainly plausible that as the cook in these households she had poor hygiene practices and contaminated the food in other ways. Food poisoning does not equate to an "infection" and a cluster of cases in one location is not a case of 'passing it on'. It is a case of everyone ingesting the same toxin from a common source.

It is also difficult to exclude a more devious origin of the promoted story which is one of the famed lynchpins for germ theory. The paucity of verifiable material raises the possibility that the events that took place have been exaggerated or distorted. Even George Soper's account in the *Bulletin of the New York Academy of Medicine*, on which the whole 'superspreader' notion hinges, was not published until three decades after the alleged affair.

Relevant to this theme, ViroLIEgy's Mike Stone has completed in-depth research into the development of germ theory in the late 1800s.[72] He pointed out that in order to keep the germ model intact, logic and the scientific method were conveniently ignored through the introduction of the asymptomatic carrier:

> *When Koch made his famous postulates that must be fulfilled in order to prove any microbe causes disease, his logic and common sense told him that a "pathogenic agent" should not be found within those who are healthy. Unfortunately for Koch...he regularly found the "pathogenic" microbes (specifically the bacteria for tuberculosis, cholera, and typhoid) in cases of those who had no disease. Thus, he could never satisfy his first postulate* [the microorganism must be found in abundance in all organisms suffering from the disease but should not be found in healthy organisms] *in order to claim that any microbe he discovered were the true causes*

> *of disease. Not wanting to give up his fame, fortune, and prestige, Koch bent his own logic and allowed for the unfalsifiable concept of asymptomatic carriers in order to keep his findings intact.*[73]

Death of "Whistleblower" Doctors

The media have developed a pattern of promoting "whistleblowers" in the early stages of an alleged pandemic. They are widely celebrated for their apparent efforts to alert the world about a new disease but are then claimed to fall victim to either censorship or lose their lives to the very same disease they were warning about. The story gains even more traction if the media-promoted whistleblower is also a doctor. In 2003 during the alleged "SARS" pandemic, the role was filled by the physician Carlo Urbani. He is widely known as the discoverer of SARS but as *Wikipedia* states, "shortly afterwards, he himself became infected and died."[74] There are no references following this claim and *Virus Mania* exposed that his cause of death was not even properly investigated:

> *At the end of March 2020, the Italian newspaper Corriere Adriatico recalled the story of medical doctor Carlo Urbani, who died shortly after he created the term SARS on March 29, 2003. The headline of the article reads: "Carlo Urbani's wife, the SARS doctor: 'His lesson is useful for the whole world, but only half understood.' Indeed, much of the world didn't understand the lesson, which, of course, is different from what Urbani's wife meant. The real lesson is that one should not blindly trust a few promoted virologists and that no virus tunnel vision should not be attached to the research into the causes of diseases.*[75]

In 2020, when COVID-19 ("SARS-2") was in its early stages of promotion, there was a remarkably similar story. This time it involved an ophthalmologist working at Wuhan Central Hospital, Dr Li Wenliang (see also "Day 1" of the time line in this book's foreword). His reported death was headlined with much fanfare in mainstream platforms everywhere - one example being Australia's *ABC News* on the 7th of February, 2020:

> *A Wuhan hospital says a Chinese doctor who blew the whistle on the outbreak of coronavirus only to be reprimanded by police has died from the virus, amid confusion over earlier reports of his death and then resuscitation...Dr Li said he was diagnosed with the coronavirus on January 20...Dr Li sent a message to medical staff advising them to wear masks and protection to avoid infection after he noticed several patients presenting with a virus similar to the deadly SARS epidemic.*[76]

Dr Li was only 34 years old and was not reported to have any significant underlying health problems, so it was an extremely unusual "case". While this book will outline why there is no evidence for "infectious disease" pandemics, even if they did exist why did Dr Li become a victim? The *Bulletin of the World Health Organization's* published study in October 2020 estimated a COVID-19 infection fatality rate of 0.05% in people younger than 70 years.[77] And in under 40-year-olds, the death rates in so-called COVID cases were significantly lower than this. Even on their own terms, he did not fit the right demographic.

The *ABC News* story went on to report that, "China has been accused of suppressing information about the coronavirus," but paradoxically linked the *ABC* webpage to the Twitter feed of the communist Chinese government's own media platform *People's Daily, China*.[78] Here it was clear that the Chinese government was not holding back on promoting the "epidemic" and the "novel coronavirus" as they broke the news of Dr Li's death to the entire world. Another Chinese government platform, the *Global Times* tabloid, also presented Dr Li as a "whistleblower" who was,

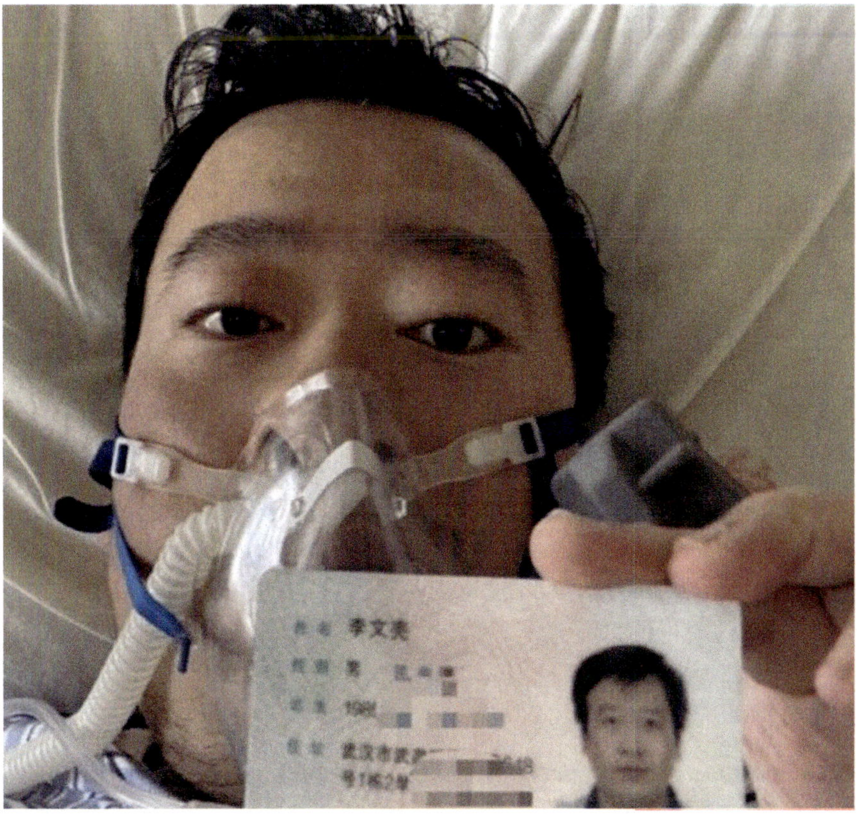

People's Daily, China *published this photo of Dr Li Wenliang, with the caption: "We deeply mourn the death of #Wuhan doctor Li wenliang, who unfortunately got infected with novel #Coronavirus while battling with the epidemic. After all-effort rescue, Li passed away on 2:58 am, Feb. 7." Strangely, he was holding up his identification card for the photo opportunity, presumably a short time before his death was announced by the government's media platform.* Source: https://twitter.com/PDChina/status/1225513842807099394

"reprimanded by local police."[79] However, it was subsequently divulged in the same article that, "a top epidemiologist at the Chinese Center for Disease Control and Prevention (CCDC) said in a recent interview with *Global Times*' editor-in-chief Hu Xijin that we should highly praise these whistle-blowers." Despite what many in Western countries have been led to believe, the Chinese government played their part in publicizing the COVID-19 show including the use of "lab leak" and "cover up" gambits.

Indeed, the residents of New York City were apparently well-informed of the alleged cover up attempts and had a memorial service in Central Park to honor Dr Li within a few days of his death. The *New Yorker* ran a feature article on the 11th of February, 2020, for the, "doctor who tried to warn China about the coronavirus":

> *Residents of the city of eleven million found ways to mourn the loss of Li in solitude. Some cried out his name from high-rise apartments, creating a hymn of sorrow; some drove their sedans and S.U.V.s slowly through empty streets, with the hazard lights on. In New York City, Mei Qiqi, a graduate student in international educational development at Columbia, cried for half an hour straight upon seeing the news on Thursday, and immediately changed her WeChat avatar to a black ribbon.*[80]

The article went on to quote several people who believed that freedom of speech could be compromised for those that were *promoting* the alleged severity of the COVID-19 situation! Like Carlo Urbani we will probably never know what killed Dr Li Wenliang because the only information available to the public is through these peripheral articles. What is clear is that mainstream corporate media platforms and the Chinese government were actively promulgating the deadly pandemic narrative in the early days.

On the other hand, those of us that questioned the science behind the pandemic narrative experienced something quite different. Starting in early 2020 we were subject to "fact-checking" pieces, smear articles, de-platforming, shadow banning and prosecution attempts.

Prepare the Public with Hollywood Blockbusters

Several high-budget Hollywood films have featured storylines that contain many of the themes that eventually play out as "reality" in the corporate media. One was the 1995 production *Outbreak*, starring Dustin Hoffman, Rene Russo, and Morgan Freeman.[81] The film opens with an onscreen quote, "the single biggest threat to man's continued dominance on the planet is the virus," which is attributed to molecular biologist and Nobel laureate Dr Joshua Lederberg (1925–2008). It is unclear how he reached such a fanciful claim which in reality appears as fictional as the plot line that follows. The film is based on the premise that deadly diseases are poised to jump out of the jungle should mankind get too close for his own good. Many of the themes are now highly recognizable, particularly after the COVID-19 era, as can be seen in the following summary of the plot:

- The zoonotic[82] origins of the outbreak, in this case from an African monkey. (More on the fallacies of 'zoonosis' in chapter 2.)
- A rapidly mutating virus with different strains.
- Airborne transmission, with infections occurring with the greatest of ease.
- A 'super-spreader' event in a movie theatre.
- Government scientists in hazmat suits and supplied with apparent testing equipment.
- The possibility that the agent could be used as a biological weapon.
- "Antibodies" providing protection against the virus and being employed as a cure.
- The militarization of the response and restrictions on freedom that are apparently required to reach a solution.

The film is as patently absurd as the COVID-19 narrative that was foisted on the world. This is because humans have been co-existing in harmony with animals for an eternity, but we are now supposed to believe that they are suddenly one of the major threats to our existence.[*83] It seems very

Mysterious pneumonia kills 3, infects 9 in Argentina: 'Similar to COVID'

By Adriana Diaz

September 1, 2022 | 2:53pm | Updated

The New York Post*, 1st of September, 2022: "Mysterious pneumonia killed three people in Argentina this week in a new alarming outbreak of an unknown deadly virus." The inserted computer-generated image is presumably supposed to represent the "virus" and the map suggests where it was discovered. The body of the article contained nothing to establish that any "deadly virus" had been found.*

strange given that even on their own terms, "infectious" diseases such as polio and diphtheria all but disappeared in the last century.[84] By the early 1980s, most people in the developed world were spending little time worrying about such concerns. Nevertheless, the alleged "HIV" epidemic and its doomsday predictions kept the wind in the sails of government agencies such as the CDC and the UK Health Security Agency in the 1980s and 1990s.*[85] The current claim of zoonotic diseases is set to drive the future narrative, with the doom-laden implication that pandemics could occur at any time and with the greatest of ease. Such dire pronouncements by the authorities will no doubt serve to keep much of society in an unnecessary state of fear.

An example of the corporate media pushing a sketchy plot as though it was reality was exemplified in a September 2022 *New York Post* story headlined, "Mysterious pneumonia kills 3, infects 9 in Argentina: 'Similar to COVID'".[86] The first line reads, "fears of a new deadly viral outbreak have begun to spread after three people died in Argentina this week from a mysterious case of pneumonia." Somehow "fears" are taken to mean 'scientific evidence' and the story quickly runs away on unestablished premises. All that was known was that some people had pneumonia and based on the fact that many of the usual tests came back negative, it was asserted there must be a mysterious virus at work. Even within the medical establishment's allopathic paradigm of germs being the *cause* of pneumonia, they acknowledge that they cannot find a germ in around half of the cases.[87] So what has precipitated the change to declare that if the current tests are not positive, new viruses must be to blame?

It was claimed that the condition in Argentina was very similar to COVID-19. This is meaningless as the WHO has stated that a confirmed case of COVID-19 is simply a positive PCR or rapid antigen test - there are no specific symptoms or signs that are required.[88] More contradictions followed in the *New York Post* reporting:

> *Samples of the unknown virus have reportedly been sent for testing to the Malbran Institute in Buenos Aires and Argentina's National Administration of Health Laboratories and Institutes. Local officials are also examining the water and air conditioning units in the area to test for possible poisoning. The most recent victim of the virus was a 70-year-old woman who died Thursday. She had been admitted to the*

> *clinic where the infected health professionals worked ahead of a procedure. The elderly woman has been suspected to have been "patient zero" but* [Tucumán health minister Luis] *Ruiz clarified that those facts are still "being evaluated."*[89]

It is not clear how they already knew they had a virus when the samples had not yet been tested. It is one of the oldest tricks in virology to assert that a virus has been found or "isolated," simply by taking a sample from someone that has already been declared to have a "viral" illness. They even admitted that environmental poisons had not yet been examined before illogically proclaiming that a recently deceased woman was a "victim of the virus".

The fear narrative was stepped up another notch when the article's last sentence linked to a story concerning a recent state of emergency that was declared in the U.S. with regard to monkeypox. We had anticipated such an announcement and three months earlier had published a light-hearted article to address the nonsense of the brewing "Monkeypox Mythology".[90]

Chapter 2 - Scapegoats for Disease

"Anyone can get sick from a zoonotic disease, including healthy people. However, some people are more at risk than others and should take steps to protect themselves or family members. These people are more likely than others to get really sick, and even die, from infection with certain diseases."

—The CDC's statement on 'Zoonotic Diseases'.[91]

"The single biggest threat to man's continued dominance on the planet is the virus.—Joshua Lederberg, Ph.D., Nobel laureate."

—*Outbreak* (the film,) 1995.[92]

Invent a Disease and Blame it on Animals

Some of the most captivating headlines in pandemic promotions involve the unproven theory that diseases are jumping from animals into humans, a process called 'zoonosis'. This dramatic claim is loaded with all the fear-inducing elements of a double threat: not only are there nasty germs, but the animals around us are reservoirs brimming with such germs. According to public health agencies these microbes can be present in perfectly healthy animals but then mutate and unexpectedly jump out to attack the human race. The CDC website states that, "zoonotic diseases are very common, both in the United States and around the world. Scientists estimate that more than 6 out of every 10 known infectious diseases in people can be spread from animals, and 3 out of every 4 new or emerging infectious diseases in people come from animals."[93] However they do not provide any direct scientific citations for us to check these fantastic claims.

The EcoHealth Alliance, presided over by Dr Peter Daszak, is one of the chief promoters of these zoonotic threat storylines. The organization has portrayed a scary scenario for humanity with regard to their postulated "Disease X":

> *Miles from the nearest city, deep in the dark recesses of a cave in Guangdong Province, it waits. Perhaps it silently stalks from high in the canopies of trees nestled along the Kinabatangan River. Or it lies dormant in one of the thousands of species native to the Amazon. Disease X. This is not science fiction, it's real.*[94]

It is not clear how a disease that does not exist can be "real" but at least they went on to concede, "we have no idea what Disease X can do, because we don't know what Disease X is." We are informed that the solution is to secure funding to the very real amount of "just $1.2 billion dollars" for the Global Virome Project, an organization in which Daszak also happens to sit on the leadership board.[95] This shows how postulating fictitious fears about 'viral disease' is incredibly lucrative in monetary terms and helps claimants to create beneficiaries, like the Global Virome Project.

According to a *CNN* report, "Daszak is a virus hunter. Over the past 10 years, he has visited over 20 countries trying to prevent the next big pandemic by searching bat caves for new pathogens. More specifically, new coronaviruses."[96] It is beyond the scope of this book to dissect the scientific publications related to these activities. This has been published elsewhere.[97] We already know that the alleged "coronaviruses" have never been physically isolated or proven to exist as contagious entities. The claims of discovering "pathogenic" abilities are through pseudoscientific techniques, including the nonsensical practice of grinding up bat intestines and injecting this toxic mixture directly into the brains of newborn rats in uncontrolled experiments.[98] One does not need to be a virologist to

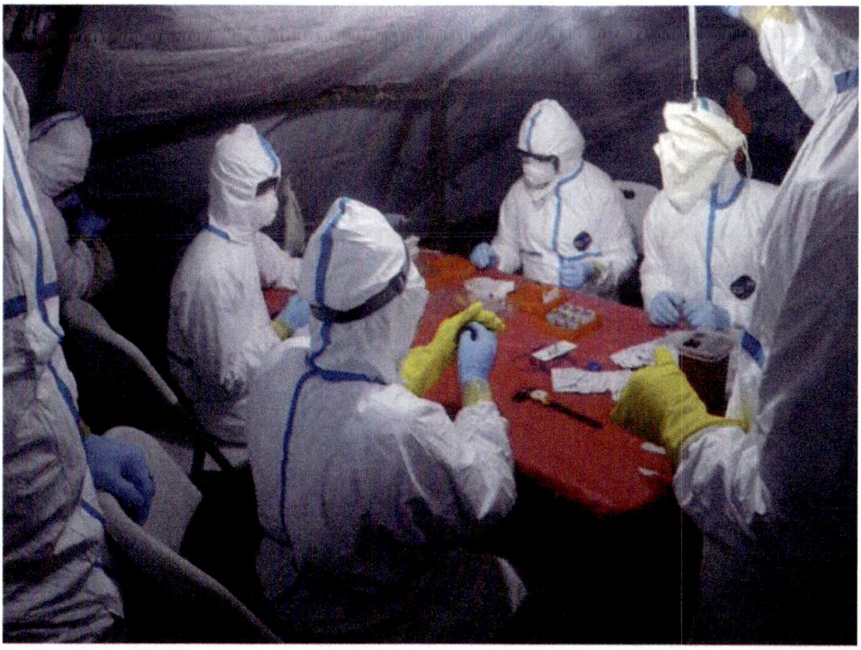

The public are presented with images of people in hazmat suits and masks, who are apparently collecting samples from bats in Chinese caves. A CNN *headline* on *the 26th of April, 2022, proclaimed: "The virus hunters who search bat caves to predict the next pandemic." It doesn't require the actual existence of pathogenic viruses but such images are an effective way to sustain a fear narrative throughout the world.* Source: *CNN*, Photograph: Smithsonian institute.

appreciate that such experiments can never prove the claimed existence of coronaviruses. Nevertheless, these foundational departures from the scientific method are generally ignored and the public are presented with an unending stream of dramatic fear-inducing headlines regarding an unending potential for pandemics to spring from animals.

Blame SARS on Bats with no Evidence

In January 2020, there were a series of stories promulgated by the corporate media that helped stoke the emerging 'COVID-19 pandemic' narrative. One involved a video purporting to show a Chinese woman eating a cooked whole bat in a restaurant. In the *Daily Mail's* coverage it was inaccurately claimed that, "scientists link the deadly coronavirus to the flying mammals," when nothing of the sort had been established.[99] In fact, a few lines into the story it was even stated that, "scientists now fear it may have spread to humans from snakes or bats." In other words, it was pure speculation. Nothing had been shown to spread, let alone something that had jumped from animals to humans. A narrative had now been created and the video sparked outrage around the world with millions of people convinced that Asian culinary habits were the cause of the claimed COVID-19 pandemic.

It was not the first time hapless bats had been blamed for causing human "SARS" (Severe acute respiratory syndrome). According to *Wikipedia*, SARS is, "a viral respiratory disease of zoonotic origin caused by the virus SARS-CoV-1."[100] The claim that the disease came from animals was based on *Wikipedia's* statement that, "the viral outbreak was subsequently genetically traced to a colony of cave-dwelling horseshoe bats in Xiyang Yi Ethnic Township, Yunnan." A review of the pivotal study,[101] that included Peter Daszak as a co-author, actually revealed that no virus or contagious agent was found in any humans or bats. All they found was that an indirect (antibody) blood test they had designed was positive in six out of 240 people who lived near bat caves. This apparently led them to draw the conclusion that it provided "likely" evidence that the bats were a source of human infection. It is quite a stretch to claim that a chemical reaction of a notoriously non-specific and highly dubious laboratory test in a few samples provides evidence that people are being infected by bats.

The authors also stated that none of the six subjects could, "recall any clinical symptoms in the past 12 months, suggesting that their bat SARSr-CoV infection either occurred before the time of sampling or that infections were subclinical or caused only mild symptoms." This is simply

Daily Mail AUSTRALIA News

Home | U.K. | U.S. | News | World News | Sport | TV&Showbiz | Femail AU | Health | Science | Weather | Video | Travel | DailyMailTV

Monkeypox | Covid-19 | Russia-Ukraine War | Breaking News | Sydney | Melbourne | Brisbane | New Zealand | Wires Login

Revolting footage shows Chinese woman eating a whole bat at a fancy restaurant as scientists link the deadly coronavirus to the flying mammals

- A video clip shows a young woman sinking her teeth into a cooked bat
- Another video shows diners preparing to eat soup made with animal
- A new strain of coronavirus has killed 25 people and sickened more than 800
- Scientists fear it may have spread to humans from snakes or bats
- Wuhan, where the virus originated, has been put under lockdown
- Two more Chinese cities are shutting down transport in response
- Coronavirus symptoms: what are they and should you see a doctor?

Site Web Enter your search Search

Follow Daily Mail | Subscribe Daily Mail | Follow @DailyMail | Follow Daily Mail | Follow @dailymailuk | Follow Daily Mail

Poll

On average, how often do you shop online?

WEEKLY MONTHLY LESS

The Daily Mail's *big story on the 24th of January, 2020. Many of the readers were unlikely to be aware that the various claims were pure speculation. However, it was made to look authentic by adding the word 'scientists' to the headline. The unsubstantiated story quickly spread around the world and millions of people were led to believe that Asian eating habits had triggered a new disease in humans.*

making the observations fit their desired theory, that is, a virus must be to blame. Comically, the authors added, "it is worth noting that all of them [the six "positive" people] had observed bats flying in their villages," which would hardly be surprising given that they all lived near bat caves. They did not care to mention how many of the 236 people who tested "negative" had also seen flying bats. It is just one of the examples in which the unscientific methods clearly failed to support the zoonotic "infection" narrative. However, the misleading journal claims lead to parroted news headlines that subsequently become reinforced and embedded in public perception to help to create, propagate and fuel the virological dogma.

Slaughter Millions of Animals to Drive the Fear

Zoonotic storylines are used by government authorities to extract large sums of money from their citizens in the name of "bio-security" and "border protection"[102] under the guise of 'regulating' citizens' consumer behaviors to favor vested interests.[103] Additionally, they often involve hysterical reactions and the mass slaughter of domesticated animals under the guise of public safety. As the book *Virus Mania* stated with regard to the alleged 2003 Dutch "Bird Flu":

> *Dozens of operations that had delivered chickens or feed from the Netherlands in the days before were put under official observation. Immediately, the search for a virus began using indirect test procedures—and look at that! The very next day, there was an announcement that a highly pathogenic virus of the type H7N7 had been found. "Over the following four months, 26 million chickens in the Netherlands, around 2.5 million in Belgium, and approximately 100,000 in NRW* [North Rhine-Westphalia] *were gassed with carbon dioxide, poisoned by lethal injection, electrocuted or manually slaughtered," according to Hans Tolzin, editor of the German vaccination publication* Impf-Report, *who did extensive analysis of the event...But the existence—or even the dangerousness—of this so-called H7N7 virus was likewise never proven.*[104]

Such atrocious stupidity may be culpable or it may be ignorant, but it cannot be both. By 2022 more mass slaughters were taking place in the U.S. poultry industry. *The Guardian* reported that, "outbreaks of the disease, also known as bird flu, have wreaked havoc across Europe and the U.S. this year, with 38 million birds killed in the U.S. so far."[105] Once again it was a man-made crisis with cases of "highly pathogenic avian influenza" being statistically created by testing samples from bird throats with a reverse transcription-polymerase chain reaction (RT-PCR) process. The PCR simply amplifies short sequences of genetic material and provides no proof of any 'virus', let alone a "highly pathogenic" one. An arbitrary level must be set for a "positive" result but this does not equate to the diagnosis of a disease. The typical information that comes with such PCR "test" kits, simply provides data about how reliably the kits detect the genetic sequences they are designed to detect.[106] There is no information provided to show what capability the kits have to detect any particular disease. So the "flu outbreaks" are nothing more than some positive results *after* the tests are rolled out.

Of course some birds do get sick but it has not been scientifically demonstrated that microbes are *causing* them to become sick or that there is a contagious element at play. In the case of what is termed 'avian influenza', the proposed pathogen, an influenza virus, has not even been shown to exist. Instead, we are told to believe it exists and is causing illness, simply through the detection of some selected genetic sequences. The stark and undeniably unwholesome reality of the conditions of many commercial poultry farms is such that the birds are continuously subjected to all kinds of stress including highly-restrictive indoor confinement, overcrowding, unnatural diets and a plethora of toxic pharmaceuticals such as vaccines and antibiotics. There is no need to blame their subsequent ill health on invented viruses.

As if these animal welfare abuses were not enough, the culling narrative is being used to terrify the public into believing that a "bird flu" is poised to jump out of the poultry industry to cause a deadly human pandemic. Instead of investigating the underlying causes of disease in the birds, the "solution" from the so-called health authorities is to slaughter entire flocks. Often this involves the barbaric technique of ventilation shutdowns where the airflow to the poultry sheds is cut off and the temperature is increased to lethal levels.[107]

It is not only birds that have been slaughtered in such horrific numbers. In 2001, during the alleged foot-and mouth "outbreak" in the United Kingdom, Neil Ferguson was part of a team at Imperial College London,

Killing in the name of...? As a result of the "bird flu virus" claims, many of the mass poultry killings in the US are carried out through "ventilation shutdowns": the birds are suffocated by cutting off their air supply and increasing the temperature to a lethal level. All of the deaths can then be blamed on a "deadly virus" which was never shown to exist. Photograph: Jo-Anne McArthur/We Animals Media.

"creating mathematical models used to inform the UK Government of the most effective methods of preventing the spread of foot-and-mouth-disease [FMD]."[108] Their models "informed" the British government to order the senseless incineration of more than 6 million mostly healthy cows and sheep, costing the UK economy billions of pounds and destroying untold livelihoods.[109] Not one of the animals were at risk of transmitting an imagined virus and the small number of "clustered" livestock that showed any signs of illness could only be said to had shared common environmental conditions. However, the germ adherents remain fixated on their destructive models. For example, to help maintain the viral illusion, an animal version of "asymptomatic transmission" was introduced in the form of a "carrier state" for FMD that can purportedly persist in livestock and wild ruminants for years.[110] It never seems to occur to them that their tests are not detecting a disease-causing virus. Just like people, the reasons why animals get sick should be looked for in their living conditions.

Blame the Pox on Gay Men (and Animals Again)

By 2022, the corporate media was taking stories of disease contagion to hitherto unseen levels. In mid-August, the *Daily Mail* reported that a gay couple in Paris had given monkeypox to a dog that shared a bed with them.[111] This time the concept of zoonotic diseases had been flipped on its head and it was proposed that humans were now transmitting germs to animals. The "science" concerning how this had happened was reported to be based on the following social media post:

> *"I'd suggest the dog probably licked the ill human and also licked its own b*tt," said MD Lynora Saxinger, a professor in the Division of Infectious Diseases at the University of Alberta on Twitter, adding there were "high viral loads in saliva with oral lesions."*[112]

The article claimed that a PCR test had been used to confirm the dog had monkeypox. However, a review of the scientific literature revealed that the monkeypox PCR kits had no established capabilities for diagnosing an illness and thus the relevance of a positive result to the subject was unknown.[113] The *Daily Mail's* story went on to claim that, "genetic sequencing showed the strain of the disease was an identical match with the disease that had infected its owners." This was conflating the detection of certain genetic sequences (in a closely-confined shared environment) with an imagined contagious virus. The virologists have claimed that these genetic sequences are specific to a monkeypox virus. However, there is a major problem with this claim: there are no scientific publications that show the sequences come from inside a virus.

Daily Mail AUSTRALIA News

Home | U.K. | U.S. | News | World News | Sport | TV&Showbiz | Femail AU | Health | Science | Weather | Video | Travel | DailyMailTV

Monkeypox | Covid-19 | Russia-Ukraine War | Breaking News | Sydney | Melbourne | Brisbane | New Zealand | Wires Login

Italian greyhound belonging to gay couple in Paris catches monkeypox after sharing bed with its infected owners, scientists reveal

- The Parisian couple developed sores a week after having sex with other men
- Their Italian greyhound also developed ulcerations and pustules on the stomach
- Genetic sequencing showed the strain of the disease was an identical match
- Doctor suggested the dog may have contracted the disease by licking lesions

By TOM BROWN FOR MAILONLINE
PUBLISHED: 01:57 AEST, 15 August 2022 | UPDATED: 02:01 AEST, 15 August 2022

Site Web Enter your search Search

Follow Daily Mail | Subscribe Daily Mail | Follow @DailyMail | Follow Daily Mail | Follow @dailymailuk | Follow Daily Mail

Poll

On average, how often do you shop online?

Another example of the Daily Mail *sensationalizing the 'contagion' headlines, this time on the 15th of August, 2022, with 'monkeypox'. Once again the word 'scientists' was added to make it appear conclusive. However, there were signs the public were not as captivated by such stories. The* Mail's *"Chinese woman eating a whole bat" story garnered more than 350,000 shares over a few days in 2020. By contrast, the monkeypox story had only 3,500 shares over a comparable period.*

Unlike the *New York Post* which used a computer-generated image for their story about the recent "mysterious pneumonia" in Argentina,[114] the *Daily Mail* included a real electron microscope image purporting to show monkeypox viruses. However, as described in the caption, it was simply a sample of human skin showing tiny vesicles. The findings could of course be *associated* with a disease condition — for example, the vesicles may result from the body's attempts to get rid of unwanted substances. If the claim was being made that these particles are viruses, then further experiments would need to be carried out to show that they are infectious and able to cause disease in another person or animal through simple contact. No such experiments can be found in the scientific literature and yet the medical establishment, assisted by its unquestioning and paid for play media acolytes, promulgate these narratives as though they are scientific facts.

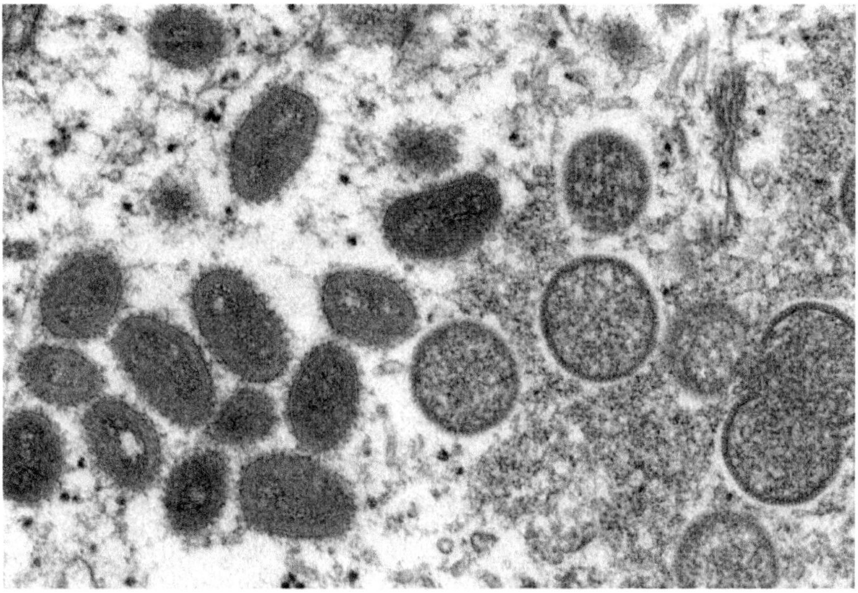

The Daily Mail *featured this electron microscopy image in their 15th of August, 2022 monkeypox story involving two gay men and a dog. The CDC reported that it, "depicted monkeypox virus particles, obtained from a clinical sample associated with the 2003 prairie dog outbreak. It was a thin section image from of a human skin sample. On the left were mature, oval-shaped virus particles, and on the right were the crescents, and spherical particles of immature virions." However, there was no explanation as to how it was established that these are infectious particles that cause disease.* Source: CDC, Public Health Image Library, ID#: 22664.

Suggest the Disease came from a Lab (and Animals Again)

During the COVID-19 era, one of the worst-kept "secrets" was the theory that a virus had come from a laboratory, whether intentionally released or by accident. The notion captured a great deal of attention as it invoked frightening ideas about "engineered pathogens" and "bioweapons," similar to some of the themes in the film *Outbreak*. However, the same scrutiny regarding biological realities and scientific evidence needs to be applied in the examination of these stories as well.

There was also a widespread belief that information regarding virus laboratories was being heavily suppressed by various governments and Big Tech. However, the "lab leak" story was already in place in early 2020 and featured in multiple mainstream media platforms over the entire alleged pandemic. For example, *The Sun* published a story on the 19th of April, 2020, titled, "COVID CRISIS - Shocking photos inside Wuhan lab show broken seal on unit storing 1,500 virus strains including bat coronavirus."[115] The story featured photographs said to come from the Wuhan Institute of Virology and it painted the following picture:

> *The startling images from the city where the virus broke out were published by the state-owned China Daily on Twitter last month before being swiftly deleted...The picture of the fridge-freezer shows a flimsy loose seal on the door, as a lab worker pulls out a chilled box containing deadly samples while wearing gloves and a mask. It was revealed earlier this month minister* [sic] *fear the deadly pandemic could have started after a leak from a lab.*

However, the story of how these pictures surfaced was very suspicious in itself. The same pictures had originally been publicly released via *China Daily's* Twitter account on the 29th of May, 2018 before news reports stated they "re-emerged" in early 2020.[116] One may only speculate why a news outlet controlled by the communist Chinese government would release the pictures not once but twice, and then allegedly take measures to "cover up" their actions?

There was a short period where these stories were "suppressed" but in mid-2021 platforms such as Facebook changed their official policies to allow the Wuhan Institute of Virology "gain of function" story and similar material to be posted once again. Around the same time, the United States Senate was openly talking about these matters in press conferences[117] and

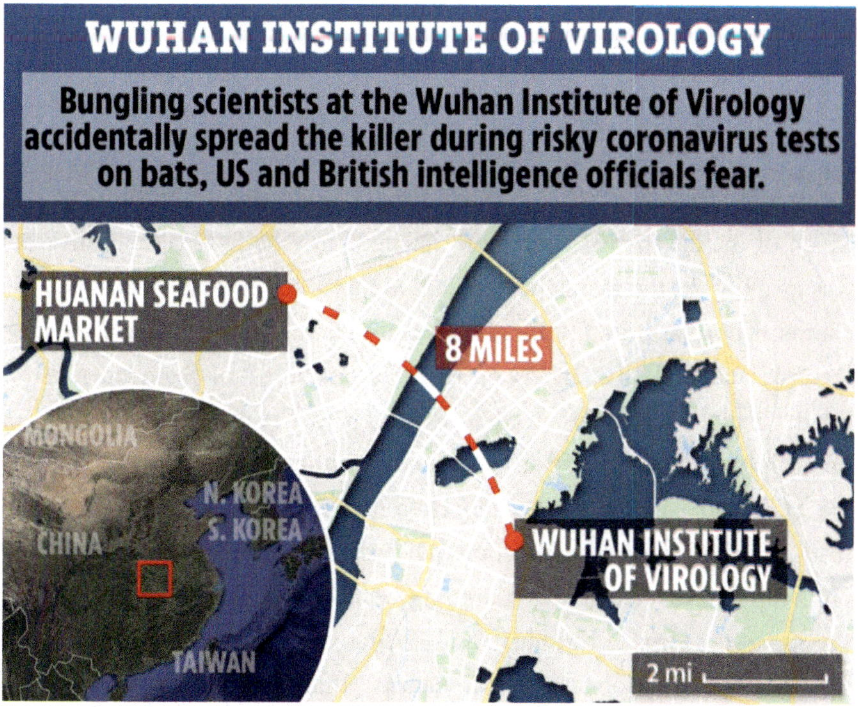

An image that appeared in The Sun's *"COVID CRISIS" story on the 19th of April, 2020. It is presented as if a "killer" [virus] exists, has come from experiments on bats, and leaked from the laboratory. However, the word 'fear' at the end of the sentence relegates the entire story to pure conjecture. It is all without a crumb of scientific evidence.*

that should have raised suspicions about the "cover up" allegations, even in the less skeptical.

By mid-2022, the 'lab leak' hypothesis was being heavily promoted once again. On the 18th of June, 2022, *The Mail* reported that the WHO's Director-general Tedros Adhanom had, "recently confided to a senior European politician that the most likely explanation was a catastrophic accident at a laboratory in Wuhan, where infections first spread during late 2019."[118] It was suggested that his change in position had come about due to the, "absence of any compelling evidence of 'zoonotic' spread," never mind that there had been no demonstration of the spread of anything, full stop. The origin narrative had come full circle, from labs to wet markets to bat caves and back to labs again — as long as all roads led to the novel "coronavirus" on went the headlines with relentless fear mongering.

Much of the alternative media also latched onto the lab leak narrative but was as guilty as the mainstream media in parroting unestablished scientific claims. The platform for the Children's Health Defense, *The Defender*, featured an article by Dr Joseph Mercola on the 8th of September, 2022, titled, "Fauci's Team Involved in Research to Create Deadly Version of Spanish Flu Virus."[119] The article opened with the claim that, "scientists in the U.S. and Canada, with support from Dr. Anthony Fauci's National Institute of Allergy and Infectious Diseases, resurrected the Spanish flu virus through reverse genetics, arguing we need to make a more dangerous version of the virus to be able to make better vaccines for it — even though the Spanish flu no longer exists in nature." It all sounded like an alarming prospect, except for the fact that nobody has ever seen a specimen of the Spanish flu "virus". As detailed in *Virus Mania*:

> *In 1997, a paper by Jeffery Taubenberger's research team appeared in* Science, *claiming to have isolated an influenza virus (H1N1) from a victim of the 1918 pandemic...The genetic analysis of pulmonary tissue form the single soldier was based on the assumption that certain genetic sequences (RNA sequences) are characteristic of all flu viruses. That is, it is theorized that there are certain proteins in flu virus shells, the RNA sequences of which were ultimately claimed to have been discovered using PCR.*[120]

In other words, they never found an actual virus in the long-dead soldier's lungs. They simply found genetic sequences that were assumed to come from the postulated virus. So when Dr Mercola claimed that a Spanish flu virus had been "resurrected" he was simply referring to test tube experiments that had introduced genetic sequences said to come from the imagined virus.

Dr Mercola's next concern that the scientists had suggested making a more dangerous version of the "virus" is similarly groundless. Instead of driving fear into his readers perhaps he could have explained the claim that, "their reverse-engineered Spanish flu virus — even at the highest doses tested — was not lethal enough to kill the macaque species selected for the experiment." The experiment in question involved large-volumes of biological soup (said to contain their "engineered virus") being poured directly into the lungs of small monkeys. As would be physiologically expected, this invasive and unnatural experimental procedure caused an inflammatory response in the lungs of some of the monkeys. It was subsequently concluded that this non-specific reaction represented evidence of an "infection". However, despite the physical assaults none of the monkeys showed any significant signs of influenza or became particularly unwell. So an inevitable question must be asked: why the production of sensationalized headlines that invoke fear in the audience?

The nonsense of this experiment titled, "Pandemic 1918 Influenza Virus Does Not Cause Lethal Infection in Rhesus or Cynomolgus Macaques,"[121] can be summarized as follows:

1. There was no evidence provided of an actual virus in the biological soup administered to the monkeys.
2. It was an unnatural exposure route (i.e. pouring the liquid directly into their lungs is something that does not happen in nature).
3. The monkeys did not manifest the usual symptoms and signs of influenza.
4. There were non-specific inflammatory reactions in the lungs (i.e. the same reaction could have been caused by pouring any foreign liquid into their lungs).

5. No control experiment was performed where the same volume of biological fluid, without the alleged virus, was poured into other comparable monkeys.

The last point alone means that the experiment was not following the scientific method. So, even if this silly procedure *had* caused the monkeys to become unwell with an influenza-like illness, it would be scientifically meaningless and would have provided no evidence of an influenza "virus" at work. This is typical of all the animal experiments said to provide evidence of viruses. Unfortunately, the cultivated current belief develops further fear-laden hyperbole that such things are being "engineered" in laboratories. The fact is there is no evidence for the 'thing' to start with.

This also touches on the wider issue of senseless animal experiments that do not advance scientific knowledge or well-being for any life on earth. It is unfathomable to the authors how scientists manage to gain funding and ethics approval for experiments that are cruel in nature and fail to follow the scientific method. As pointed out in a 2014 *British Medical Journal* analysis concerning the abysmal state of affairs:

> *When we searched for systematic evidence to support claims about the clinical benefits of animal research we identified only 25 systematic reviews of animal experiments, and these raised serious doubts about the design, quality, and relevance of the included studies…if poorly conducted studies produce unreliable findings, any suffering endured by animals loses its moral justification because their use cannot possibly contribute towards clinical benefit.*[122]

The scale of animal experimentation is probably greater than most people think. For example, it was estimated that by 2005, over 115 million animals were being used annually in laboratory research.[123] In the authors assessment, the use of almost all of these animals contributes nothing of value towards human health. This scourge exacted upon animals is an indicting blight upon humanity.

The Washington Post Connects no Dots

On the 19th of September, 2022, in their "Ask a Doctor" series, *The Washington Post* published an article, "Why are so many viruses popping up again?"[124] The author Jay Varma, a professor of population health sciences at Weill Cornell Medicine, gave his five reasons for why, "the microbes appear to be winning now." His first claim was that, "humans are encroaching into animal environments, such as forests and jungles, at a greater frequency," and used COVID-19/the "coronavirus" as his example of a disease that most likely came from bats. We dealt with the silliness of this nonsensical claim at the start of this chapter. He also referred to a 2021 computer modeling study that was funded by the French National Research Agency (ANR).[125] The ANR happens to be the national operator of the 'France 2030' program, which is in alignment with the World Economic Forum's 'Agenda 2030'.[126] So perhaps there were no surprises that their modeling study supported limitations on agriculture by alleging an unscientific claim that such practices lead to new disease outbreaks in humans.

Varma's second reason was that "humans are growing, trading and consuming animals in greater numbers." This is not a cause of human disease and is in complete contradiction to the historical data. In countries such as the United States, the United Kingdom, New Zealand and many others, farming has been in operation for centuries with no evidence that this has harmed humans in the ways claimed. Varma expects us to believe that if poorer countries now emulate these first world practices, it will cause health problems for the entire world.

The third reason given by Varma was that, "humans are concentrating in cities more than ever before," and he claimed that this facilitated person-to-person spread of disease. At this point we would request that he shows us any scientific publication that demonstrates such transmission of disease. This completely missing evidence is something that will be explored in the next chapter.

Varma's fourth reason appeared to be a further grasp at straws when he stated that, "humans are moving more." No data was provided as to how this made people more unwell and triggered pandemics. Once again it is a theme of various globalist organizations that promote restrictions on freedom of movement, both in domestic and international travel. In November 2019, an Imperial College London partner organization 'UK FIRES' published a report titled, "Absolute Zero - Delivering the UK's climate change commitment with incremental changes to today's technologies."[127] Not only did they require beef and lamb to be "phased out" by 2050 (related to Varma's second reason,) but they also stated that, "the [aviation] industry faces a rapid contraction." This remarkable prediction was made just before the dawn of the COVID-19 era when airline flights were massively curtailed through government policies. These policies were sold to the public through more ludicrous modeling from Professor Neil Ferguson and Imperial College London with their recommendations to enforce social distancing and lockdown entire nations.[128] (Ferguson did not appear to fear the "deadly coronavirus" himself. He was caught *in flagrante delicto*[129] visiting the house of his mistress on several occasions in March and April of 2020 while hypocritically promulgating the British government's 'stay-at-home' message in public.[130])

Back to Varma's fifth reason that was, "climate change has supercharged all of these factors," followed by his advice that, "you can also contact elected officials and ask them to support measures that strengthen public health and mitigate climate change." In essence, after two and a half years of COVID-19 power grabs and public health tyranny, his article was an advertisement to lend more support to these political responses. He also introduced the equally dubious notion that 'climate change', whatever he was meaning that to be, was causing alleged disease outbreaks in humans.

Fear-inducing "Viruses" Like Ebola...that Never Arrive

The mass media has a habit of making sure people are very aware of diseases that the average person has no chance of ever experiencing. One of the most-feared is so-called viral hemorrhagic fever, the most famous of which is Ebola, also known as Ebola virus disease. It is alleged to be one of the most deadly and infectious viruses ever known. Like many other such "viral" diseases, Ebola was unknown to mankind until it supposedly jumped out of the jungle and started killing people in Africa in 1976. However, a look at the Ebola entry on *Wikipedia* makes interesting reading:

> ***It is believed*** *that between people, Ebola disease spreads only by direct contact with the blood or other body fluids of a person who has developed symptoms of the disease...Although* ***it is not entirely clear*** *how Ebola initially spreads from animals to humans, the spread* ***is believed*** *to involve direct contact with an infected wild animal or fruit bat...Animals* ***may*** *become infected when they eat fruit partially eaten by bats carrying the virus. Fruit production, animal behavior and other factors* ***may*** *trigger outbreaks among animal populations...The natural reservoir for Ebola has* ***yet to be confirmed****; however, bats* ***are considered*** *to be the most likely candidate. EBOV* [Ebola virus] ***is thought*** *to infect humans through contact with mucous membranes or skin breaks.*[131] [authors' emphasis]

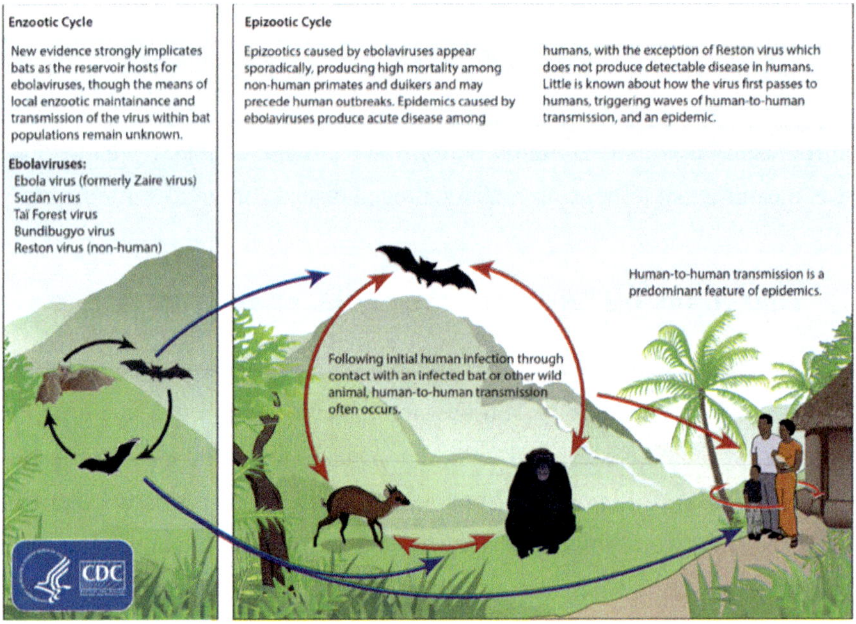

The CDC produced this illustration for the public, purportedly showing how the "Ebola virus" jumps out of the jungle and into the human population. However, this remains pure speculation and to this day no disease has been shown to transmit and no virus has been isolated from an animal or a human. Source: CDC, EbolaCycle.png.

There appears an awful lot of speculation rather than scientific evidence that a transmissible germ is at work. Furthermore, the clinical diagnosis of Ebola virus disease (EVD) raises more than a few problems given the non-specific nature of the symptoms:

> *Early symptoms of EVD may be similar to those of other diseases common in Africa, including malaria and dengue fever...The complete differential diagnosis is extensive and requires consideration of many other infectious diseases such as typhoid fever, shigellosis, rickettsial diseases, cholera, sepsis, borreliosis, EHEC* [Enterohemorrhagic Escherichia

> coli], *enteritis, leptospirosis, scrub typhus, plague, Q fever, candidiasis, histoplasmosis, trypanosomiasis, visceral leishmaniasis, measles, and viral hepatitis among others. Non-infectious diseases that may result in symptoms similar to those of EVD include acute promyelocytic leukemia, hemolytic uremic syndrome, snake envenomation, clotting factor deficiencies/platelet disorders, thrombotic thrombocytopenia purpura, hereditary haemorrhagic telangiectasia, Kawasaki disease, and warfarin poisoning.*[132]

So this introduces the problem of how Ebola is diagnosed and differentiated from all these other conditions. The CDC state that the three main methods are virus isolation, antibody tests, and the PCR.[133] In this context it should be pointed out that the word 'isolation' does not mean what most people understand it to mean. Instead, the "isolation of ebola" describes a virological process where a crude human sample is taken and then: (a) mixed with monkey kidney cells to see if the cells react, (b) injected into the brains and abdomens of baby mice to see if it kills them, or (c) injected into the abdomens of young guinea pigs to see if it kills them.[134] Most people would agree that the results of the above experiments would not mean that you had "isolated" anything, in fact, in each case you would have more things than you started with. Similarly, the antibody tests derived from these kind of experiments cannot be used to prove something that was never found in the first place. In any case, nothing has been established through scientifically controlled methods. (The experiments cited above mention "control cultures" only in the monkey kidney experiments but provided no details of their nature. Furthermore, there was no independent variable that could be identified as their samples contained crude mixtures, not "isolated viruses".)

These days the main diagnostic tool for alleged ebola is the PCR (for detecting small genetic sequences) and more recently rapid antigen tests (for detecting proteins). The problem with both of these is the same as any "viral" diseases: if the claimed virus has never been isolated how were the genetic and protein tests matched to it? It is a product of the virologists circular reasoning where detecting these small genetic or protein fragments means there is a virus…because the virus is said to contain these bits. The stunning reality is that the physical isolation of any virus has never taken place to enable a determination of their very existence to be made.

However, whether the virologists want to claim they have "isolated" something or have produced tests that purport to detect this something, there remains a major problem with their hypothesis: why does Ebola not spread? The outbreaks are essentially limited to clusters in destitute African countries but the alleged highly infectious virus never appears in first world countries. There are cases like that of Craig Spencer, a New York doctor who became unwell a week after returning from Guinea where he was working with Doctors Without Borders in 2014.[135] At that time, the *New York Times* documented his steps over a six day period:

> *He departed Guinea on a flight to Brussels…He departed Brussels and arrived in New York City. He was screened at Kennedy International Airport and reported no symptoms…he ate at the Meatball Shop…he walked on the High Line and stopped at Blue Bottle Coffee…he got off the High Line at 34th Street and rode the 1 Train to the 145th Street Station…he went on a three-mile run along Riverside Drive and Westside Highway…he went to the Community Supported Agriculture farm share at Corbin Hill Farm…he rode the A and the L trains to bowl with two friends at the Gutter in Williamsburg…He left the bowling alley at about 8:30 p.m., returning to Manhattan in an Uber taxi…He first reported a low-grade fever of 100.3 at 10:15 a.m. Medical workers, wearing full protective gear, picked him up from his home in*

> *Harlem…Shortly after 1 p.m., he arrived at Bellevue Hospital Center.*[136]

Despite Spencer's travels about the city over several days, not one other person in New York came down with Ebola. The explanation offered for this is that, "people infected with Ebola cannot spread the disease until they begin to display symptoms, and it cannot be spread through the air. As people become sicker, the viral load in the body builds, and they become increasingly contagious."[137] This convenient story apparently involved remarkably specific knowledge of the disease given all the aforementioned speculations regarding Ebola.

Wikipedia has a "List of Ebola outbreaks" page where all of the recorded incidents of Ebola are in poor African countries apart from a tiny minority. Of these, as of September 2022, there were only two deaths amongst people who were based outside of Africa at the time they were said to be "infected," and both were in Russia.[138] The first was in 1996 in the Sergiev Posad laboratory as described by the *Washington Post* in a 2014 article:

> *She was an ordinary lab technician with an uncommonly dangerous assignment: drawing blood from Ebola-infected animals in a secret military laboratory. When she cut herself at work one day, she decided to keep quiet, fearing she'd be in trouble. Then the illness struck. "By the time she turned to a doctor for help, it was too late," one of her overseers, a former bioweapons scientist, said of the accident years afterward. The woman died quickly and was buried, according to one account, in a "sack filled with calcium hypochlorite," or powdered bleach.*[139]

The second death was also said to have occurred in a laboratory accident in 2004 as reported at the time in *Science*:

> *A Russian scientist working on an Ebola vaccine died last week following a lab accident. On 5 May, Antonina Presnyakova, 46, pricked her hand with a syringe after drawing blood from infected guinea pigs in an ultrasecure biosafety level 4 (BSL-4) facility at the Vektor Research Institute of Molecular Biology, a former bioweapons lab near Novosibirsk, Russia. She was hospitalized immediately, says a lab official, developed symptoms 1 week later, and died on 19 May.*[140]

Apart from these second-hand reports, there is no other evidence that has been made available for us to analyze exactly what happened to these two women. Neither of the stories provided any adequate scientific information and essentially remained at the level of hearsay.

More details were made available in the (nonfatal) case of Geoffrey Platt, a British laboratory technician said to have, "contracted Ebola in an accidental needlestick injury," at the Porton Down campus in 1976.[141] The authors have previously refuted the claims that he was infected with anything and exposed the uncontrolled experiments that were presented as evidence for a "virus" at work.[142]

The most straightforward conclusion for the reason why the "highly infectious" Ebola disease has never spread around the world is because there is nothing to spread. Based on current statistics, an individual in a developed country is more likely to be struck by lightning twice than killed by Ebola disease, whatever that may be. There are plenty of reasons why people get sick in destitute areas from the multiple environmental toxicities and stressors they are exposed to. Unfortunately, the toxicologists and nutritionists are not given a seat at the table when the "virus hunters" have taken center stage and convinced others into thinking that their pet deadly germ is the only cause of such diseases.

Chapter 3 - The History of Misplaced Beliefs

"It was even known by 1945 that DDT is stored in the body fat of mammals and appears in the milk. With this foreknowledge the series of catastrophic events that followed the most intensive campaign of mass poisoning in known human history, should not have surprised the experts. Yet, far from admitting a causal relationship [for polio and other diseases] so obvious that in any other field of biology it would be instantly accepted, virtually the entire apparatus of communication, lay and scientific alike, has been devoted to denying, concealing, suppressing, distorting and attempts to convert into its opposite, the overwhelming evidence."

—Morton S. Biskind M.D., 1953.[143]

What Human-to-Human Transmission?

It is possible that medical authors such as Professor Jay Varma (chapter 2: *"The Washington Post Connects no Dots"*) are naive to the fact that the claimed transmission of *disease* via microbes has never been established in appropriately designed and controlled scientific studies. The authors can attest that during their training as doctors, the concept of such disease transmission was presented as dogma rather than demonstrated to be based in experimental evidence.

Perhaps the most spectacular failure to show transmission of a disease commonly thought to be highly contagious were the 1918 Spanish Flu experiments. These took place at Gallops Island, Boston and were conducted by the Public Health Service and the U.S. Navy under the supervision of Dr Milton Rosenau.[144] As described by Rosenau in his summary report that was published in the *The Journal of the American Medical Association* in 1919:

> *The volunteers were all of the most susceptible age, mostly between 18 and 25, only a few of them around 30 years old; and all were in good physical condition. None of these volunteers, 100 all told in number, had "influenza;" that is, from the most careful histories that we could elicit, they gave no account of a febrile attack of any kind during the winter, except a few who were purposely selected, as having shown a typical attack of influenza, in order to test questions of immunity, and for the purpose of control.*[145]

The clinical experiments that were performed by Rosenau's team can be summarized as follows:

1. Material was taken from the lungs of people said to be victims of the Spanish Flu and made into a liquid. This was then sprayed in large volumes into the eyes, nose, throat and lungs of the volunteers.
2. Mucous secretions were obtained from the nose, throat, and lungs of diseased individuals and around 1ml of this was placed directly into the nostrils and throats of the volunteers.
3. Part 2 was repeated, this time with 6ml, enough that some of the mucous secretions were swallowed by the volunteers.
4. Material was transferred directly from nose to nose and throat to throat with swabs.
5. Blood was taken from diseased individuals and 10ml of this was injected into some of the volunteers.
6. Mucous was obtained from sick individuals, passed through bacterial filters and then 3.5ml of the filtered fluid was injected under the skin of the volunteers.
7. Volunteers shook hands with patients in Spanish Flu wards, sat close to them for prolonged periods, breathed in their exhalations, and had their faces coughed on. They each repeated this same interaction with ten hospitalized patients in total.

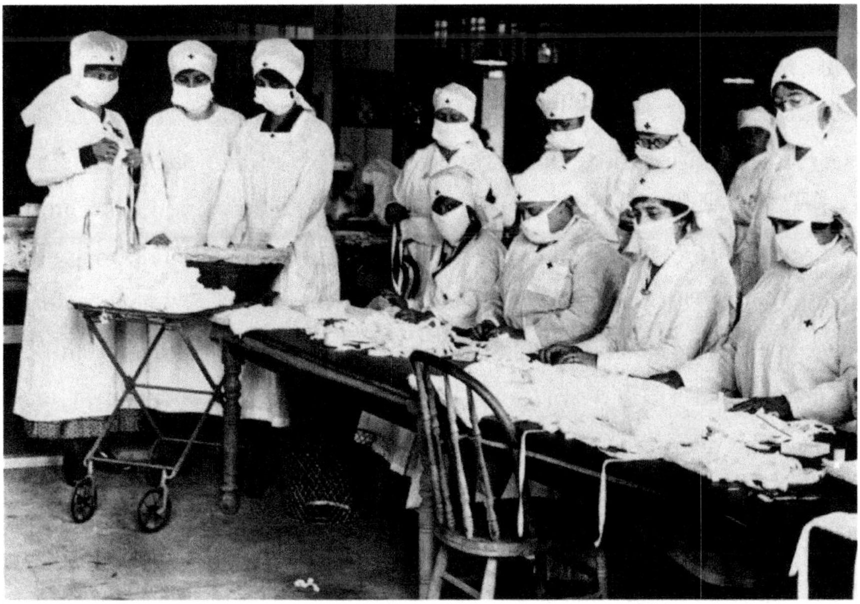

Women working for the Red Cross make face masks during the Spanish flu pandemic in 1918. No disease could be shown to pass between human without masks on so what was the point? Source: Bettmann Archive/Getty Images.

And what was the result of these incredible experiments? Not one volunteer developed influenza or became ill in any way. To this day the concept of human-to-human transmission of influenza remains a hypothesis, or more accurately a refuted hypothesis given the repeated experimental failures.[146, 147] In what can only be described as a scientific scandal, the medical establishment remains remarkably silent and complacent on these pivotal experiments. For example, the 500-page *Textbook of Influenza* published in 2013 mentions "transmission" of the condition several hundred times and yet provides no evidence of a clinical study to support this claim.[148] Even more conspicuous is the fact that Rosenau's and other similar human studies were completely omitted from the textbook - an omission that should have been of great interest to the editors of a textbook dedicated to influenza. Equally conspicuous are the public records of Dr Rosenau. An obituary that appeared in the *American Journal of Public Health* in May 1946 made no mention of his crucial research into influenza.[149] Similarly, Rosenau's *Wikipedia* page makes no mention of his work with the U.S. Navy and what are some of the most important clinical experiments involving alleged contagion ever performed.[150] The widely-held belief that influenza is a transmissible illness via a microbe can simply not be substantiated in any of the scientific publications. In 1919 it was evident that Rosenau was shocked at the results of his own experiments but unfortunately the medical community chose to ignore his profound conclusion:

> *As a matter of fact, we entered the outbreak with a notion that we knew the cause of the disease, and were quite sure we knew how it was transmitted from person to person. Perhaps, if we have learned anything, it is that we are not quite sure what we know about the disease.*— Dr Milton J. Rosenau[151]

But Can't You Catch a Cold?

We have been raised in a world where most of the medical industry and the public take it for granted that "viral" illnesses are contagious. There is a complacency that further investigations into direct evidence that viruses cause disease or even exist appear unnecessary. People are getting sick with similar clinical illnesses and seem to be passing it onto those around them, so what more is there to know? Take the common cold, for example. As publications such as the *New York Times* stated in 2003:

> *Colds, of course, are caused by any of several hundred different strains of virus. People get more colds in the winter at least in part because nasty weather drives them indoors to*

make extremely close contact with one another's infectious mucus.[152]

These days, "catching a cold" is commonly understood to mean that a "viral infectious disease" has taken hold of someone's throat and upper airways, with the responsible invader being one of "well over 200 viral strains".[153] But the original meaning of the word 'cold' was well established before germ theory took hold in the late 1800s.[*154]

It did not refer to the transmission of illness between humans.

The word dates back to the 1530s meaning, "indisposition involving catarrhal inflammation of the mucous membranes of the nose or throat."[155] Originally, the term simply referred to the signs and symptoms observed when a person was exposed to cold environmental conditions. 'Catching' derived from, "you'll catch your death [of cold]" which again simply meant that you could become sick and potentially die if you went out and became wet and cold. No virus required.

However, by the 1950s, the common cold had morphed into what was believed to be a contagious viral illness, with "rhinoviruses" being frequently implemented as the culprit. There was even a Common Cold Unit (CCU) that operated near Salisbury in the United Kingdom from 1946-1990 to, "study methods of cultivating and transmitting colds in human volunteers".[156] The history of the facility was described by author Beth Greenhough in 2008:

The hospital was converted into 12 flats, each housing 2 volunteers, and other spaces for recreation rooms, administrative, research and catering facilities. The first volunteers arrived on 17th July 1946, beginning a research effort that lasted over 44 years and involved (among other

> *things) around 20 000 volunteers, a wide range of scientists working on respiratory viruses, medical and catering staff, tissue culture technologies and selection of carefully cultivated pedigree cold viruses.*[157]

Most volunteers regarded their time at the CCU as akin to being at a holiday camp with free food and accommodation, as well as some bonus pocket money. As reported by the *BBC* in 2019 in a headline titled, "Why thousands went on holiday to the Common Cold Unit," the typical 10-day stay was welcomed by housewives, among others, who often went there for a rest.[158] The CCU was funded by British tax payers through the Medical Research Council, a division administered by the Government of the United Kingdom.[159]

Many of the CCU's experiments were of dubious scientific merit, and they often "infected" subjects with crudely mixed cultures placed directly into the nasopharynx (upper part of the throat). With such experiments, the CCU scientists did not once demonstrate that it was viruses that were infecting and causing disease in the study participants. That was because they could not find actual viral particles in the fluids of any of the volunteers. Additionally, they often needed to employ other factors to increase the chances of causing a cold:

> *...only one in three volunteers, on average, usually developed a cold, despite, over the lifetime of the unit, some rather extreme experiments in making humans more susceptible. These included chilling volunteers, deserting them on an island for three months to decrease their immunity, and shutting them in wardrobes while spraying them with fake sneezes.*[160]

Some of the incidental claims by the CCU's researchers were equally dubious. Clinical administrator Dr. John Wallace wrote about the nonsensical circular benefits of participating in the experiments in a letter to volunteers:

> *Our virologists are expert at giving volunteers a dose of the virus which produces at worse a slight illness, but at the same time gives protection against a natural infection by that particular virus.*[161]

Virologist David Tyrrell led a team at the CCU and made the first description of what was said to be a human coronavirus in 1965 in an article published in the B*ritish Medical Journal.*[162] At the time, the sample was known as 'B814' and was obtained from a "boy with a typical common cold in 1960". But how did they know that viruses were present in their mixture? Citing only indirect findings and without evidence of an independent variable (the claimed "virus" particles), they reported that:

> *These experiments indicate that the infectivity of B814 can pass a bacteria-tight filter, is inactivated by ether, and can induce colds in volunteers given sufficient antibiotics to cure a fully developed infection with the Eaton agent (M pneumoniae). These results showed that B814 is a virus, not a mycoplasma, and that it is not an adenovirus, enterovirus, or rhinovirus because it is ether-labile.*[163]

Subsequently, electron micrograph images of the sample, already asserted to contain viruses, were taken by Scottish virologist June Almeida and published in 1966.[164] The virus hunters wrote in *Nature* magazine in 1968 that the:

> *Particles are more or less rounded in profile... there is also a characteristic 'fringe' of projections...recalling the solar corona... which they suggest should be called the coronaviruses.*[165]

The story was sold to the world that these "coronaviruses" caused the common cold, but examining the methodology they were employing reveals that they were making a considerable number of assumptions.

By the 1960s, virologists had generally abandoned trying to directly isolate viruses from humans and had turned to the new trend of virus cultures to undertake 'isolation'. In the introduction of a 1962 paper, "Virus Isolations From Common Colds Occurring In A Residential School," the authors state that,"the viruses can be cultivated in rolled tissue cultures of human embryo-kidney cells maintained at 33°C. They produce a focal cytopathic effect."[166]

This is clearly a deceptive use of the word "isolation" because cytopathic effects (CPEs) refer to the microscopic appearances of the cells breaking down. The same effects can be observed in test tubes simply by stressing the cells when transferring them into new mediums and with the addition of toxic compounds such as antibiotics. The presence of a virus was never directly established, and there was certainly no physical isolation taking place. The researchers did not appear to be concerned that even with their loose definition of the word "isolation" they only saw CPEs in 18 out of 59, or 30%, of colds, although they said this could be due to the culture cells used.[167] They had some success stressing human embryo-kidney cells and causing CPEs, but it is hard to imagine what this cell type or this process has to do with common colds.

It was also admitted that, "we were unable to collect washings from boys without colds." As is so often evident in virology, the paper relinquished a disciplined scientific method because a suitable control group was not being used for comparison. They conceded that, "as we had no specimens from boys without colds there was no epidemiological evidence that the viruses isolated were actually causing the illnesses observed" and then went on to claim that, "such evidence has been obtained by others."

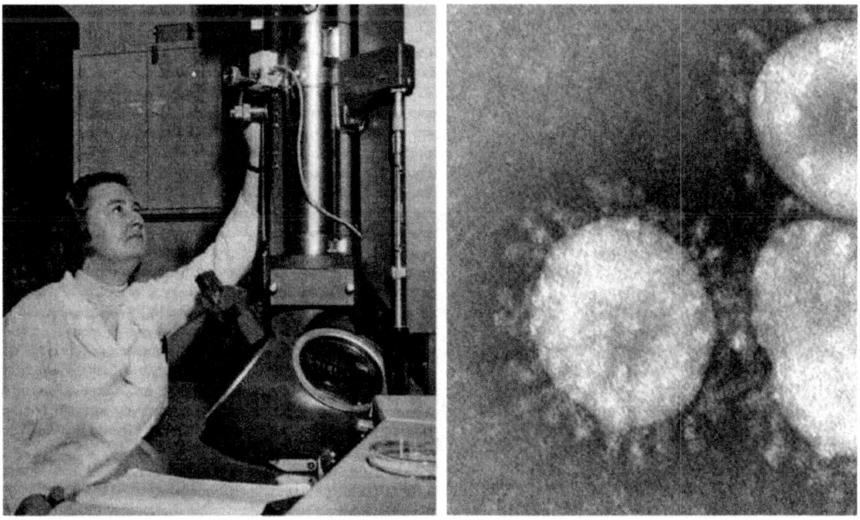

In the 1960s, electron microscopist June Almeida (left) was given cell culture mixtures from the Common Cold Unit's director David Tyrrell. She was asked to find the "viruses" and they declared that these apparent vesicles (right) were "coronaviruses". There were no control experiments in place and there was no demonstration that the particles were infectious or caused disease in humans. Source: *Wikipedia.*

However, "such evidence" was not apparent in the cited papers either, as none of them demonstrated that the particles they called viruses were either infectious or the cause of disease. Moreover, the lack of valid controls meant much of their work could not be considered scientific. At best, they were making some amusing observations about snot!

Perhaps because of the complete failure to find actual viral particles that could transmit between humans and cause the common cold, the CCU inevitably found other research areas more attractive though arguably, equally unfruitful. By the 1960s, the CCU became increasingly involved in the new trend of "culturing" viruses in the laboratory and contributed to the ever-growing list of viruses purported to cause the common cold.[168] It was one of the several teams that enthusiastically announced that they were discovering various rhino-, adeno-, parainfluenza-, and of course corona- "viruses".[169] Now we are told that over 200 strains of viruses are apparently implicated in the common cold.[170] All that these researchers showed was that by mixing a patient sample with abnormal cells and then utilizing different test tube techniques to stress them, various nano-particles could be seen in the breaking-down biological soup.

From these uncontrolled experiments, whole families of "viruses" were created, contributing to the generally accepted notions in medicine that these *in vitro* (test tube) particles were: (a) present in living humans, and (b) the cause of the common cold. But, clearly, neither of these fundamental observations was proven by the CCU, nor have they been proven since. And yet most people believe the common cold is definitely a viral condition: they would probably even say it is a scientific "fact" or "principle".

Amongst its other activities, the CCU was also trying to find a vaccine for colds. However, after 44 years as director of the CCU, David Tyrrell conceded that, "they have studied immunity to rhinovirus and coronavirus colds down to the molecular level, though this has not yet resulted in the production of a vaccine."[171] For virus hunters, their fixated mindset does not allow for the possibility that the common cold may not be caused by a virus. This is a tragic mindset that hinders our understanding about the real causes of illness and our best ways to health.

Despite remaining optimistic about the future of "antiviral" medications, when the unit closed down in 1990, Tyrrell went on to admit that, "studies of synthetic antivirals in volunteers for decades [had] yielded meager results."[172] Without a touch of irony, one of the obituaries for Dr. Tyrrell stated that, "though he never found a cure, he discovered almost everything we know about cold viruses."[173] However, it remains unclear what, if any, actual tangible benefits for human health came out of the 44-year existence of the CCU. One of the reasons the unit was set up was to reduce the impact the common cold has on the economy — which is estimated to run into tens of billions of dollars annually for some countries.[174] Clearly, it failed in that objective.

Indeed, "almost everything we know about cold viruses" cannot be said to have translated into any meaningful health or economic improvements for the public. Additionally, perhaps the British taxpayers would not have been happy to fund the CCU's so-called human transmission experiments at the facility had they known about the complete failure of previous transmission attempts with influenza dating back to 1918. (Daniel Roytas' book *Can You Catch A Cold?: Untold History and Human Experiments* provides a comprehensive overview of the human studies involving colds and flu as well as possible mechanisms at play if they are not contagious conditions.[175])

Blaming Nutritional Deficiencies on Germs

By the late 1800s germ theory had firmly taken hold in the world of medical science, largely through the widespread promotion of Louis Pasteur's and Robert Koch's claims. The prized goal of 'magic bullet'*[176] countermeasures was here to stay. Despite inconsistencies in their theories and failures of their "treatments" against alleged dangerous germs, their influence was immense as outlined in *Virus Mania*:

> *At the end of the 19th century, when Pasteur and Koch became celebrities despite their scams, the general public had hardly a chance to brace itself against microbe propaganda. Medical authorities, who adhered to the microbes = lethal enemies theory, and the rising pharmaceutical industry already had the reins of power and public opinion firmly in their hands...From*

> *this point on, scientists tried to squeeze virtually everything into the model "one disease—one cause (pathogen)—one miracle cure," something that prompted one failure after another.*[177]

Beriberi is serious condition that can result in disorders of the nervous system including weakness and even paralysis due to damage to the peripheral nerves. The brain can also be impaired in a similar way to the toxic effects of alcohol, in fact, beriberi is associated with alcoholism. There is also a "wet" form of beriberi which results in heart failure and swelling of the legs. The disease can manifest in infants, with the severest cases turning blue and then dying of heart failure.

Beriberi was described at least as far back as 600AD in traditional Chinese medicine scripts.[178] Chinese practitioners knew that the condition could be deadly and had recognized that certain foods were useful in its treatment. In more modern times Japanese naval physician Takaki Kanehiro was tasked with investigating beriberi in the 1880s due to the heavy toll the disease was taking on seamen during long voyages.[179] He discovered that increasing the amount of barley, meat, milk and vegetables reduced the number of cases dramatically. However, his remarkable discovery was ignored because the prevailing belief amongst the establishment doctors of the time was that it was an infectious disease.

The idea that it was caused by a microbe was given further wind in its sails through a 1894 report by Dr Max Glogner, which was translated into English and published in the *Indian Medical Gazette*. In typical fashion, it had already been asserted in advance that a rogue germ was responsible for the condition — the only real question for Glogner was deducing *which* particular germ was to blame:

When we compare this great and important resemblance between beriberi and malaria on epidemiological and therapeutic grounds, the conclusion is near that the cause of the disease may also possess similarity; that is, that beriberi is not a bacterial disease but a protozoic disease. Already numerous inquirers during the last ten years have occupied themselves with the etiology of this sickness...All, with the exception of Eijkman and Fiebig, have found micro-organisms in the blood, and some in the organs, of beriberi patients, which they are inclined to bring into etiological relation with the disease...It is not unlikely that these organisms poison the body by means of the production of an especially poisonous matter, which appears to possess an especially strong chemical affinity for the nervous system.[180]

Glogner was so convinced that a microbe was causing beriberi that he thought quinine, a chemical being used in the treatment of malaria, was also of great benefit to his patients.*[181] However, all of these medical men were completely misguided in their 'germ warfare' pursuits and should have paid attention to the vitally important dietary findings of Takaki and the Chinese health practitioners centuries earlier.

In the early 1900s it was "discovered" that beriberi was a deficiency syndrome, specifically of thiamine, also known as vitamin B_1. In other words, it is something that can be readily corrected through dietary measures. How many thousands of people had suffered and died due to the neglect of failing to consider the real underlying causes of disease while being blinded by germ theory tunnel vision? As we shall see, this fallacious belief in 'one disease - one germ' continues to this day and is one of the most harmful beliefs in the medical system.*[182]

Blaming More Dietary Problems on Germs

Pellagra is a disease that has been characterized by the four "D's": diarrhea, dermatitis, dementia, and death.[183] These days it is usually only seen in the developing world and is strongly associated with poverty. Historically the disease plagued Europe including being endemic in Northern Italy in the late 1800s with over 100,000 Italians being affected by pellagra. While it was known to be associated with the consumption of diets limited to mostly maize, many of the germ theorists of the day ignored nutritional factors. In their false paradigm, they were too busy debating whether the disease was caused by microbes contaminating the crop or if it was transmitted by a parasite carried by insects.

One of the leading Italian "pellagrologists" was Louis Sambon, a germ theory enthusiast who claimed that tropical illnesses, including even sunstroke, could be explained by dangerous microbes.[184] As detailed in 2015 by medical historian Professor David Gentilcore, Sambon had already decided that pellagra was caused by a germ and it was yet again, just a question of which one it would turn out to be:

> *Maize might come into it, but only indirectly, Sambon remarked: "Probably, therefore, it is in the maize field that the peasant comes in touch with the specific agent of pellagra, and possibly through the agency of some biting fly."...If the protozoan responsible for the disease had not yet been identified, the role of the Simulium* [black fly] *in the transmission of pellagra was "almost a certainty."*[185]

Not to be outdone by Sambon, professor of pathology Guido Tizzoni claimed to have isolated a bacterium from individuals with pellagra in 1912. However, like Sambon's elusive parasite, Tizzoni's proposed bacillus (*Streptobacillus pellagrae*) was soon found to be an illusion.

Unlike many European countries, who had been battling pellagra for centuries, the United States' devastating experience with the disease was just beginning at the start of the 20th century. As outlined by Gentilcore:

> *Pellagra seemed to appear from nothing in the United States in the early 1900s, so fast indeed that it was regarded as an infectious disease. What else could explain its sudden appearance and quick spread?...If long experience with pellagra had taught the local, family doctor in Italy that maize and poor diets had to be linked in some way, the average U.S. practitioner thought of pellagra as a disease one "caught"—from family, neighbors, or ancestors.*[186]

The U.S. maize industry and vested interests were concerned that any perceived association of pellagra with maize-based diets could be bad for business and gave support to the infection hypothesis. In 1910, with hundreds of thousands of cases in the South, the State of Illinois set up a commission to study pellagra. Despite Sambon's lack of evidence for an infectious agent, the commission's report favored his claims and rejected a dietary cause.[187]

As suggested by Chris Leslie in the paper, "'Fighting an Unseen Enemy': The Infectious Paradigm in the Conquest of Pellagra," the media also played a role in promoting the myth that a deadly contagious agent was spreading, as well as the associated fallacies that were built upon this:

> *The public's fear of pellagra was inflamed by newspaper reports of the rapidly spreading disease, which suggested that eighty percent of those infected would die..."Some had destructive tendencies; they might pull out their eyebrows or try to set their houses on fire. Others feared for their safety, imagining that the neighbors planned to assassinate them"...*

> *The public's impression of the disease definitely leaned to the side of the infectious agent. The Literary Digest reported in 1913 that there was ample evidence to discard the dietary factor. The writers announced that the ancient Italian doctors were mistaken about the basis of pellagra in spoiled corn and they were sure that pellagra was an infectious disease imported from Italy along with the "hordes of immigrants who have arrived in the last 30 or 40 years."*[188]

Although many North American physicians did not believe that a microbe was responsible for pellagra, some were still relentlessly pursuing an imagined parasite. Like Glogner's claim that quinine could treat beriberi, Edward Jenner Wood preposterously claimed in his 1912 publication that the poison arsenic could be used successfully to treat patients "infected" with pellagra:

> *As the idea of the protozoal origin of pellagra has grown in favor, the use of arsenic has been more generally resorted to in the hope that it would have the effect that it was found to have in trypanosomiasis. One of the main arguments in favor of an animal parasitic origin of pellagra was that these arsenic derivatives had such a decidedly favorable effect.*[189]

Not to miss an opportunity, Charles Davenport, one of the founders of the American eugenics movement, also brought his preconceived ideology into the pellagra debate, claiming in a 1916 paper that it was a hereditary disorder.[190] Never mind that this was a year after Dr Joseph Goldberger had presented his conclusive research to the U.S. Surgeon General demonstrating that the disease was due to a nutritional deficiency and it could be easily cured by dietary improvements.[191] In the late 1930s the deficiency was deduced to be niacin, a form of vitamin B_3. By this stage it was over 200 years since the Spanish physician Gaspar Casal had first described pellagra in 1735 and noted in his writings that the origin of the disease was from a poor diet.[192] The story of pellagra is illustrative of the recurrent medical themes in far too many diseases: blaming it on germs and other ill-conceived ideologies, driving up fear and employing toxic 'therapies', all the while sustaining industry dogma and the surrounding interest groups. The end result for the population is the untold suffering, economic hardship, shortened lives and sickness created by delays in understanding the true causes of disease.

Blaming the Effects of Environmental Toxins on Germs

The orthodox medical literature has a difficult time attempting to explain polio within its germ theory framework. It is claimed that "poliovirus" is highly contagious, passing from person to person by entering the body through the mouth and then shedding in the feces.[193] However, it is also said that while the "virus" fails to do anything to the vast majority of people, in some it can cause devastating paralysis and even death. This interesting behavior is conveniently put down to the degree of "immunity" that allegedly happens to be in the person's possession at the time.[194] Apart from the virologists' usual problems of not being able to demonstrate that a virus has been physically isolated and shown to cause polio, the historical patterns of outbreaks are also more than a little suspicious.

Although there are accounts of what is believed to be polio in some ancient depictions (see also case classification issues below), prior to 1900 it was not considered a disease of any significant burden to humanity. But then for some reason the pattern completely changed:

> *Outbreaks reached pandemic proportions in Europe, North America, Australia, and New Zealand during the first half of the 20th century. By 1950, the peak age incidence of paralytic poliomyelitis in the United States had shifted from infants to*

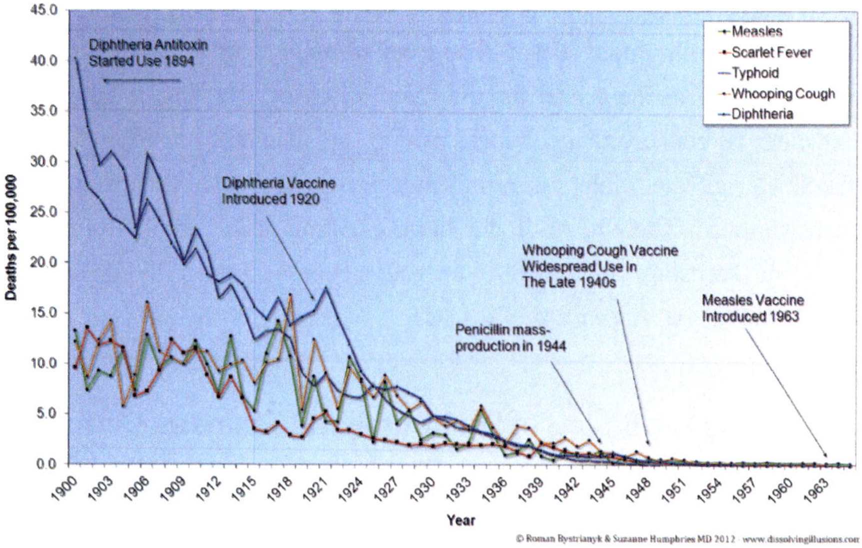

The incidence and mortality of once common childhood diseases continued to fall dramatically after 1900 in the United States. On the other hand polio epidemics were just beginning. Source: https://dissolvingillusions.com/graphs-images/

> *children aged five to nine years, when the risk of paralysis is greater; about one-third of the cases were reported in persons over 15 years of age. Accordingly, the rate of paralysis and death due to polio infection also increased during this time. In the United States, the 1952 polio epidemic became the worst outbreak in the nation's history. Of the nearly 58,000 cases reported that year, 3,145 died and 21,269 were left with mild to disabling paralysis.*[195]

This was of course in contrast to the burden of other childhood diseases which had all decreased dramatically over the 19th century and continued their retreat over the 20th century. As standards of living improved with sanitation, secure food sources and access to clean water, infant mortality plummeted and children's health was improving in multiple ways in first world countries. So why did a polio "virus" then start ravaging the population? The polio epidemic reached its peak in the U.S. in 1952 and a common misconception is that the subsequent decline was explained by the introduction of vaccines. However, this is inconsistent with the facts as Jonas Salk's inoculation was not introduced until 1955.

The actual explanation of polio does not require a germ, let alone one that has not even been shown to exist such as "poliovirus". In fact, the symptoms attributed to polio can all be induced by chemical toxins, including pesticides. And as outlined in *Virus Mania*, this had been known for a long time:

> *In 1878, Alfred Vulpian, a neurologist, had provided experimental evidence for the poisoning thesis when he discovered that dogs poisoned by lead suffered from the same symptoms as human polio victims. In 1883, the Russian Miezeyeski Popow showed that the same paralysis could be produced with arsenic. These studies should have aroused the scientific community, considering that the arsenic-based pesticide Paris green had been widely used in agriculture to fight "pests" like caterpillars since 1870...Within a short time, however, lead arsenate became the most important pesticide in the industrialized world's fruit cultivation. It was not the only toxic substance used in agricultural industries. In 1907, for example, calcium arsenate was introduced in Massachusetts and was used in cotton fields and factories. Months later, 69 children who lived downstream from three cotton factories suddenly became sick and suffered from paralysis. Meanwhile, lead arsenate was also being sprayed on the fruit trees in their gardens. But microbe hunters ignored these legitimate "cluster" factors, and instead continued searching for a "responsible" virus.*[196]

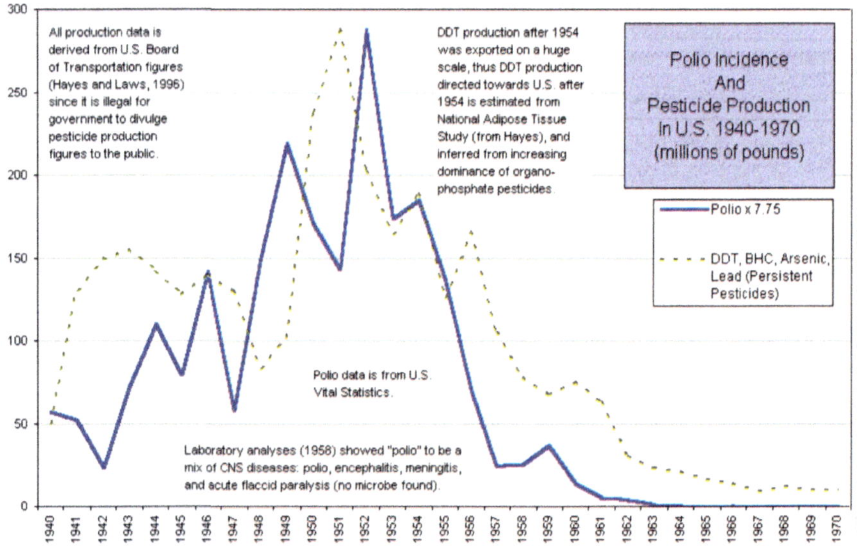

The incidence of polio in the United States was closely matched to the use of toxic pesticides. The end of the epidemic was not the result of polio vaccines as they did not come into use until 1955. Source: Jim West, harvoa.org

The polio epidemics can be traced back to the widespread use of these pesticides as well as the increasing use of DDT which peaked in many first world countries in the middle of the 20th century. In countries like the U.S., restrictions on the use of DDT began in the 1950s, before its use was almost completely banned in 1972. After that DDT was exported to third world countries, some of which then also had polio epidemics. Jim West has been one of the researchers at the forefront of investigating the relationship between environmental toxins and polio and his charts show some of the striking correlations he has unearthed. The incidence of polio was also influenced by the way it was classified, particularly after the introduction of the vaccines. This type of manipulation of case numbers to suit a narrative was dealt with in chapter 1. In this instance, cases that would have previously been called polio were reclassified to other neurological conditions such as multiple sclerosis, cerebral palsy and

Guillain–Barré syndrome. Such deception made it appear as though the vaccines had helped eradicate polio.

Polio is an example of a man-made health crisis that was swept under the carpet by blaming a (not even shown to exist) microbe and hiding what really happened to the many victims. It is telling that the *Wikipedia* page for polio makes not one mention of the extensive scientific research linking chemical toxins to the symptoms of polio and blames the whole thing on a "virus".[197] Once again the real causes for disease are ignored and the public pays a very heavy price. (A more detailed account of the polio scandal is presented in chapter 2 of *Virus Mania*, and F. William Engdahl's 2022 essay, *Toxicology vs Virology – Rockefeller Institute and the Criminal Polio Fraud.*[198])

"Treatments" that Cause the Disease?

Rabies is a rare disease, so rare that the vast majority of doctors will never see a single case of the condition in their lifetimes. From 2000 through to 2020, there were only 52 human cases in the United States, making it one of the rarest diseases known to mankind.[199] Despite this fact, the specter of rabies haunts the human imagination and a large proportion of the population believes that a single bite from an animal comes with a high risk of "catching" the disease. Probably as a result of this fear, rabies is frequently cited as both evidence for infectious disease (caused by a "virus") and the need for vaccines.

Louis Pasteur is credited with the development of the rabies vaccine in the late 19th century after his public declaration that it had been successfully trialled in dogs preceding the then, first human trial. *Wikipedia* states that Pasteur, along with compatriot, Émile Roux,

> *developed the first rabies vaccination in 1885. Nine-year-old Joseph Meister (1876–1940), who had been mauled by a*

> *rabid dog, was the first human to receive this vaccine. The treatment started with a subcutaneous injection on 6 July 1885, at 8:00pm, which was followed with 12 additional doses administered over the following 10 days.*[200]

The subsequent recovery of the young peasant Joseph was put down to Pasteur's alleged "treatment" which was a convenient explanation for what actually took place. The first issue is that rabies is a *condition* and whoever makes the diagnosis makes their decision based on a subjective selection from a collection of symptoms and signs. There is no objective test that can be performed and independently verified. Joseph had received at least a dozen bites from the dog but there was no way to know that he had or was going to develop rabies. Instead, as was reported, "upon examining the boy's wounds, Drs Vulpian and Grancher concluded that he almost surely faced death from rabies."[201] Therefore, despite Joseph being *without symptoms*, it had already been decided that any intervention that was administered at this point could be declared as life-saving.

The second issue is the nature of what was injected into the boy. Pasteur's "transmission" experiments in animals were typically carried out by injecting tissue from a diseased animal into another animal with the claim that the diseased tissue contained an "infectious" agent. His experiments were not scientifically controlled and this type of exposure route does not require the existence of a germ to damage or kill the recipient animal. Pasteur's vaccine was simply a variation of these experiments: he took spinal cord material from a dead rabbit, then "attenuated" the imagined germ by drying the tissue for around a week, and injected this into Joseph. The theory was that the claimed germ was weakened by this process which would allow the boy to become "immune" to the disease.

This dubious practice of inoculation with disease products to supposedly prevent disease in others persists until this day. Whether people believe it to be a valid health measure or not, it can be shown that the widely claimed success stories for Pasteur's rabies vaccine were fallacious. After his long-hidden journals were finally disclosed in the mid-1970s, it was apparent that his public announcements about the successful treatment of rabies in dogs were fraudulent. In the 1995 book, *The Private Science of Louis Pasteur*, author Gerald Geison revealed that, "the survival rates for the two sets of dogs fall into the following ranges for the dogs treated by Pasteur, 50 to 78 percent, for the untreated control dogs, 57 to 71 percent."[202] In other words, there was no evidence that his rabies shot was of any use at all.

In fact, it was probably even worse. As Dr Montague Leverson reported in 1909, the widespread use of Pasteur's rabies vaccines in France corresponded with a dramatic increase in the number of cases of the condition that it was supposedly preventing:

> *During twenty-three years preceding the use of the anti-rabic serum there were 685 deaths from rabies in all France, or an average of 30 per annum. But since the use of the anti-rabic inoculations the average has risen to 100 per annum, in place of 30, with a continually increasing number each year, so that according to the official returns the number of deaths from rabies in France for the year ending in June, 1907, was just about 300. In truth, as Professor Peter said, in his address to the Academy of Medicine, Paris, on the 11th of January, 1887, "M. Pasteur does not cure rabies he imparts it!"*[203]

Geison had already written an article in 1978 outlining the overblown claims about the risk of humans developing rabies and the role of the rabies vaccine in treating victims of animal bites:

> *In any case, most victims of rabid animal bites could forego treatment without experiencing any untoward consequences in*

> *the future...In vaccinating the victim of an animal bite against rabies...one can never be sure that the subject of treatment has in fact contracted the disease. And one can therefore never be sure whether the treatment is even potentially beneficial to him or to anyone else.*[204]

However, the enduring rabies mythology means that many people are convinced of the need for a vaccine if they have been bitten by an animal. As a consequence, if they do develop symptoms of rabies following such an injection, it can of course be blamed on the rabies "virus" rather than the purported treatment. Once again, it cannot be emphasized enough that there are much better actions to take to improve health instead of worrying about things that will almost certainly never affect us. The illogical beliefs about rabies and the oft-repeated claim that the condition must be caused by a "virus" prompted us to publish the video, "What About Rabies?" in 2022.[205]

Don't Worry if the Germ Even Exists

Although the debate about whether there is evidence of particular viruses usually takes place in the scientific community and online forums, on occasion the dispute can make its way into court. In 2011, German microbiologist Dr Stefan Lanka offered a reward of €100,000 to anyone who could prove the existence and the size of the alleged measles virus by means of a scientific publication.[206]

Believing that he had collated the required proof, physician David Bardens submitted six publications to claim the prize. However, as Dr Lanka had specified a single publication, he replied that the conditions of his offer had not been fulfilled. Bardens then sued Lanka, and in March 2015, the Ravensburg Land Court ruled that Lanka had to pay the €100,000, including interest.[207] However, Lanka appealed against this ruling and won the case before the Stuttgart Higher Regional Court in February 2016.[208] Bardens appealed against this ruling to the Federal Court of Justice *Bundesgerichtshof* (or 'BGH', the highest court in Germany) but the appeal was dismissed in December 2016, and Lanka kept his money. In the end, it was ruled that none of the six publications could singly prove the existence of a measles virus. As Dr Lanka explained in January 2017:

> *Five experts have been involved in the case and presented the results of scientific studies. All five experts...have consistently found that none of the six publications which have been introduced to the trial, contains scientific proof of the existence of the alleged measles virus. In the trial, the results of research into so-called genetic fingerprints of alleged measles virus have been introduced. Two recognized laboratories, including the world's largest and leading genetic Institute, arrived at exactly the same results independently. The results prove that the authors of the six publications in the measles virus case were wrong, and as a direct result all measles virologists are still wrong today:*
>
> *They have misinterpreted ordinary constituents of cells as part of the suspected measles virus. Because of this error, during decades of consensus building process, normal cell constituents were mentally assembled into a model of a measles virus. To this day, an actual structure that corresponds to this model has been found neither in a human, nor in an animal. With the results of the genetic tests, all thesis of existence of measles virus has been scientifically disproved.*[209]

It should have been worrying for the virologists that the "evidence" for the measles virus remains on such shaky ground.

A brief examination is merited of the six papers that were submitted in the court case to expose the foundational lack of proof of one of their most famous viruses. The papers were as follows and they also serve to reiterate our earlier discourse around "viruses" and the Common Cold Unit:

1. "*Propagation in tissue cultures of cytopathogenic agents from patients with measles*" by Enders & Peebles, 1954[210] – In this experiment, the alleged measles virus was added to a cell culture, and the observed cytopathic effects (CPEs) were attributed to the virus. CPEs indicate disease of cells and include changes in their appearance and shape as they break down. PROBLEM: No control experiment was done, and it is now known that it is possible to observe these effects in the test tube without even adding an alleged virus to the culture. The authors did warn that, "it must be borne in mind that cytopathic effects which superficially resemble those resulting from infection by the measles agents may possibly be induced…by unknown factors."
2. "*Studies on measles virus in monkey kidney tissue cultures*" by Bech, 1958[211] – This was another cell culture experiment in the laboratory with CPEs attributed to a virus. PROBLEM: The same issues as the first paper.
3. "*Electron microscopy of measles virus replication*" by Nakai & Imagawa, 1969[212] – The authors obtained electron micrograph images of particles inside cells and claimed they were measles viruses. PROBLEM: The particles were not characterized in any other way. In no part of the experiment was it determined that the particles were infectious or had any capacity to cause disease.
4. "*The molecular length of measles virus RNA and the structural organization of measles nucleocapsids.*" by Lund, et al., 1984[213] – The authors claimed to have produced images of "purified virions." PROBLEM: The particles that were photographed could only be said to be vesicles of unknown biological role. They were not demonstrated to be viral in nature, i.e., infectious and the *cause* of disease.

5. "*Structure, Transcription, and Replication of Measles Virus*" by Horikami & Moyer in *Measles Virus*, 1995[214] – In this consensus review, the authors describe the measles virus "genome". PROBLEM: The "genome" was generated from fragments of genetic material in test tubes and assembled into a hypothetical model using computer software. It was not established that the genome existed in nature or that the genetic material came from a "virus".
6. "*Analysis of Morphology and Infectivity of Measles Virus Particles*" by Daikoku et al., 2007[215] – The authors produced electron micrographs of cell cultures and claimed they showed measles virus particles budding from the cells. PROBLEM: the particles were not differentiated from harmless extracellular vesicles. (Note: the authors betrayed themselves by earnestly reporting that the "virus" particles ranged from 50 to 1000 nm in size - which is a preposterous range as viruses are alleged to result in faithful replicas of themselves. It would be equivalent to adult humans having offspring that ranged in height from 5 feet to 100 feet tall!)

While some critics of the court verdict have argued that it was simply the result of the semantic formulation of Dr. Lanka's required proof, it must be recognized that science is most particular regarding its use of accurate, explicit language and the adequacy of techniques to support a hypothesis. The merit or otherwise of a publication is quickly discerned by the precision of the language and methods employed. It is thus unscientific to conclude that even together, these papers could prove the existence of a disease-causing virus. In fact, at the court proceedings, Professor Andreas Podbielski, head of the Department of Medical Microbiology, Virology and Hygiene at the University Hospital in Rostock, stated that with regard to the six presented papers, none of the authors had conducted *any* controlled experiments following internationally defined rules and principles of good scientific practice.[216] Hence, the claim that the measles virus exists lacks any foundation in the scientific literature.

Just keep in mind that these papers were presented as the *best* six publications regarding the alleged proof of the existence of the measles virus. As you can see, they fell far short of proving anything. It is nevertheless unlikely that we will see any serious attempt by the virology establishment to provide the missing evidence. While tens of thousands of published papers are said to relate to the measles virus, most of them simply *assume* that the virus exists. As Dr Lanka outlined:

> *...they are the only publications in the entire field of about 30,000 technical articles about "measles" in which a reference to the accepted existence of the measles virus is made. However, all the tons of other papers, which nobody can ever finish reading, assume "a priori" the existence of the measles virus and always refer to citations of citations, which are finally and exclusively based on the alleged "evidence" supplied by Enders on the 1st of June 1954.*[217]

It was also noted at the trial that the Robert Koch Institute (RKI), the highest German authority in the field of infectious diseases, had failed to perform tests to scientifically substantiate the existence of the alleged measles virus and to publish these findings. Interestingly, the RKI has claimed it has in its possession internal studies on the measles virus but refuses to hand over or publish the results![218] Dr Lanka continued:

> *With the Supreme Court judgment in the measles virus trial any national and international statements on the alleged measles virus, the infectivity of measles, and on the benefit and safety of vaccination against measles, are since then of no scientific character and have thus been deprived of their legal basis.*[219]

But despite these events in 2016 exposing the lack of evidence for the existence of a measles virus, just a few years later, the German parliament passed into law the "Measles Protection Act" to make immunization mandatory for children and staff in kindergartens and schools, medical facilities, and community facilities from March 2020.[220] Seemingly, the lack of proof that the measles virus exists is ignored by the policymakers while they act as enablers for the distribution of Big Pharma's unnecessary products. (A full account of the measles court case can be found in Dr Lanka's 2017 essay "go Virus go".[221] An English translation of the essay has been published by John Blaid and Northern Tracey.[222])

Death-dealing Drugs Marketed as "Life-saving"

The pharmaceutical industry has a very unusual position in our society. It sickens, kills and maims in numbers so vast that any other civilian industry would likely be shut down permanently in a matter of weeks. What keeps it alive is the contrived narrative that it provides all of us with "life-saving" drugs and that standards of health improve when we have easy access to their plethora of chemical products. By 2020, the pharmaceutical industry's revenue had reached US$1,228.45 billion and was projected to keep growing at a compound annual growth rate of 1.8%.[223] Pfizer alone reported a 92% growth in revenue to US$81.3 billion for the year 2021, largely on the back of its COVID-19 vaccine 'Comirnaty' which was purchased in massive quantities by governments around the world.[224]

This kind of revenue and the pervasive influence of the industry throughout the medical system has put Big Pharma in a position of almost total control of its desired narratives. Dr Peter Gøtzsche wrote in his 2013 book, *Deadly Medicines and Organised Crime: How Big Pharma Corrupted Healthcare*, "virtually everything we know about drugs is what the companies have chosen to tell us and our doctors."[225] He goes on to detail numerous examples of doctors and other whistle-blowers who have exposed pharmaceutical fraud and subsequently faced punishing consequences from one of the most powerful cartels in the world. The mirage of "safe and effective" is one that is maintained at all costs and ending a doctor's career sends a strong message to others who question the narrative.

The reality is that while there are a small number of pharmaceuticals (for example, synthetic insulin in a diabetic crisis) that are life-saving, the majority of the population does not need to take any of these products at all. People get sick because, amongst other things, they are deficient in nutrients, good water, and exercise. Just as importantly they can suffer from deficiencies in their psychological and spiritual states.[*226] It is extremely rare to get sick because of a deficiency of drugs in the body! And yet the medico-pharmaceutical industry have convinced most people that there is at least one of their products (and usually several) that need to be taken on a regular basis. Sometimes this may seem as innocent as a nasal spray, a steroid cream or some paracetamol (acetaminophen) tablets. However, none of these are treatments: they only cover up symptoms and interfere with the body's healing attempts. The short term relief they provide can manifest as an even more serious problem in the future.

New Zealand's Dr Ulric Williams was a physician who abandoned almost all of his allopathic pharmaceutical prescriptions half way through his practicing career. After realizing the true nature of the chemicals he had been taught to administer, he wrote in the 1930s that:

> *Almost all drugs are poisonous. Many are venomous. Few are even temporarily admissible. None would be required if natural requirements were complied with. Were we not taught not to "think," the stupidity of swallowing or injecting noxious substances with a view to ridding ourselves of the consequence of wrong thinking and living, would hardly need emphasis.*[227]

Unfortunately, since that time the number of pharmaceuticals being consumed in most parts of the world has risen dramatically. By 2018, around half of the US population was taking at least one prescription drug during each month, with around a quarter taking three or more drugs during a typical month.[228] Keep in mind that this does not include Over-the-Counter (OTC) medication consumption which is much higher. Children are also highly medicated with a study as far back as 1994 reporting that, "during the past 30 days, 53.7% of all 3-year-old children in the United States were given some OTC medications" and, "the high prevalence of use has occurred despite the dearth of scientific proof for the effectiveness of certain classes of OTC medications and the risks associated with improper use."[229] The US Food & Drug Administration provides the public with the blanket reassurance that OTC drugs, "are safe and effective when you follow the directions on the label and as directed by your health care professional."[230]

However, there is no evidence that the vast majority of this pill popping has overall benefits for the population and in many instances the results are literally deadly. Dr Peter Gøtzsche noted in *Deadly Medicines and Organised Crime*:

> *Our drugs kill us on a horrific scale. This is unequivocal proof that we have created a system that is out of control. Good data are available, and what I have made out of the various studies is that around 100,000 people die each year in the United States because of the drugs they take even though they take them correctly. Another 100,000 die because of errors, such as too high dose or use of a drug, despite contraindications...The European Commission has estimated that adverse reactions kill about 200,000 EU citizens...This means that in the United States and Europe: drugs are the third leading cause of death after heart disease and cancer.*[231]

Perhaps we could add that it cannot be claimed that most of the drugs could be taken "correctly" at all. When a pharmaceutical enters the body there is one general response and that is elimination of the chemical intruder. "Magic bullets" do not exist outside of drug company spin and nature's processes do not benefit from the introduction of these artificial contaminants. The manufacturers and their distributors may proffer various explanations about how drugs work, such as it acting on a particular cell receptor or intracellular pathway. Whatever theories gain acceptance within the medico-pharmaceutical industry the effects of many drugs can only be said to be a result of the body's attempts to eliminate them. As Dr Ulric Williams tried to warn us almost a century ago - in most instances it is not correct to take any drugs at all if the goal is true health.

Chapter 4 - Pandemics of Testing

"It starts making you believe in the sort of Buddhist notion that everything is contained in everything else. If you can amplify one single molecule up to something you can really measure, which PCR can do, then there is just very few molecules that you don't have at least one single one of in your body."

—Kary Mullis, inventor of the PCR process.[232]

"[Then] they chose a highly sensitive method, the polymerase chain reaction (PCR)...Where terminally ill people were previously reported, now mild cases and people who are actually perfectly healthy are suddenly included in the reporting statistics."

—Christian Drosten on 'MERS', 2014.[233]

"As May 2020 drew to a close and mass testing continued to ramp up, it should have been obvious to anyone paying attention that what we had was a testing pandemic rather than a 'viral' one... Even the mainstream media had difficulty hiding the fact that asymptomatic cases were the majority of the positive cases as well as the fact that the more testing that was done, the more cases that would ultimately be 'found.'... If the tests went away, so, too, did the 'pandemic'."

—Mike Stone of *ViroLIEgy*.[234]

PCR Already Known to Cause False Pandemics

In April 2006, a crisis unfolded in the Dartmouth-Hitchcock Medical Center in New Hampshire. One of the staff members, Dr. Brooke Herndon, a medical specialist of internal diseases, developed a non-stop cough for several weeks.[235] Because relentless coughing can be a symptom of pertussis or whooping cough, an infectious diseases specialist speculated that it could be the start of an epidemic. They believed it was confirmed when more and more health care workers started coughing over the next few weeks.

The hospital took drastic action, and almost 1,000 staff were put off work. A new rapid test kit was rolled out, and their worst fears were realized when 142 people, or around 15%, tested positive for pertussis. Thousands of people were given antibiotics, and 3,599 doses of a recently approved pertussis vaccine were administered, covering 72% of the hospital staff in a mass immunization campaign.[236] There were considerable disruptions to normal hospital services, including a loss of beds available for intensive care. However, then came the big surprise when it became apparent by the end of the year that the whole thing was a false alarm. Not one case of pertussis was confirmed with the established "gold standard": that is identifying the bacteria *Bordetella pertussis* from a patient sample. (This "gold standard" test also has a problem and will be addressed in the next section.) Medical journalist Gina Kolata outlined what happened with the new test kits in the *New York Times* in 2007:

> *At Dartmouth the decision was to use a test, P.C.R., for polymerase chain reaction. It is a molecular test that, until recently, was confined to molecular biology laboratories... Now, as they look back on the episode, epidemiologists and infectious disease specialists say the problem was that they placed too much faith in a quick and highly sensitive molecular test that led them astray. Infectious disease experts say such tests are coming into increasing use and may be the only way to get a quick answer in diagnosing diseases like whooping cough, Legionnaire's, bird flu, tuberculosis and SARS, and deciding whether an epidemic is under way.*[237]

Dr Trish Perl, an epidemiologist at John Hopkins advised that there was no good data on pseudo-epidemics caused by over-reliance on these molecular tests. In the 2007 *New York Times* piece, she said, "it's a problem; we know it's a problem...My guess is that what happened at Dartmouth is going to become more common."[238]

However, despite such an abysmal track record, many health authorities now claim that the PCR is the investigation of choice to diagnose pertussis. For example, the New Zealand Ministry of Health once required the formal isolation of the implicated bacterium *Bordetella pertussis* to count as a confirmed case of pertussis. However, in 2012 the Ministry changed the criteria and declared that:

> *Laboratory definitive evidence for a confirmed case requires isolation of Bordetella pertussis or detection of B. pertussis nucleic acid* [via PCR], *preferably from a nasopharyngeal swab...PCR should be considered the* ***diagnostic method of choice****, unless the presentation is delayed until 4 weeks after onset of symptoms, or 3 weeks after the onset of paroxysmal cough.*[239]

So why on earth would a process that they acknowledge produces so many false positives be increasingly recommended as the preferred test?

Medical researcher Hilary Butler postulated that there could have been an ulterior motive behind introducing the dubious test into the new case definition:

> *People who want to 'create data,' to provide government officials or media with supposed 'gold standard evidence' purportedly showing an increase in whooping cough cases. Is the new diagnostic criteria driven by their need to increase*

> *their 'control' over people, and advocate yet more whooping cough booster vaccines for everyone?*[240]

These suspicions would not have been allayed by an article that appeared on the 1st of April, 2007, in *Relias Media,* which provides continuing medical education for physicians in North America and advertises itself as, "the trusted source for healthcare information." Despite Robert McLellan, the medical director of Dartmouth-Hitchcock employee health, admitting there had been no pertussis outbreak, the article concluded with the following *non sequitur*: "the Dartmouth case points out the benefits of pertussis vaccination of health care workers."[241] It is unclear what benefits were actually provided as the "outbreak" had nothing to do with pertussis. Perhaps they were claiming that the fake epidemic would have been a real epidemic without the vaccines? However, such a claim is not supported by the historical data as chapter 6 will explain.

The incident at Dartmouth also highlights the habit of the medical industry to overestimate the benefits of rolling out medical interventions, including vaccines, during such situations while underestimating potential adverse outcomes. Far too many health professionals make overstated positive claims about vaccines without checking the existing evidence base. In 2019, veteran pharmaceutical investigator Prof. Peter Gøtzsche assessed the evidence regarding the DTP (diphtheria, tetanus, and pertussis) vaccine and commented that:

> *The most important principle in medical ethics is: First, do no harm. I believe that the DTP vaccine should not be used unless being one of the interventions in a large randomized trial...It is the duty of a manufacturer of a drug or vaccine to demonstrate in randomized trials that it works and has a positive benefit to harm balance. This has not been done for the DTP vaccine...I therefore believe no one should be offered*

> *this vaccine without full informed consent that includes information that the vaccine is likely to increase total mortality.*[242]

As a little segue, the currently recommended pertussis vaccine for adults in the United States is the Tdap (tetanus, diphtheria, and acellular pertussis) vaccine.[243] Like the DTP vaccine, there are no randomized control trials that support the CDC statement that, "adults should receive a booster dose of either Tdap or Td (a different vaccine that protects against tetanus and diphtheria but not pertussis) every 10 years, or after 5 years in the case of a severe or dirty wound or burn."[244] Indeed, many readers will be familiar with the experience of being pressured to take a tetanus shot when seeking medical attention for an acute wound. The practitioners promoting these injections are almost universally unaware that there is no sound evidence behind their use and the recipient is put at risk of adverse events.

Returning to the Dartmouth experience, what went so wrong with the use of the PCR for clinical diagnostics? Again, one must keep in mind the limitations of the PCR: it simply amplifies selected genetic sequences. So here are some of the possibilities of why there was a 100% false-positive rate at the Dartmouth-Hitchcock Medical Center (those already aware of the flaws in germ theory may want to skip to the next section):

1. Many people may have small numbers of *Bordetella pertussis* in their lungs the bacteria may be dead or in such small numbers as to not indicate illness or grow a "positive" culture. However, the PCR is so sensitive that it will show a positive result.
2. The PCR may have reacted to other Bordetella bacteria species such as *B. holmesii* or *B. bronchiseptica.*[245]
3. There was contamination of the target DNA. This could come from environmental surfaces or during the collection of the clinical specimens.

4. The PCR tests were being run at high cycle counts (e.g., greater than 35), resulting in nonspecific amplification. In other words, the target sequences were not even present in the samples, but the result was positive.
5. The target genetic sequences were not specific to *Bordetella pertussis* and may be found in other organisms, including those outside the Bordetella genus.
6. Any number of technical errors with regard to the specimen collection process and laboratory processing.[246]

However, there is another more important possibility to consider, related to point 1 above. The PCR may have inadvertently falsified germ theory in demonstrating that *Bordetella pertussis* is not the *cause* of the condition known as whooping cough. This gets to the root of the problem of why people get sick. There is certainly an association between whooping cough and the *presence* of *Bordetella pertussis* or at least the presence of more of this particular bacterium than usual. However, this does not mean that having some of the bacteria in our lungs will make us sick. And it is certainly not evidence that it is a contagious disease.

The PCR Exposed Whooping Cough's Faulty Science

In its "Whooping cough" entry, online encyclopedia *Wikipedia* plainly states, "pertussis is caused by the bacterium *Bordetella pertussis*" and provides a single reference for the claim.[247] The reference is a CDC webpage, and like many public health authorities, it emphatically states that, "pertussis, a respiratory illness commonly known as whooping cough, is a very contagious disease caused by a type of bacteria called *Bordetella pertussis*."[248]

The CDC webpage cited two references for its claim. The first reference was a 2004 epidemiological paper that simply interviewed family members to identify the "source" of the alleged infection in 264 out of 616 (43%) infant cases.[249] The second CDC reference, "Transmission of *Bordetella pertussis* to Young Infants" was a prospective study investigating 404 "contacts" of 95 infant pertussis cases.[250] The methodology in this paper involved diagnostic evaluation (including PCR and a blood test) being performed on all participants independent of symptoms. It concluded that the "source" had been identified in 48% of cases. In other words, despite their trawling efforts they were unable to identify the alleged source in over half the cases, and if they did find the "source," the supposed culprit could be completely well. More crucially, neither study possessed suitable methods to determine if the bacteria *caused* disease or whether humans could transmit the *condition* of pertussis.

It is also noteworthy that this second paper makes the claim that, "pertussis vaccination has reduced the number of notified cases in industrialized countries from peak years by more than 95%." This is deceptive because vaccines could not have been a significant factor for the dramatic decrease in disease *burden* that has been witnessed. As documented in the book *Dissolving Illusions*, by the time widespread pertussis vaccination was introduced in the 1950s, whooping cough had become a mild disease, and mortality had plummeted by over 90% in the US and 99% in the UK.[251]

Additionally, in a 1995 letter from Victoria Romanus at the Swedish Institute of Infectious Disease Control, there was the indication that nationwide deaths from whooping cough were only 0.6 children per year from 1981 to 1993 in Sweden when there was no national vaccine program.[252] Clearly the pertussis vaccines were not responsible for the massive reduction in deaths which is what most of the public have been led to believe. (The authors recommend that the reader consults *Dissolving Illusions* where similar conclusions are demonstrated for the relationship of vaccines to all the best known childhood diseases.[253])

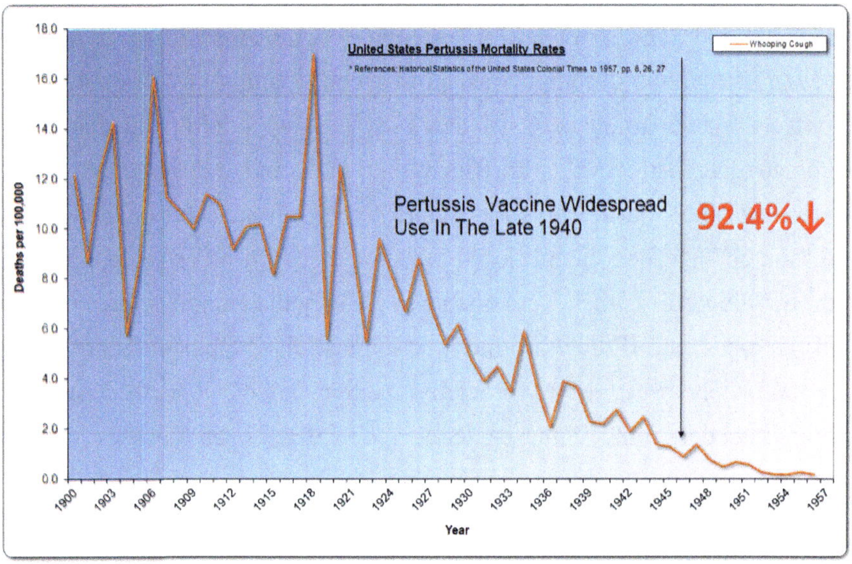

Decline in whooping cough mortality far preceding the national vaccination programs commenced in the late 1940s for the United States. Source: Roman Bystrianyk, https://dissolvingillusions.com/

From these two studies the CDC cited it is simply not possible to conclude that; (a) *Bordetella pertussis* is the causal agent for whooping cough or that, (b) human to human transmission of disease occurs. At most, it can be concluded that the presence of the bacteria possesses an association with the clinical picture of whooping cough and that sometimes there are clusters of illness in people sharing common environmental conditions.

It is already apparent that the use of the PCR to detect "cases" is highly dubious. Even if the PCR has very specific primers and is done with the utmost care, what is the clinical significance of finding some genetic sequences from the bacteria? The bacteria may be already dead, or if alive, simply present in such small numbers that they will cause no problem for the lungs. Crucially, the PCR itself cannot determine whether an individual is well or unwell in these circumstances.

If we examine the history of the apparent identification of the bacteria responsible for whooping cough, we can see that the idea of a "contagious pathogen" was imagined very early on. In 1765, Swedish doctor Nils Rosen von Rosenstein, considered one of the pioneers in the field of pediatrics, commented that:

> *The true cause of this disease must be some heterogeneous matter or seed which has a multiplicative power as is the case with smallpox...we find that it is communicated by infection and that a part of it is attracted by the breath down into the lungs.*[254]

Then in 1901, when the focus on germ theory had become much stronger, Marcus Hatfield, Professor of Diseases of Children at the Chicago Clinical School, wrote:

> *Contagiousness is great, a chance meeting, a few moments conversation, or a seat next to the sick child is generally sufficient to convey the disease, which may also be carried upon linen, or clothing soiled with the expectoration of one suffering from whooping cough...It is generally conceded that a microorganism is the exciting cause of pertussis, but its natural history has not yet been definitely settled, although since 1867 bacteriologists have at short intervals been discovering the alleged peccant microbe.*[255]

Belgian microbiologists Jules Bordet and Octave Gengou took up the challenge to confirm the alleged offending microorganism, and in 1906 it was declared that they had found it, as described in this 2010 account by Patrick Guilfoile:

> *Bordet and Gengou initially took respiratory secretions from a five-month-old infant who had whooping cough and placed*

> *the material on their growth medium. Many small bacteria, now identified as Bordetella pertussis, grew on the plate. Subsequently, they placed plates containing this medium under the mouths of children who had whooping cough, during a coughing spell, and isolated the same pathogen from these other patients.*[256]

Hence, from 1906 onwards, *Bordetella pertussis* has generally been considered the causal agent of the clinical condition known as whooping cough. However, what was described by Bordet and Gengou did not establish that this bacterium was inhaled by people to *cause* illness. Instead, they simply found it in the respiratory secretions of some individuals who had a persistent cough. The relentless coughing is merely an indication that an abnormal state exists in the respiratory tract. Their only significant finding was an *association* with the presence of, or at least increased amounts of *Bordetella pertussis*.

In the modern era, animal studies have been cited as apparent evidence that *Bordetella pertussis* causes whooping cough. However, these studies can hardly be said to establish any such claims when one examines the methodology. For example, the researchers were "infecting" rhesus macaques by introducing concentrated bacterial cultures directly into their nostrils and lungs via endotracheal tubes while under ketamine anesthesia.[257] Following this procedure, which cannot be said to replicate anything that would happen in nature, they concluded that:

> *All four monkeys were infected, as demonstrated by our ability to isolate B. pertussis from nasopharyngeal washes from day 3 until approximately day 15 postinoculation. Two of the four monkeys developed a significant rise in white blood cells (4- and 6-fold). One of the two monkeys with an elevated white blood cell count developed a mild cough that persisted for several days.*[258]

In summary, half of the monkeys had a rise in their white blood cell count, which would be an expected inflammatory response when foreign material is poured directly into their lungs, and only one developed a cough, which again would be expected by the artificially-induced lung irritation. They then claim they had "demonstrated" infection by finding the bacteria in the same place they had poured them into, for the following two weeks. Even more "success" was achieved by making baby baboons cough by injecting the concentrated bacterial brew directly into their lungs. However, there was no control group of animals to see whether simply pouring other types of brews directly into their lungs would result in similar effects. In other words, none of these experiments followed the scientific method and there was no determination that a bacterium was the cause of the symptoms.

Yet other experiments that claim to demonstrate "infection" with pertussis among baboons also labour under dubious interpretations. In a 2014 US Food and Drug Administration study, young baboons were "infected" with *Bordetella pertussis* by again pouring concentrated bacterial cultures directly into their lungs.[259] They found that co-housing these "infected" baboons with other baboons caused the latter to become "colonized" with *Bordetella pertussis*. But these "colonized" baboons did not develop whooping cough or become unwell. Instead, the researchers simply detected the bacteria in their respiratory tracts. Further, the degree of colonization was indistinguishable between the animals that had been vaccinated and those unvaccinated, an inconvenient result for the claim that the vaccines offer protection.

So, despite the declaration that *Bordetella pertussis* was named as the cause of whooping cough in 1906, more than a century later, there does not appear to be a single scientific publication that establishes that this is in fact the case. It remains entirely probable that when an individual becomes unwell, they are more likely to have an overgrowth of bacteria such as *Bordetella pertussis* due to the changing terrain, including dying cells, in the respiratory tract. And despite the claims that "people with pertussis usually spread the disease by coughing or sneezing,"[260] it has never been demonstrated that spraying the bacteria into the air can make any nearby humans or animals sick. Studies of the nasal microbiome in healthy volunteers have shown that there are always billions of bacteria present, and some are even termed "pathogens."[261] Obviously, the mere presence of these microorganisms is insufficient to cause disease alone.

Unfortunately, germ theory tunnel vision means that mainstream researchers continue to create new narratives to explain the glaring inconsistencies and the manifestly unscientific vagaries of their research. For example, in 2020, a pertussis systematic review paper found that many "cases" had minimal or no symptoms and concluded that, "the studies included in this review report a high incidence of asymptomatic and mild/atypical infection among household contacts of pertussis cases."[262] This echoed another paper from 2015 that stated, "asymptomatic transmission is the most parsimonious explanation for many of the observations surrounding the resurgence of *B. pertussis* in the US and UK."[263] Surely implying that entirely healthy people are now "infected" or have become carriers of disease is starting to stretch the theory very thin?

For many researchers, however, adherence to germ theory continues to cement the tendency that all roads to lead to vaccines. For example, a 2013 paper on "Pertussis resurgence" advises us, "to select vaccines and vaccination strategies that are most effective" and goes on to claim, "pathogen adaptations reveal weak spots in the bacterial defense and hence point to ways to improve vaccination."[264] Trying to explain the mild persistence of whooping cough through "pathogen adaptation" and waning vaccination immunity is simply another case of the germ theorists trying to fit observations of the natural world into their model. The consequence of this impaired theory is that it fails to identify and correct the real causes of illness.

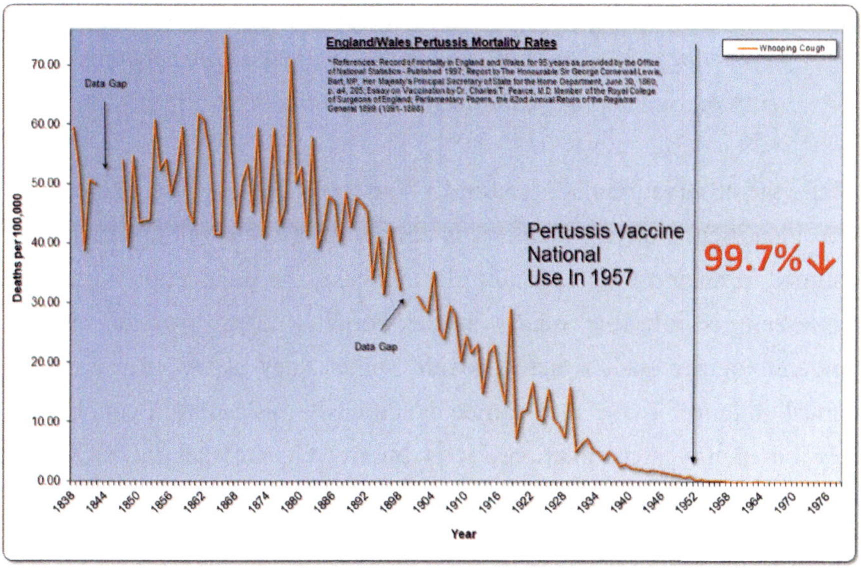

Decline in whooping cough mortality far preceding the national vaccination programs commenced in the 1950s for England and Wales. Source: Roman Bystrianyk, https://dissolvingillusions.com/

On that account, what is the conceivable cause of whooping cough if it has never been proved that this bacterium alone can cause the disease? Due to the persistent research and confirmation bias that centers on the Bordetella model, that question remains unanswered. However, we can reasonably suspect that various environmental and nutritional factors contribute to the individual's 'terrain' and thus susceptibility to illness.*265 Unfortunately, studies tend to focus on factors such as household contacts rather than the underlying physical characteristics of the cases. For example, a 2017 epidemiological study concluded that:

> *Sharing a household with a young adolescent was a significant risk factor for pertussis in adults and older teenagers. The primary focus of the childhood pertussis vaccination programmes is to prevent infant disease. Although evidence is emerging that adolescent vaccination does not*

> *provide indirect protection to infants, our results highlight the importance of children aged 10–14 years in pertussis transmission to older adolescents and adults.*[266]

While the observation that, "sharing a household with a young adolescent" was identified as a risk factor, it is simply an association and cannot be claimed to demonstrate causation. In this case, the implication is that the adolescent is infecting others in the house with *B. pertussis*. While epidemiological studies may provide some clues as to what may be contributing to disease, they can be dangerously misleading if conclusions rely on unproven assumptions. It is highly relevant that the CDC has reported around 90% of whooping cough cases occur in the developing world.[267] While the CDC claims this is due to low vaccination rates, it ignores the stark reality that children in the developing world have much higher rates of nutritional deficiencies and exposure to a host of potentially compromising environmental factors.

It is also known that with regard to fatal cases of whooping cough, the children have significantly lower birth weight and younger gestational age compared to non-fatal cases.[268] It is a tragedy that more data has not been gathered surrounding underlying physical, nutritional, and toxicological factors. This appears particularly so with regard to "conventional" treatments such as antibiotics. Even a *Cochrane Collaboration Review* concluded that:

> *The findings of this review suggest that administration of antibiotics for the treatment of whooping cough is effective in eliminating B. pertussis from patients with the disease to render them non-infectious but does not alter the subsequent clinical course of the illness...There is insufficient evidence to determine the benefit of prophylactic treatment of pertussis contacts. Prophylaxis with antibiotic was significantly*

> *associated with side effects and did not significantly improve clinical symptoms, whoop, paroxysmal cough, number of cases who develop culture positive B. pertussis or paroxysmal cough for more than two weeks in contacts older than six months of age.*[269]

The only criticism we would add to this otherwise accurate conclusion is that eliminating *B. pertussis* in patients would, "render them non-infectious," which is a blatant example of illogical circular thinking. As the scientific evidence shows, no patient has ever been shown to be "infectious" regardless of whether the bacteria can be found in the person or not. In other words, there is no evidence that people "pass on" or "catch" whooping cough.

What is the Polymerase Chain Reaction?

Before 2020, the polymerase chain reaction, or PCR, was far less well known to the public, and even to much of the medical community, who had little engagement with or knowledge of the process. However, with the alleged worldwide "pandemic" of COVID-19, the PCR became a household name. Hundreds of millions of people around the world had samples taken, usually via a nasopharyngeal swab, which was then said to be tested for the presence of the SARS-CoV-2 "virus". We will explore why this is not scientifically correct, as well as the even more absurd claim that the tests could detect a new disease called 'COVID-19' in people. It is in this regard we will outline the PCR process in order to appreciate what the PCR is capable of doing, what its limitations are and what it is not capable of doing. This will show how readily the test may be misinterpreted or indeed, misused.

To fully understand how the COVID pandemic was manufactured, one necessarily needs to understand the basic science concerning the PCR process. Perhaps the single most important fact to come-away with is that the PCR is a biological laboratory 'tool' – it is not in itself a diagnostic or clinical test. The simplest way to imagine what the PCR does is to think of it as a biological photocopier designed to precisely replicate molecular chains in large numbers. In the following four paragraphs we will summarize the scientific theory underpinning the reverse transcription-polymerase chain reaction (RT-PCR) and provide some foundational knowledge that lifts the veil of mysticism surrounding seemingly ominous words like 'reverse transcriptase' and 'polymerase'. We completely sympathize with readers who may wish to skip over these more technical paragraphs.

* * *

Polymerase is the name of an enzyme that catalyses (brings about) the formation of a polymer (or long-chain molecule) from smaller units. In this case, we are talking about deoxyribonucleic acid (DNA), the genetic material present in most living organisms. The smaller units of DNA are nucleotides, of which there are four types: cytosine (C), guanine (G), adenine (A), and thymine (T). A 'Chain Reaction' means that the process is carried out multiple times in sequence. The amplification means that a minuscule sample of DNA, which cannot be detected with typical laboratory tests, is multiplied millions of times to produce sufficient material to allow for identification.

DNA cloning techniques were being used prior to the PCR method, but they were cell-based, typically requiring a host bacterium to amplify the genetic sequences, which were very time-consuming.[270] The laboratory process could extend over weeks or months, which was also very expensive and greatly limited the practicality and suitability of the process for any useful applications. The history of PCR started in 1976 with the discovery of *Taq* DNA polymerase. The enzyme was found in *Thermus aquaticus* – a bacteria discovered living in hot springs in Yellowstone National Park.[271] Because the enzyme could withstand temperatures of 95 degrees centigrade, it was suitably robust for the thermally dependent PCR process. Prior to this fresh enzyme would have to be added at every single PCR cycle. In the 1980s Kary Mullis realized how to put *Taq* Polymerase to use for the PCR and the enzyme became commercially promoted. Mullis was awarded the Nobel Prize in Chemistry in 1993 and is generally considered the inventor of the PCR method.[272]

Once a specimen is obtained, for example, from a nasal swab, the PCR process starts with heating the sample. This is said to separate the double-stranded DNA into two pieces of single-stranded DNA. Primers are then added, which are short pieces of engineered DNA (typically 18 to 24 bases long) designed to flank a limited target section of DNA for amplification.[273] The polymerase enzyme then synthesizes a new DNA strand that is complementary (a mirror image) to the target DNA section. This essentially completes a cycle, and the amount of target DNA has been doubled. The cycle then starts again, but this time with around twice as much target DNA as the first time. This is typically repeated 25-40 times which results in exponential amplification of material being produced. For example, after 40 cycles, around 1,000 billion copies would be made from a single initial molecule of DNA. However, *Taq* DNA polymerase has a certain number of errors when it replicates the DNA, so higher cycle numbers are more likely to produce inaccurate results.

Some alleged viruses, such as SARS-CoV-2, are said to have genetic material consisting of ribonucleic acid, or RNA, which introduces an additional issue for the PCR. The PCR only works effectively with DNA which means that before starting the actual PCR process, the target RNA must be converted to complementary DNA (cDNA) with the enzyme reverse transcriptase. This is known as the reverse transcription polymerase chain reaction, or RT-PCR (not to be confused with the other RT: "Real-

Time”-PCR). During the conversion process from RNA to cDNA, the amount of DNA obtained with the same RNA base material can vary widely, even by a factor of 10, equivalent to three to four PCR cycles, which can significantly impact how results are interpreted.[274]

PCR Cycles	Copies	
1	2	
20	1,048,576	(1 million)
25	33,554,432	(33 million)
37	137,438,953,472	(137 billion)
40	1,099,511,627,776	(1 trillion)
45	35,184,372,088,832	(35 trillion)

The exponential amplification of the Polymerase Chain Reaction (PCR) is truly astounding. Even if there is only a single molecule in the original sample, trillions of copies can be rapidly created. Hence the results need to be interpreted with caution. The claim that the PCR can determine whether an organism such as a human has an “infectious” disease or is “contagious” has not been substantiated through the scientific method. Instead it has been claimed through circular reasoning and the belief that the PCR can validate itself. (For example, some sequences of unknown origin have been called “viral” so it is claimed that detecting these sequences means that a “virus” exists and is causing an infection.)*

**In reading this book, Dr M.C.J. McGrath eloquently remarked that, “the monstrously magnified result has the effect of turning a whispered hint into a bullish roar, inverting uncertainty into imagined certainty while simultaneously conveying an illusion of authoritative ‘science' and providing justification for an infinite constellation of controlling social interventions. The manufacturing of ‘cases’ is the very backbone of the gaslighting illusion of a ‘pandemic’, whose definition by the WHO is now meaningless, constituting no more than a readily ‘transmittable’ idea.”*

* * *

It is important to keep in mind that despite the incredible achievement and development of the PCR, along with technical improvements over the decades, the nature of what the PCR can do has not changed: it simply amplifies *selected* target genetic sequences. It cannot confirm where the genetic material came from, whether it came from an intact organism, or whether a human is "infected" by something. For example, you could be provided with a swab from a man named "Bill" and then detect DNA with the PCR. But from this, you would not be able to draw any conclusions about whether he was dead or alive, a whole human being or "he" was a few cells that had been preserved in a jar for the past century.

The danger we have already commented upon previously, namely that a test may be misinterpreted or indeed, misused is of profound concern when used as a 'tool' to dictate the behavior of populations. It can be seen that this powerful tool can be misapplied at a national and even global level, as indeed became apparent at the dawn of the COVID-19 era, where the PCR results were used to justify severe measures against entire populations. In the case of New Zealand, the detection of some nucleotide sequences in a single person was used by Prime Minister Jacinda Ardern to justify the lockdown of the entire nation in August 2021.[275] This could obviously never have been done in the pre-COVID era. Governments worldwide apparently became obsessed with the PCR case numbers and had no regard for what the results actually meant, which was very little.

One of the few leaders to go against the international "case" hysteria was Tanzania's President, John Magufuli. As reported by *Africa News* on the 6th of May, 2020:

> *On Sunday President Magufuli, who has consistently downplayed the effect of the virus shocked the world when he said animals, fruits and vehicle oil had been secretly tested at the laboratory. Now, take a read at some of the specific things*

> *he said had been tested. A papaya, a quail and a goat. All of them he says had been found to be positive to Covid-19.*[276]

Instead of admitting there might be a problem with the way the PCR was being used, the corporate media and platforms such as *Wikipedia* smeared Magufuli as a "COVID-19 denier," even going as far as suggesting he died of COVID-19.[277] If he was not killed, the irony remains how could they allege the diagnosis using the same falsified PCR test that Magafuli had already demonstrated was incapable of making a clinical diagnosis?

The PCR revolutionized several areas including forensic science, genetic studies and metagenomics.[278] (Not that these applications have been without misinterpretation either.) However, Kary Mullis did not believe the PCR was suitable for diagnosing illness in humans, as he explained during a "Corporate Greed & AIDS" talk in Santa Monica, California in 1997:

> *That could be thought of as a misuse: to claim that it is meaningful. It tells you something about nature and what is there. To test for that one thing and say it has a special meaning is, I think, the problem...PCR is just a process that allows you to make a whole lot of something out of something. It doesn't tell you that you are sick, or that the thing that you ended up with was going to hurt you or anything like that.*[279]

Mullis passed away on the 7th of August, 2019, at the age of 74, around six months before the explosion in the international use of the so-called SARS-CoV-2 PCR tests. In April 2020, David Crowe, author of 'The Infectious Myth' commented on what he thought Kary Mullis would say about this wholesale use of the PCR in entire populations:

> *I'm sad that he isn't here to defend his manufacturing technique, Kary did not invent a test. He invented a very*

powerful manufacturing technique that is being abused. What are the best applications for PCR? Not medical diagnostics. He knew that and he always said that.[280]

Why was SARS-2 (COVID-19) Bigger than SARS-1?

As was detailed in chapter 1, COVID-19 was a bait-and-switch operation where the moniker 'SARS' or severe acute respiratory syndrome was attached to an alleged novel "virus". As the name suggests, SARS was supposed to be a *severe* lung condition, something that is never experienced by the vast majority of the population. While the causes of SARS and whether it is even a specific entity can be debated, it is apparent that the case numbers were always going to be low by definition. At the end of the alleged 18 month "outbreak" in 2004 there were less than 8500 cases and less than 800 deaths worldwide. To put this in perspective, there are around 1.35 million worldwide road traffic deaths per year.[281]

In April 2020, *Healthline* published an article with the title "COVID-19 vs. SARS: How Do They Differ?"[282] They listed the common symptoms of COVID-19 as, "fever, cough, fatigue, shortness of breath, muscle aches and pains, headaches, diarrhea" and the common symptoms of SARS as, "fever, cough, malaise, shortness of breath, body aches and pains, and headache." In other words, it would be impossible to distinguish the alleged specific disease entities on symptoms alone. So how did the second "pandemic" have thousands of times more cases than the first one when they were both supposed to be related to each other?

The *Healthline* article then introduced two ideas which became pivotal in creating the appearance of a pandemic:

SARS-CoV-2 appears to be transmitted more easily than SARS-CoV...According to the Centers for Disease Control

> *and Prevention (CDC), research suggests that SARS-CoV-2 can be transmitted by people who are not showing symptoms of illness, which is rarely seen with a SARS-CoV infection.*

The first suggestion subsequently became the "superspreader" narrative and the second became the "asymptomatic transmission" narrative. The article does not provide any scientific citations which established such claims and instead makes appeals to authority in the form of the WHO and the CDC. However, neither of these so-called authorities has ever produced scientific evidence for the existence of disease-causing infectious particles ("viruses") known as SARS-CoV-1 or SARS-CoV-2 so how were the narratives sustained let alone the nonsense of 'superspreaders' and 'asymptomatic transmission'?

Dr Claus Köhnlein, a *Virus Mania* co-author and physician based in Germany, had seen this ruse unfold previously with the HIV/AIDS scandal decades earlier and explained it in straightforward terms in 2020:

> *I came across my first AIDS patient who was suffering from a lymphoma...and all of a sudden it was told, "he has AIDS now." And I asked, "how come he has AIDS now? Yesterday he was suffering from a lymphoma." And they told me, "well, he has a positive HIV test." And I said, "well, ok but that's not a new epidemic. It might be* ***an epidemic of a new test because it was not a new clinical disease****, this lymphoma." And years later I recognized that* ***the whole thing was a test pandemic*** *- it went around the world like COVID-19 today by our testing. There were no new clinical diseases.*[283] [authors' emphasis]

This cuts right to the heart of the matter and explains how apparent pandemics are created out of thin air. There does not need to be a virus and there does not need to be a new clinical disease entity: all that is required is a new test and the cases will follow. Around 2003 during the alleged SARS outbreak there were no widely-deployed tests available. Doctors were only registering cases if they saw a severely unwell and febrile patient with significant shortness of breath that typically led to hospitalization. Not only that, but it was reserved for cases that could not be "explained" through other respiratory illness tests. A PCR test did eventually appear during the SARS episode but was not widely available and was not incorporated into any screening or routine use.

Fast forward to 2020 and PCR tests were deployed in the hundreds of millions. People were encouraged to get tested and rather than a diagnosis of exclusion as SARS had been, COVID-19 was the *anticipated* diagnosis. If you had the snivels or felt in the least bit unwell then you were instructed to present for a test promptly. The messaging was drilled into the public on a daily basis by governments and their sponsored medical institutions: 'test, test, test'. Cold and flu cases disappeared and were reclassified as COVID-19 cases through a testing pandemic, as explained by Dr Köhnlein.

It cannot be emphasized enough that the PCR is a manufacturing tool for molecular amplification that has actually become a tool for the amplification of social control. It is a way of amplifying a particular genetic sequence that is selected by the design of primers, as was explained earlier in this chapter. It does not "test" for anything, apart from whether a particular genetic sequence is present no matter in how minuscule an amount. A few molecules present in a sample are generally of no relevance to a large organism such as a human and yet the PCR can produce a "positive" result, such is its power of amplification. It is outrageous to claim that any positive result represents a "viral infection" - otherwise it would also have to be concluded that pieces of fruit, the soil, and sewers also have such "infections" as testing them with the same PCR can produce the same result. Even with microbes that have been shown to exist, such as bacteria, it would be similarly irrational to claim that the detection of some of their genetic sequences by the PCR would mean that the individual has a bacterial infection. In and on the human body there are trillions of bacteria, in fact, with bacterial cells expected to outnumber the human cells.[284]

By 2021, lateral flow tests, also known as rapid antigen tests (RAT) started replacing the PCR as a purported SARS-CoV-2 detection tool. As explained by Dr Mark Bailey, these tests had no more capability than the PCR to detect an imagined virus or diagnose a clinical condition:

> *Unlike the PCR, which amplifies selected genetic fragments, RAT purports to detect a protein, currently the "SARS-CoV-2 nucleocapsid" or 'N'-protein. There are no published papers proving the existence and biochemical properties of a pathogen termed SARS-CoV-2, so the protein cannot be claimed to have any specificity to a "virus" – it is simply a protein class found in some humans and mammalian tissue culture experiments. The typical test kit contains a membrane onto which a few drops of nasal-derived fluid are placed. The fluid is drawn along the membrane and mixes with a fixed "anti-SARS-CoV-2 antibody" (read: something that will react with the non-specific N-protein) conjugated with gold. If this reaction occurs a visible bar is produced on the strip. But what does this actually mean?*[285]

However, one major difference from the PCR was that the RATs were made even more widely available to the public and they could be used as home kits. In countries like New Zealand, the cases from these home kits surged with the subsequent testing frenzy.[286] Nothing even remotely close to this testing hysteria took place during the SARS-1 era.

Now we had entered a brave new world where clinically unvalidated test strips "diagnosed" the cases without sound science or common sense. It is easy to see on this fact alone why the number of COVID-19 cases were always going to be far greater than SARS. Indeed, when *Healthline* stated that, "SARS-CoV-2 appears to be transmitted more easily than SARS-CoV," the key word is 'appears'. When the PCR and RATs are rolled out into the community, no virus is required to create the *appearance* of transmission.

How to Create "Virus Genomes"

One of the most confusing aspects for the public is the illusion that viruses can be grown in a laboratory. By definition, a virus is supposed to be an obligate intracellular parasite, meaning that it cannot reproduce outside of a host cell. So to grow postulated viruses, the process needs to be done either in a living organism (*in vivo*) such as a laboratory animal, or in an artificial proxy environment (*in vitro*) such as with cell cultures in a test tube. This is an important difference from growing known to exist micro-organisms such as bacteria. Bacteria do not require host cells to be cultured and can be grown in media containing basic building blocks and energy sources such as water, protein components, salts, and carbohydrates. This allows us to be much more confident that we are dealing with a truly isolated species in the petri dish with regard to both the appearances under the microscope and the biochemical characteristics of the bacterium, including its genetic makeup. However, there can be no such confidence when examining the methodology of "growing" alleged viruses.

With regard to "viral" cultures, we will use the CDC's flagship paper "Severe Acute Respiratory Syndrome Coronavirus 2 from Patient with Coronavirus Disease, United States," published in June 2020,[287] to illustrate the typical process and highlight the problems as well as the circular thinking. First, they state that they collected, "clinical specimens from a case-patient who had acquired COVID-19 during travel to China and who was identified in Washington, USA." This introduces the first problem: how do we know that this specimen contains the alleged pathogenic virus? The purported COVID-causing pathogen 'SARS-CoV-2' was not seen and physically isolated from the patient's swab specimens.

There has been no step leading up to this point that demonstrated: (a) the existence of the particle SARS-CoV-2, and (b) that if it does exist, it is *causing* the disease "COVID-19". Instead, we are informed that, "the CDC confirmed that the patient's nasopharyngeal and oropharyngeal swabs tested positive for 2019-nCoV [later named SARS-CoV-2] by real-time reverse-transcriptase–polymerase-chain-reaction (rRT-PCR) assay."[288] In other words, they are saying that by detecting some pre-decided target genetic fragments with the PCR, the existence of the "virus" is already confirmed, and the patient is known to have it even before they look for it!

They then proceeded to culture the "virus" in the laboratory and conclude that said virus is present if they observe cytopathic effects (CPEs). We know from earlier chapters that CPEs are nothing more than the abnormal appearances of stressed cells under the microscope that indicate they are breaking down and dying. In this case, their "culture" was performed with a mixture including Vero cells, fetal bovine serum, antibiotics, and antimycotic (antifungal) agents.

It is worth exploring these various components to understand the subsequent claims made through this methodology:

1. **Vero cells** are derived from the kidney of an African green monkey and have been in use since 1962.[289] The cell line is aneuploid, meaning that they have an abnormal number of chromosomes, and continuous, meaning the cells can be replicated indefinitely. They are favored by virologists as they grow quickly (thus demonstrating lots of cellular "effects"). However, even some virologists question the use of cells unrelated to the type that the virus is actually supposed to infect.[290] The European Collection of Authenticated Cell Cultures Laboratory

Handbook also warns that, "transformed cell lines present the advantage of almost limitless availability, but the disadvantage of having retained very little of the original *in vivo* [in living organism] characteristics."[291] In summary, they are using highly abnormal monkey kidney cells in a test tube to "demonstrate" the imagined effects of the alleged virus in the airway cells of living humans.

2. **Fetal bovine serum (FBS)** is obtained from fetuses taken from pregnant cows during slaughter. It is commonly harvested using a cardiac puncture without any form of anesthesia, so fetuses are possibly exposed to pain.[292] The RSPCA has called for an end to this practice and suggested alternative products.[293] FBS is comprised of serum albumin (protein), amino acids, sugars, lipids, and hormones. Although the serum should be devoid of cells, it is likely to contain variable freely circulating bovine DNA and RNA contaminating the culture.[294]
3. **Antibiotics** are used in viral cell cultures to kill potential bacterial contaminants that came with the patient specimen. In fact, all throat and respiratory swabs would be expected to contain various bacterial species. Even if the antibiotics kill bacteria, components such as their genetic traces may remain in the mixture. Antibiotics are also potentially nephrotoxic, meaning they can be toxic to the Vero monkey kidney cells, particularly if the cells are stressed in other ways. Thus, there does not need to be any virus to cause the breakdown of the cells.
4. **Antimycotic agents** are antifungals and are used similarly to antibiotics, killing any potential fungi that came with the patient specimen. Killing the fungi still leaves components such as their genetic fragments in the mixture. Antimycotics such as amphotericin are also toxic to kidney cells, which can again contribute to the observed CPEs.

So, at this point, it is apparent that the culture contains genetic material from the human subject (from their throat and nasal cells), the monkey

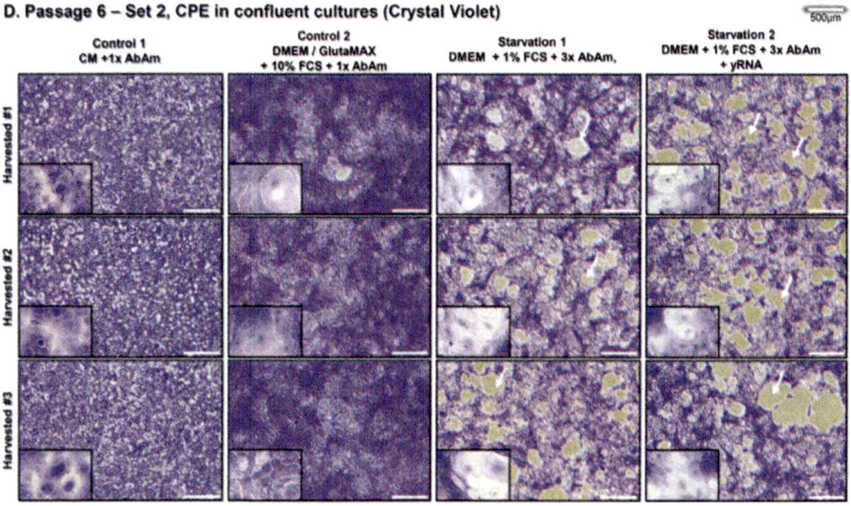

Dr Stefan Lanka demonstrated that cytopathic effects (CPEs) appear by simply stressing the cells with antibiotics and "passaging" (see text below) - no virus required. Even more dramatic CPEs were seen by adding yeast (far right images). Source: https://coldwelliantimes.com/eilmeldung/kontrollexperiment-phase-1-mehrere-labore-bestatigen-die-widerlegung-der-virologie-durch-den-cytopathischen-effekt/

cells, the FBS, as well as potentially other genetic fragments from any other micro-organisms that came along for the ride. The importance of this will become apparent when we look at the process of sequencing a "genome" they attribute to SARS-CoV-2.

Often at this point, there is a failure to see any CPEs in the test tube, which seems strange as the suspected virus is supposed to be very aggressive and has been given all the nutrients and host cells of its wildest dreams. Then 'passage 1' is performed where some of the culture mixture is removed and placed in more monkey kidney cells with reduced nutrients and extra doses of antibiotics and antifungals. The culture is then observed over several days again to see if CPEs will now appear. This "passaging" is another questionable technique used by the virologists because it is a process that further stresses the cells - a stress that may well cause CPEs in and of itself. Incredibly, even the manufacturers of the laboratory products admit that there are no standardized parameters surrounding how passaging should be done:

> A *straightforward method for determining the passage number of a cell line does not exist. A review of the literature on passage-related effects in cell lines demonstrates that the effects are complex and heavily dependent on a host of factors such as the type of cell line, the tissue and species of origin, the culture conditions and the application for which the cells are used.*[295]

Apparent CPEs are not the only problem with passaging because the process can also alter the genetic expression of the cells in the test tube. A study in 2010 revealed that when certain human cells were passaged, their RNA had changed by up to 10% following 5 passages.[296] So the technique itself can result in different genetic sequences being detected, which is again something that commercial laboratory suppliers such as the American Type Culture Collection have issued warnings about:

> *"There is agreement that the number of passages should be minimized to reduce the possibility of phenotypic variations, genetic drift, and contamination as much as possible, but standards organizations differ as to how many passages are acceptable."*[297]

This certainly confirms the earlier research of geneticist Barbara McClintock, who showed that "shocks" to cells can form new genetic sequences that were not previously detectable. Clearly these sequences arise from the cells themselves and cannot be viruses. She gave an explanation for this observation in her 1983 Nobel prize speech: "Our present knowledge would suggest that these reorganizations originated from some "shock" that forced the genome to restructure itself in order to overcome a threat to its survival."[298] In other words, the detection of an apparently novel sequence does not equate to a "novel virus".

Back to the CDC's flagship paper "Severe Acute Respiratory Syndrome Coronavirus 2 from Patient with Coronavirus Disease, United States," published in June 2020. In this study, once the desired CPEs had been observed, the "viral lysate," (the broken up cells in the mixture), was used "for total nucleic acid extraction," to start sequencing the coronavirus "genome". But here there exists a major problem. At no stage was a virus actually demonstrated or isolated. Instead a soup of broken-up cells and contaminants with all sorts of genetic fragments was used. So you can see that their following statement, "we extracted nucleic acid from isolates," is misleading in that the "isolates" are simply referring to their soup of culture brew – they have in no way established that the RNA being detected comes from a virus or that it causes a disease referred to as COVID-19.

And how did they know which genetic sequences they should be looking for in the first place? The paper stated that they, "designed 37 pairs of nested PCRs spanning the genome on the basis of the coronavirus reference sequence (GenBank accession no. NC045512)." GenBank is an open-access database that contains the genetic sequences of thousands of organisms, including many purported virus sequences. So they went to GenBank to find out in advance which sequences to amplify with the PCR. But how was it established that GenBank accession number NC045512 is the SARS-CoV-2 genome?

Now we get into the circular reasoning loop of modern virology…

This particular sequence was published by the Chinese team of Fan Wu on the 3rd of February, 2020, in a paper titled "A new coronavirus associated with human respiratory disease in China."[299] The researchers purportedly obtained a specimen from a 41-year-old man who was admitted to the Central Hospital of Wuhan on the 26th of December, 2019, with bilateral pneumonia and, despite no new or definitive clinical features, a condition later called "COVID-19". The specimen was crude bronchoalveolar lavage fluid (washings from the lungs), so it contained a mixture of human cells and potentially all sorts of other micro-organisms and genetic fragments.

From this mixed sample, they found tens of millions of different sequences (termed "reads") and then put their computer software to work to see how they could fit all the reads together. To do this "fitting," the software searched for "contigs" or areas where different fragments appear to have overlapping sequences. The software employs probability algorithms to "establish" these overlaps. Of the hundreds of thousands of hypothetical sequences generated in this fashion, they identified that the longest "continuous" sequence the computer could create was about 30,000 bases long, so they concluded that this must be the length of the "viral" genome.

But why would that be the case? They have a hypothetical model with no way to check that it exists in its full length outside of their simulation. And even if it did exist in nature, how did they jump to the conclusion that it must be viral and the *cause* of a disease? At best they have a hypothesis and that is as far as *any* alleged virus genome has made it in the entire history of virology.

Fan Wu's team reported that their hypothetical sequence was 89.1% similar to "a bat SARS-like coronavirus" designated 'SL-CoVZC45'. Firstly, 89.1% isn't actually that similar when comparing genetic sequences - for example, humans and chimpanzees share about 96% of their genome and we can agree that they are remarkably different.[300] Perhaps 89.1% sounds "similar" when the virologists permit their alleged coronavirus genomes to vary by as much as 50%.[301] But this is just a blatant case of allowing the purported ‘characteristics’ of these “viruses” (extreme genetic variation, size, 'infectivity', 'lethality', clinical manifestations, and anything else one cares to include) to have a conceptual flexibility that may be fitted to an invalid model. Secondly, how was the so-called bat coronavirus sequence originally obtained? It was another hypothetical computer sequence placed on GenBank in 2018 also generated using the same techniques just discussed. In summary, once these sequences are deposited on the database and called “viral,” other virologists go out and “find” similar ones. As the Reverend J.F. Berg once stated: “My opponent’s reasoning reminds me of the heathen, who, being asked on what the world stood, replied, ‘On a tortoise.’ But on what does the tortoise stand? ‘On another tortoise.’”[302]

So, we’ve opened the door into the world of “virus genomes” and how they are created, without any proof that the genetic material comes from a virus. Hypothetical genomes are then used as the template for subsequent hypothetical genomes to follow. In any case, the CDC’s “genome” which was designed in advance based on a GenBank sequence, still adds nothing further to any proof of the existence of a claimed contagious and disease-causing particle termed ‘SARS-CoV-2’.

The CDC paper reported that CPEs were, “not observed in mock infected cells,” but as is typical, they failed to document the details of that experiment. (They also failed to disclose these details to the public on direct request.[303]) For a valid control experiment in this setting, it should have been repeated with the same human-derived specimen but without the claimed viral particles. Only in that way would the alleged virus be an independent variable; only in that way can a scientist implicate the virus and no other factor as the cause of the pneumonia.*[304] However, this appears to be an impossibility for the virologists as they have never been able to physically isolate (and thus remove) virus particles from these specimens in the first place. As we mentioned in the ‘Settling the Virus Debate’ Statement:

> *Perhaps the primary evidence that the pathogenic viral theory is problematic is that no published scientific paper has ever shown that particles fulfilling the definition of viruses have been directly isolated and purified from any tissues or bodily fluids of any sick human or animal.*[305]

In the absence of being able to perform such a properly controlled experiment, the virologists could still test samples from both well individuals and those who were unwell with highly-comparable respiratory diseases that were deemed not to be COVID-19 or "viral" in cause. Every sample should be exposed to the same passaging and stressors as the case sample to test for CPEs. However, the virologists have a habit of conspicuously avoiding these experiments and this unscientific approach extends to the genome sequencing process as well.

As a final note, the CDC researchers attempted to "infect" various human cells with their so-called COVID-19 samples. After all, COVID-19 is supposed to be a human respiratory disease, not a monkey kidney disease. As is so frequently the case, the other cell lines failed to produce the cytopathic effects they were looking for, and they concluded, "the results indicate that SARS-CoV-2 maintains a similar profile to SARS-CoV in terms of susceptible cell lines."[306] Indeed, kidney cells are designed to process mostly sterile blood, not deal with respiratory secretions and all kinds of inhaled particles. Perhaps they should consider the possibility that an alleged virus is not infecting any cells at all and they are going about things the wrong way by selecting abnormal cell types from other organs that simply have a high propensity to "react" in test tubes.

Evidently, much of virology has departed from the earlier attempts to nail down direct evidence of viruses. Now that they are ensconced in their indirect methods, are virologists trapped deep inside Plato's Cave just watching dancing shadows on the wall?

Chapter 5 - Press Release Science

"The old motto about 'speaking truth to power' is overrated. Power, as he points out, quite probably knows the truth already, and is mainly interested in suppressing or limiting or distorting it. We would do better therefore to instruct the powerless."

—Christopher Hitchens.

"In the past few years, you have been living within an escalating hybrid war. Globally, we have witnessed overt media control and propaganda campaigns; censorship, including arrests of people speaking in public; monitoring of all electronic communications and physical contact tracing; brutally enforced lock-down and masking requirements, with people being beaten, handcuffed and arrested, even in their homes..."

—David Rogers Webb, 2023.[307]

"Today, most doctors realize they're really working for the pharmaceutical industry, which in turn controls the news and colludes with the federal government to push as many drugs and vaccines as possible on the public. These doctors don't ask questions. They scrap their Oath to first do no harm, and they collect paychecks."

—Jon Rappoport, 2023.[308]

Programming the Public

It can be hard to imagine just how different life was in the early 1980s. Children during this period received much fewer vaccinations and the influenza vaccine was rarely distributed to the wider public in most countries. Human "coronavirus" vaccines had not progressed further than the ideas board of the Common Cold Unit. The word "anti-vax" (originally 'anti-vacks' recorded in 1810–15 in a letter by Edward Jenner[309]) was not commonly used and those choosing not to have vaccines were not demonized. In first world countries most families were not particularly focussed on "infectious" diseases as such conditions had largely disappeared. When they did occur, the mortality rates were extremely low. For the vast majority of parents such diseases were considered a mild inconvenience with their child spending a few days at home at worst.

The horizon appeared bleak for vaccine manufacturers whose "successes" had already peaked in the eyes of the public. Additionally, the role of public health institutions looked increasingly superfluous - rising living standards, knowledge about hygiene, and common sense offered far more benefits to health than any of their tax payer funded "experts". Something was urgently needed to focus the attention of the population once again, returning the vested interests of the medico-pharmaceutical industry to the limelight. And then a new "virus" arrived…in the form of a televised press conference as was detailed in *Virus Mania*:

> *American virologist Robert Gallo and US Health Minister Margaret Heckler stepped in front of the cameras on 23 April 1984, with an important message: "Today we add another miracle to the long honor roll of American medicine and science. Today's discovery represents the triumph of science over a dreaded disease. Those who have disparaged this scientific search—those who have said we weren't doing enough—have not understood how sound, solid, significant medical research proceeds." The media immediately passed the news on to their audiences, without questioning what kind of "medical research" had led these scientists to believe what would soon become the dogma of the AIDS establishment:*

> *that AIDS can only occur in the presence of a viral infection, and that the virus dramatically destroys the patient's helper cells (T cells). Gallo and Heckler then promised that an AIDS vaccine would be ready by 1986.*[310]

It marked a new era of so-called medical science where alleged discoveries would be broadcast directly to the public before a process of rigorous scrutiny of the material had even started. The "facts" came from the officials on the television and following their announcements, a non-negotiable narrative was set in place. Everyone was expected to follow suit, including all of the health practitioners in the system. It was not the place of your family doctor to question "the science" that had been espoused by the high priests of the medical establishment. In any case, patients had seen it on the television so it must be true. The doctor's role was being remolded to confirm what everybody already knew.

The 1980s also coincided with the rise of medical laboratory tests, the key factor in providing the "cases" that create the appearance of a new epidemic. This phenomenon of a 'pandemic of testing' was already explored in detail in chapter 4. It is enough to say here that the public promotion of any alleged epidemic must also involve a simultaneous campaign to line up everyone for testing. Often this is initially recommended only for those who have symptoms but it later expands to their "contacts" as well. As more tests are done, more cases appear providing the apparent evidence that the disease is spreading. Finally the tests are recommended to almost everyone or at least a large proportion of the community regardless of their circumstances. At this point it is declared to be a "screening test" and the disease may now be classified as 'endemic' or regularly occurring at a more predictable rate.

In 2020, we entered another new era where entire nations were instructed what to do in their daily lives via a plethora of uniform press releases from governments. It started when the WHO Director-General, Dr. Tedros Adhanom Ghebreyesus, stood in front of the international media on the 11th of March, 2020, and stated, "COVID-19 can be characterized as a pandemic."[311]

The "118,000 cases in 114 countries"[312] Director-General Tedros used to justify his declaration were simply the result of a hysterical pandemic of testing as earlier chapters in this book have revealed. Despite the contrived novel "virus" and the absence of any new disease, each WHO member state was now poised to unleash its own variation of an 'epidemic preparedness' plan on its citizenry.*[313] Here was a facade of science where governments claimed they were carefully following the advice of "experts" who were universally, a cadre of various institutional doctors and scientists hand-picked by the governments themselves. The mainstream media unsurprisingly fawned over such individuals, promoting their doom-laden models and cries to close borders, enforce quarantines, ramp up testing, and curtail civil rights.

The New Zealand government exemplified such totalitarian action and took over the airways with incessant advertisements about the COVID-19 "pandemic" both in the form of paid commercials and press conferences. An Official Information Act request revealed that the Department of the Prime Minister and Cabinet spent NZ$106,107,468, "on public information campaigns in support of New Zealand's COVID-19 response between 1 March 2020 and 31 March 2022."[314] In a country of only five million people it was an obscene amount. However, it did not end there as the government had also administered a $55 million "Public Interest Journalism Fund" for an overlapping period.[315] Unsurprisingly, the "journalism" that was funded was heavily biased towards supporting government actions, including the COVID vaccine promotions, and was vitriolic towards anyone questioning the narrative. In November 2023 it prompted the incoming Deputy Prime Minister to announce to the assembled media, "you can't defend $55 million of bribery."[316]

At one stage starting in late March 2020 the press conferences were held on a daily basis[317] and became a part of regular life for the New Zealanders who were now hypnotized into a state of virus fixation by the government show. The typical announcement included the number of cases, how many tests had been done, the "rules" regarding lockdowns and other childish nonsense about what people were permitted to do each day. Just prior to this, on the 20th of March, the then Prime Minister Jacinda Ardern made the ridiculous claim that along with her ministerial junta and COVID cabal, she was the, "single source of truth" as reported by *LifeSite News*:

> *"We will share with you the most up-to-date information daily. You can trust us as a source of that information," Ardern declared. "You can also trust the Director-General of Health and the Ministry of Health. For that information, do feel free to visit at any time to clarify any rumor you may hear covid19.govt.nz, otherwise dismiss anything else." Ardern next revealed that the government and its various appointed ministers would be the harbinger of truth and that New Zealanders were to trust no one else apart from the government. "We will continue to be your single source of truth," she said...Reporters queried Ardern on what such an example of a conspiracy theory might be, referencing rumors on social media that a COVID-19 related lockdown was imminent, in March 2020. In response, Ardern avoided the specific point but stated that such online messages "add to the anxiety people feel."*[318]

The very next day Ardern announced a new four-level COVID "alert system" and on the 25th of March the country went into a severe lockdown with major restrictions on freedom of movement and civil rights. During the 13th of August, 2020 press conference Ardern was still endorsing the 'single source of truth' narrative when she stated, "if you're someone that views politicians suspiciously, then, please, by all means, listen to the independent doctors, scientists—those who are our source of advice that we lean on."[319] Once again, by "independent" she meant the doctors and scientists that were approved by the government.

With the media bribed and millions of taxpayer dollars pouring into propagandizing, indoctrinating and gaslighting the public with their own money, Ardern even brazenly admitted what the New Zealand government were doing. In a March 2021 press conference she announced, "we drum in that messaging around the dangers of COVID pretty diligently for a full two-week period of sustained propaganda."[320]

Celebrity Cases

Mainstream media stories featuring celebrities with "new" diseases was also a practice that gained traction in the 1980s. Previously, health matters were generally dealt with privately and perhaps only shared with family and close friends. However, the pharmaceutical industry and many medical institutions realized that prominent celebrities could attract significant revenue streams for research and new drugs. Naturally the media were happy to feature such eye-catching headlines involving these "reveal all" stories as well. As outlined in the epilogue of *Virus Mania*, the practice has a track record of being highly effective:

> *In the case of HIV/AIDS, it was the Hollywood world star Rock Hudson who depicts a kind of "big bang" here. Hudson was one of the first to undergo an "HIV antibody test". This happened on June 5, 1984, just a few weeks after Gallo's TV appearance on stage...So it happened that the 1.96-metre tall*

> *image of American manhood received a "positive" test report...According to the motto: if AIDS can affect someone like Hudson, it can affect anyone, men and women alike...In 2010, the German daily newspaper Frankfurter Allgemeine Zeitung (FAZ) published the article "Rock Hudson: He gave AIDS a face" on the occasion of the 25th anniversary of the Hollywood legend's death and hit the nail on the head with it. Indeed, it was the world-famous actor who gave HIV/ AIDS a face in 1985. Unfortunately, the FAZ article failed to tell its readers how scientifically untenable the message was that Hudson had died of HIV, and in what fatal way this gave the worldwide virus hunters unimagined power.*[321]

In the case of COVID-19, Hollywood leading man Tom Hanks was one of the first major celebrities to go public with his "diagnosis". On the 12th of March, 2020, he posted the following tweet:

> *Hello, folks. Rita and I are down here in Australia. We felt a bit tired, like we had colds, and some body aches. Rita had some chills that came and went. Slight fevers too. To play things right, as is needed in the world right now, we were tested for the Coronavirus, and were found to be positive. Well now. What to do next? The Medical Officials have protocols that must be followed. We Hanks' will be tested, observed, and isolated for as long as public health and safety requires."*[322]

In essence, Hanks and his wife Rita felt, "like we had colds" because that is what they had. If they also recorded, "slight fevers" then they probably had a mild bout of typical influenza-like symptoms. COVID-19 was not a new disease aside from the fact that coronaviruses have never been shown to physically exist as contagious, disease-causing entities. The only new development was a PCR "test" that was spreading around the world, as this book has already outlined. However, Hanks had presented the new corona playbook to the world: get tested, follow the public health officials, and prepare to be isolated for as long as you are told.

TIME simultaneously promoted the story with the headline "Tom Hanks and Rita Wilson Test Positive for COVID-19"[323] (which was the 11th of March, 2020, in the United States). The online article featured a video where Queensland State Premier, Annastacia Palasczuk appeared in front of the media and announced, "Tom Hanks and Rita Wilson are being cared in one our [sic] world-class hospitals in Queensland…I've been in contact with [film director] Baz Luhrmann quite often today and he has said to me that he wants to pass on to everyone that we all stand with the people of Queensland in making sure that we comply with any restrictions…"

Once again another Hollywood representative cheerleading the developing infringements on civil rights in line with the political class. It was also unclear why Hanks and his wife required hospital-level care for what he later described as, "the blahs."[324] The *TIME* article had noted that, "the actor's 29-year-old son Chet said that he just got off the phone with his parents. 'They're both fine. They're not even that sick. They're not worried about it. They're not trippin',' the younger Hanks said."

Despite the preposterous narrative and the glaring inconsistencies, the celebrity involvement helped get COVID-19 firmly embedded in the minds of the public with the Hanks tweet allegedly receiving over 900,000 likes. It should be mentioned here that the tweet also featured something else: a photo of a biohazard plastic waste bag and a discarded latex glove. It was an odd image for Hanks to have and had all the appearances of being staged. Perhaps it was worth a thousand words, fictional as the words may have been?

Less than a month following the Hanks tweet the mainstream media was heavily promoting the illness of British Prime Minister, Boris Johnson.

FREE

METRO

CORONAVIRUS CRISIS

TUESDAY, APRIL 7, 2020

THE WORLD'S MOST POPULAR FREE NEWSPAPER

PM PUT IN INTENSIVE CARE UNIT

JOHNSON'S SYMPTOMS WORSEN 11 DAYS AFTER TESTING POSITIVE FOR KILLER VIRUS

Turn for the worse: The prime minister in a tweet last week, looking unwell

Expert care: Mr Johnson was transferred to the ICU at St Thomas' Hospital in London around 7pm last night

CORONAVIRUS patient Boris Johnson was last night moved to intensive care after taking a turn for the worse.

The prime minister remained 'conscious at this time' and had been moved as a precaution in case he needed to be put on a ventilator, No.10 announced.

He asked for his No.2 Dominic Raab, who earlier revealed they had not spoken since Saturday, to deputise for him 'where necessary'.

Mr Johnson was diagnosed 11 days ago and was admitted to hospital on Sunday after suffering persistent symptoms. Downing Street said last night: 'Over the course of this afternoon, the condition of the prime minister has worsened and, on the advice of his medical team, he has been moved to the intensive care unit at the hospital.'

by DOMINIC YEATMAN

The PM is thought to have been given oxygen at St Thomas' hospital, part of the Guy's and St Thomas's NHS trust, as doctors warned he risked contracting viral pneumonia.

Sadiq Khan, his successor as mayor of London, tweeted: 'Praying for the Prime Minister's swift recovery tonight. @GSTTnhs has some of the finest medical staff in the world, and he couldn't be in safer hands.'

Labour leader Sir Keir Starmer tweeted: 'Terribly sad news. All the country's thoughts are with the Prime Minister and his family during this incredibly difficult time.'

The SNP's Westminster group leader Ian Blackford posted: 'This is very worrying news. Thoughts and prayers with Boris, @carriesymonds and all their family.

'This is such a terrible virus that we

Continued on Page 4

The hospital admission of British Prime Minister Boris Johnson dominated the headlines in April 2020. Metro *declared it was due to a "killer virus" in their 7th of April, 2020 edition. Other publications such as* The Daily Telegraph *and* The Sun *also featured the cumulative cases and deaths attributed to the "coronavirus".*

In fact, the headlines started promoting themselves with a memorable one from the *BBC* being, "Newspaper headlines: PM's intensive care move dominates front pages" on the 7th of April, 2020.[325] Tom Hanks merely had "the blahs" which made the alleged new disease seem like a joke and nothing more than a cold. But now the fear dial was being turned up with newspapers reporting that "BoJo" was struggling for his life due to the "killer virus." For example, the following was from a *BBC* feature:

> *The prime minister, 55, was admitted to hospital in London with "persistent symptoms" on Sunday evening...A No 10 statement read: "The prime minister has been under the care of doctors at St Thomas' Hospital, in London, after being admitted with persistent symptoms of coronavirus. Over the course of [Monday] afternoon, the condition of the prime minister has worsened and, on the advice of his medical team, he has been moved to the intensive care unit at the hospital."*[326]

It was not reported to the public how it was determined that he had, "symptoms of coronavirus," due to the non-specific, if not meaningless case definition of COVID-19. The overweight Johnson is hardly a picture of good health and has previously admitted to heavy drinking and an unhealthy diet.[327] Despite claiming that he had cut down on the alcohol, ironically he was caught partying at a Downing Street gathering on the 13th of November, 2020.[328] It was at a time when the British government had imposed a strict lockdown on their citizens with the rules stating at the time that only two people from different households were allowed to mix indoors. Clearly, despite the government and media fear campaigns, BoJo and his associates were not particularly concerned about the alleged "killer virus".

Rigging the Playing Field

While the celebrity cases were promoted, it was equally important to the establishment that information and evidence counter to their narratives was suppressed. There were several notable "lead up" events to COVID-19 and one of these was the (September) 2019 Global Vaccination Summit, which will receive further commentary in chapter 6. Here the WHO and the powerful institutions associated with it were building the infrastructure to suppress anyone challenging their claims. At the summit they announced that:

> *The influence of media on public sentiment is well documented. An open media landscape plays a crucial role in democratic societies and transparent public debate. The information environment is rapidly changing, however, and new technologies – especially digital media – are increasingly vectors for large-scale anti-vaccination campaigns. This is particularly true of social media, where the 'anti-vax' movement is actively pushing the narrative that vaccines are not safe and have serious side effects...The EU is also taking action on the spread of false information about vaccination on social media. In 2018, the European Commission proposed a series of measures to tackle disinformation online, including an EU-wide code of practice on disinformation, support for an independent network of fact-checkers, and a series of actions to stimulate quality journalism and promote media literacy. The EU collaborates with online platforms, including social media and search engines, to ensure the protection of European values and security. Several of them, including Facebook, Google and Twitter, recently subscribed to a code of practice committing them to greater transparency on algorithms and sponsored content, and to introducing*

> *measures to identify and close fake accounts and enable fact-checkers, researchers and public authorities to monitor online disinformation.*[329]

The notion that there was anything close to an "open media" or any "transparent public debate" taking place in the subsequent COVID-19 era is as absurd as it is an outright bald-faced lie. The advent of 2020 saw new and epic levels of propaganda, censorship, shadow-banning, demonetizing and de-platforming with many Big Tech platforms employing "guidelines" that prohibited information that went against supra-national and government institutions such as the WHO and the CDC, respectively. Whether the material was factual and scientifically accurate or not was irrelevant. It meant that what "they" said was always 'right think', but what one was permitted to say as a counter-point on social media about issues such as face masks and lockdowns, mandates and injections could change overnight and would be deemed, 'wrong think'. On these issues, the whims of individuals such as Anthony Fauci eclipsed all else.[330]

In a similar vein, portraying claims made by the network of fact-checkers that have suddenly appeared in recent years as "independent" is also risible. In 2021 Twitter announced it would partner with the *Associated Press* and *Reuters*, two of the world's largest media conglomerates.[331] As reported by attorney and investigative journalist Megan Redshaw, the self-evident conflicts of interest in these arrangements were enormous:

> *In February, Reuters announced a similar partnership with Facebook to "fact check" social media posts. However, when announcing its fact-checking partnerships with Facebook and Twitter, Reuters made no mention of this fact: The news organization has ties to Pfizer, World Economic Forum (WEF) and Trusted News Initiative (TNI), an industry collaboration of major news and global tech organizations whose stated*

> *mission is to "combat spread of harmful vaccine disinformation." Reuters also failed to provide any criteria for how information would be defined as "misinformation" and did not disclose the qualifications of the people responsible for determining fact versus false or misleading "misinformation."*[332]

The wider mainstream media and government funded departments also joined the misinformation bandwagon. There were often huge incentives to do so and what actually qualified as 'misinformation' was unclear. This was explained by Dr Sam Bailey (on uncensored platforms) in October 2021:

> *Here in New Zealand we have government funded departments and state-sponsored media that claim to be responsible for collecting, monitoring, and educating on COVID misinformation. But when you try and pin them down on backing up their allegations of misinformation, it seems they all pass the buck and none of them can give you specific examples...I was first put on this trail by retired United States oncologist Dr Anna Goodwin...When Anna couldn't find any official definitions of "COVID misinformation" she enquired to the Health Research Council of New Zealand. She pointed out to them that, "Health Minister Andrew Little announced today that your organization has appropriated $42 million to fund 36 projects directed at addressing 'misinformation' related to the COVID-19 jab resulting in 'vaccine hesitancy' by the NZ public. She asked the HRC, "what is the definition of 'COVID-19 misinformation' for the purposes of the allotment of funding to address this problem?" They responded that, "the Health Research Council has not referred to 'COVID-19 misinformation' and none of the*

funded projects used this term, hence we do not have a definition for it."...So we head over to the 'Unite against COVID-19' government website to see if we can get an official definition there. They claim to tell us how to recognize COVID-19 misinformation. In the section "Get the Facts" they point to websites you can go to, which are all government websites. Interestingly, they say you could try, "speaking with your health provider" but fail to mention that New Zealand doctors are threatened with investigation and may lose their license if they don't universally promote the Covid shots.[333]

"Stuffing Their Mouths with Gold"

The other side of the rigged playing field was the incentivisation (often financial) for health practitioners to go along with government policies. For example, the $2.2 trillion Coronavirus Aid, Relief, and Economic Security (CARES) Act was passed by the United States Congress and signed into law by President Donald Trump on the 27th of March, 2020.[334] It included a monumental amount of money, "$130 billion in direct financial relief to the medical and hospital industries" amongst the other funding that poured into the medico-pharmaceutical complex in the name of, "the Fight Against the Coronavirus".[335] It also meant that Medicare gave a bonus 20% to hospitals when they listed a diagnosis of COVID-19 and patients could access COVID-19 tests and vaccines "free" of cost.[336]

The Association of American Physicians and Surgeons (AAPS) noted that in this hypernormalised[*337] setting a "free" COVID PCR test was, in fact, a *requirement* in the Emergency Room or upon the admission of a patient.[338] Also of grave concern was the additional 20% bonus awarded to a hospital for the use of the dangerous and useless "anti-viral" drug remdesivir.[*339] The AAPS went on to point out that Medicare and Medicaid Services implemented "value-based" payment programs that tracked how many healthcare staff received COVID vaccines, leading to their conclusion that, "we see why many hospitals implemented COVID-19 vaccine mandates. They are paid more."[340]

Also of significance was the declaration by the US Department of Health and Human Services (HHS) on the 17th of March, 2020 (and notably applying retroactively from the 4th of February, 2020) that COVID-19 "countermeasures" would be covered under the Public Readiness and Emergency Preparedness Act (PREP Act).[341] The PREP Act was passed by the US Congress in December 2005 and the egregious nature of the legislation fully manifested with COVID-19. During alleged pandemics, this Act, "specifically affords to drug makers immunity from actions related to the manufacture, testing, development, distribution, administration and use of medical countermeasures".[342] The March 2020 declaration by the HHS provided extremely broad immunity for commercial manufacturers, organizations and medical practitioners in their war against the "virus" and described counter-measures in the following way:

> *Covered Countermeasures are **any** antiviral, **any** other drug, **any** biologic, **any** diagnostic, **any** other device, or **any** vaccine, used to treat, diagnose, cure, prevent, or mitigate COVID-19, or the transmission of SARS-CoV-2 or a virus mutating therefrom, or **any** device used in the administration of **any** such product, and all components and constituent materials of **any** such product.*[343] [authors' emphasis]

The PREP Act gives the HHS secretary unilateral and sweeping powers and does not list any criteria for determining the existence of an emergency.[344] It also allows formerly in place protective legislation to be overridden and abused. For example, "if the HHS secretary designates that a vaccine is a covered countermeasure, thimerosal (a mercury containing preservative) can be used in the vaccine, even in states that have enacted such bans."[345]

Almost every country had their own legislative and financial incentive systems in place for medical practitioners and their associated industries to participate in the COVID theatre. In New Zealand, an Official Information Act request revealed that many medical centers and pharmacies administering Pfizer's Comirnaty vaccine received hundreds of thousands of dollars and some in excess of $NZ1 million.[346] It is beyond the scope of this book to detail the perversion of the medical system through funding structures. Suffice to say here that during their time in the institutionalized "system" both authors witnessed the overt influences that revenue streams have on the behavior of practitioners. In our experience it is something that most patients significantly underestimate. With the advent of the COVID era this was not a new development though it was markedly amplified.

Historically, politically motivated "health" funding was perhaps articulated most succinctly by Aneurin Bevan, the famous British politician and architect of the National Health Service (NHS). In recounting how he bribed doctors to go along with the National Health Service Act (1946) that led to the formation of the NHS, Bevan declared that, "I stuffed their mouths with gold."[347]

Persecution of Those Questioning the Narrative

The authors' Bailey have experienced severe censorship since 2020 with the majority of COVID-19 content now banned on the Big Tech platforms such as Facebook and YouTube. Questioning the use of the PCR or other alleged diagnostic tools was sometimes permitted but questioning the implementation and effects of COVID vaccines was generally not allowed. Presenting refutations of the existence of SARS-CoV-2 or other "viruses" typically resulted in strikes or complete bans on Big Tech platforms. We are frequently informed by our audience that even mentioning our names or placing links to our platforms can result in their posts being deleted or accounts being suspended.

As well as censorship from Big Tech, the attempts to control permissible material and expressed opinions have increasingly stemmed from medical regulatory bodies. Dr Sam Bailey was "under investigation" by the Medical Council of New Zealand (MCNZ) by mid-2020 and elected not to renew her practicing license in 2021. Even after this point the Council continued to make attempts to suppress her free speech. One was through the farcical claim that continuing to discuss COVID-19 and its various aspects, including vaccines, may constitute, "practicing medicine without a license." Apparently anyone else, whether they were a politician, a radio DJ, or a taxi driver could weigh in with their opinions on COVID-19 but not a fully trained doctor. Unless of course the doctor was mindlessly repeating all the claims by the government and the organizations under their influence. It is clear that practitioners that are working within the current system do not possess anything resembling autonomy and are increasingly being coerced into carrying out the agendas of governments and supra-national organizations. Sadly also, so many of them remain unquestioningly compliant and are thus complicit in the treachery.

As part of their attempts to keep all doctors toeing the government's COVID-19 line, the MCNZ issued what they called a "Guidance statement" on the 28th of April, 2021, which stated:

> *The Dental and Medical Councils have an expectation that all dental and medical practitioners will take up the opportunity to be vaccinated—unless medically contraindicated...As a health practitioner, you have a role in providing evidence-based advice and information about the COVID-19 vaccination to others. You should be prepared to discuss*

> *evidence-based information about vaccination and its benefits to assist informed decision making...As regulators we respect an individual's right to have their own opinions, but it is our view that there is no place for anti-vaccination messages in professional health practice, nor any promotion of antivaccination claims including on social media and advertising by health practitioners.*[348]

The statement was anti-scientific and illogical and would have been more at home featured in a dystopian novel along the lines of George Orwell's *Nineteen Eighty-four.* The discussion of "evidence-based information" could have been removed from the statement because the MCNZ had already decided that doctors were obliged to promote the injections. Not only that but somehow they had determined that the shots only came with "benefits". The "evidence" they provided for this proclamation was a link to the New Zealand Ministry of Health's webpage "COVID-19: Vaccines" which simply had information about the vaccine role out program and how to get one.[349] The MCNZ's "expectation" that all doctors would endorse them apparently also extended to Dr Mark Bailey. Despite permanently exiting the medical system in 2016, the MCNZ attempted to launch a potential prosecution following his initial public appearances discussing the COVID fraud. Their farcical investigation was quickly and discreetly withdrawn when they were put on notice.[350]

The guidance statement prompted New Zealand Doctors Speaking Out with Science (NZDSOS) to file a for a High Court Judicial Review of its legality. The MCNZ were clearly using their "guidance statement" to threaten doctors into submission and complicity with the government dictates. In the article "MCNZ Served Legal Papers by NZDSOS" published in August 2023, NZDSOS stated:

> *In issuing the now notorious "Guidance Statement" on Covid-19 vaccination, it firmly placed itself between patients*

> *and doctors, and their right to free speech. Furthermore, if doctors were to follow the guidance statement, they would be in breach of the MCNZ Statement on Informed Consent which was changed in 2021…Moreover, the MCNZ used its "Guidance Statement" on Covid-19 vaccination in action against doctors who questioned the country's covid response. This statement is in no way legally binding but they have proceeded as if it is, presumably to threaten other doctors into obedience. The courts have told them they should stop. We have seen no evidence of this as they continue to investigate doctors, send them to the Health Practitioners Disciplinary Tribunal and to "re-education".*[351]

Suspiciously, the MCNZ quietly "revoked" the statement a few weeks after being notified of the proposed Judicial Review. In contrast to the much publicized launch of the statement, doctors in New Zealand were not notified of its revocation with only the following excuse offered on the MCNZ website:

> *From 13 September 2023...the Medical Council of New Zealand no longer provides the guidance statement on COVID-19 vaccine and your professional responsibility as a current expectation for doctors. This follows the New Zealand Government's decision to remove vaccine mandates and other public health restrictions in connection with the COVID-19 pandemic. The Medical Council is maintaining this page as a historical record only.*[352]

It is unclear why they would revoke the statement due to the removal of the government's vaccine mandates because the statement was originally issued by the MCNZ at a time when there were no vaccine mandates in the country. The obvious explanation is that these supposedly "independent" medical institutions are in fact collaborating with the government. More evidence of this political interference was uncovered in official government correspondence from 2020 that discussed Dr Sam Bailey:

> *Furthermore, an OIA* [Official Information Act request] *has uncovered correspondence between Dr Ashley Bloomfield, the then Director General of Health, and Joan Simeon, the MCNZ CEO regarding an NZDSOS member* [Dr Sam Bailey] *making videos about covid. Ms Simeon states that there is a potential risk of harm to public health (note again she does not mention individuals but the all-encompassing public), a statement that comes very close to a medical assessment by a lay person. She goes on to state that the MCNZ would like to work with the MoH* [Ministry of Health] *in their approach to this doctor. On a side note the OIA correspondence linked above also states that the "vaccine" would be independently tested and that vaccination would not be mandatory. Both of these statements would be shown to be false, and likely knowingly so at the time.*[353]

The recent nefarious actions of medical regulators is but another arm in the measures that have been put in place merely to provide a public illusion of "evidence-based" medicine. In reality, it has become an anti-scientific proscribing of critical thinking in doctors. In addition, core to the declared axioms of 'evidence-based medicine' is the expressed acknowledgement of the taking into account of the wishes of a patient: "Patient involvement in decision making is part of the process of being an effective practitioner."[354]

The draconian control mechanisms of the medical profession that are now fully manifesting were being seeded more than a century ago. What we witnessed in the COVID era was a tightening of the noose and the attempted eradication of any remaining dissidents. As author F. William

Engdahl reported, the origins of what is now sometimes known as "Rockefeller Medicine" was carefully contrived through a "study" arranged by the Rockefeller and Carnegie families:

> *The 1910 study was titled, The Flexner Report, and its ostensible purpose was to investigate the quality of all US medical schools. The outcome of the report was, however, predetermined. Ties between the well-endowed Rockefeller Institute and the AMA* [American Medical Association] *went through the corrupt AMA head, George H. Simmons. Simmons was also the editor of the influential Journal of the American Medical Association, a publication delivered to some 80,000 doctors across America. He reportedly wielded absolute power over the doctors' association. He controlled the rising ad revenues for drug companies to promote their drugs to AMA doctors in his journal, a highly lucrative business. He was a key part of the Rockefeller medical coup that was to completely redefine acceptable medical practice away from remedial or preventive treatment to use of often deadly drugs and expensive surgeries.*[355]

"Modern" medicine was born that year and since that time doctors have been progressively brought to heel by the threat of regulation and of losing their licenses if they failed to comply with "acceptable practice.". Even if it is argued that the materializing reforms of that period helped establish "standards" with a science-based and research-centered approach in medicine, it took a relatively short time for the centralization of medical bureaucratic control. Indeed, it led to a rapid monopolization and an intersection of financial interests in "health care" in the United States and in many other countries. The keys to the kingdom were happily picked up by a small cabal under the influence of vested interests, including the emerging pharmaceutical industry.

Case Study: The Suppression of The Perth Group

The Perth Group is a private organization that formed in 1981 in Perth, Western Australia with the three original members being biophysicist Eleni Papadopulos-Eleopulos, emergency physician Valendar Turner and Professor of Pathology John Papadimitriou. For over four decades they have argued that the HIV/AIDS experts have not scientifically established any of the following:

1. The existence of a virus termed 'HIV'.
2. The specificity of 'HIV' antibody tests for 'HIV' infection.
3. The theory that 'HIV' causes the clinical syndrome AIDS.
4. That the "HIV genome" comes from an infectious particle.
5. 'HIV'/AIDS being infectious by blood or sexual intercourse.
6. Mother to child transmission of 'HIV' (and the alleged benefit of certain "anti-virals").[356]

No group has produced more detailed scientific critiques of the HIV/AIDS model and their 2017 treatise *HIV - A Virus Like No Other*, weighs in at over 60,000 words with several hundred supporting scientific citations.[357] This and the Perth Group's many other publications have refuted all aspects of the theory that a "deadly virus" is passing around and causing AIDS. And yet the vast majority of doctors have never heard of them or read even one of their works.

The incredible state of affairs is readily explained by the fact that doctors are trained to believe that 'HIV=AIDS' is settled science. Most do not know any of the historical events that took place and if they do it is restricted to the fanciful story that HIV was all worked out by the likes of Robert Gallo, Luc Montagnier and Anthony Fauci in the 1980s. How could these famous individuals and their highly-resourced institutions be completely wrong with the science?

Indeed, after two decades in the medical system neither of the authors were aware that anyone had even attempted a refutation of the HIV model, let alone produced an 83-page treatise. All we were informed in our training was that some people engaged in "AIDS denialism" as a reaction to the terrible burden of a death sentence for themselves or others.

Of course the term 'AIDS denialism' is highly disingenuous as no serious critics of the model deny that the individuals in question may become sick and even terminally unwell. The dispute is over the evidence that an infectious virus is the cause of the clinical syndrome known as 'AIDS', first *described* in the 1980s. The CDC currently lists 27 AIDS-defining conditions,[358] all of which existed prior to the alleged appearance of HIV. The only new development is the claim since the 1980s that these wide-ranging conditions can all be caused by one postulated virus and diagnosed with a biochemical test(s). (See also Dr Claus Köhnlein's comments about this phenomenon in chapter 4: *"Why was SARS-2 (COVID-19) Bigger than SARS-1?"*)

The United States National Institutes of Allergy and Infectious Disease (NIAID) website once featured a page titled "The Evidence That HIV Causes AIDS." It included a section titled "Answering The Skeptics: Responses To Arguments That HIV Does Not Cause AIDS" written in a "MYTHS" and "FACTS" format. It does not specify who they are responding to. For reasons unknown to us the webpage was taken down in 2009 but can still be found on the 17th of January capture that year on archive.org.[359] The article stated that, "nearly everyone with AIDS has antibodies to HIV," as though an "antibody" (protein) reacting in a laboratory test plate is evidence of a virus at work. They have engaged in circular reasoning by claiming that a chemical reaction is evidence of the virus…because the virus will cause this particular chemical reaction. However, there was no demonstration of a "virus" to start with.

The NIAID also make the fraudulent claims that, "HIV fulfills Koch's postulates as the cause of AIDS," and "the suspected pathogen can be isolated - and propagated - outside the host." The cited evidence is in the form of epidemiological statistics, anecdotes, and pseudoscientific animal studies. It is beyond the scope of this book to address all of the "evidence" that was on display in the article. However, in their typical fashion, The Perth Group made a succinct response to the NIAID in 2000, addressing both the key argument and the disingenuous nature of the article:

> *It is incomprehensible how a body of scientists at the National Institutes for Health in the US could present both sides of a scientific debate as a series of "MYTHS" and "FACTS". Especially without providing the names of scientists who hold the opposing view or any citations to enable the reader to investigate the matter himself. The only conclusion one can make from this behavior is that the NIH does not want their readers to learn the full story. Here we examine one very important "FACT" and leave it up to the reader to make his own judgement as to whether or not it is a "MYTH".*
> *FACT: THERE IS NO EVIDENCE A RETROVIRUS HAS BEEN ISOLATED FROM THE TISSUES OF AIDS PATIENTS. HENCE THERE IS NO GOLD STANDARD FOR ANTIBODY TESTING FOR "HIV" INFECTION AND NO PROOF A RETROVIRUS CAUSES AIDS.*[360]

In order to anticipate the establishment's hardening dogma, The Perth Group had several of their papers published in the peer-reviewed scientific journals.[361] Equally so many were rejected,[362] most often for spurious reasons that had little to do with the carefully presented scientific arguments. An example was "A critical appraisal of the evidence for the existence of HIV," which was submitted to the Royal Australasian College of Surgeons in 1997. The Perth Group have commented on the astounding excuse for rejection they received:

> *According to that journal it is editorial policy to "welcome personal views of surgeons on a variety of topics," and to publish papers on "current and controversial issues." Although both reviewers accepted the bulk of the scientific arguments and found the paper "interesting reading," they advised against publication because, in their view, an analysis of evidence for the isolation of HIV was of "no real relevance...to a surgical audience" or "would be of little interest or use to the majority of readers of the Australian and New Zealand Journal of Surgery".*[363]

In another example, the HIV theory of AIDS proposed that the "virus" was causing two principal diseases: *Pneumocystis Carinii* Pneumonia (PCP) and Kaposi's sarcoma (KS), a type of cancer that affects the skin and other organs. However, the "HIV experts" were subsequently forced to bite the bullet and declare HIV was not the cause of KS. This was because cases of KS were reported in homosexual men who did not have positive HIV antibody tests. Eleni Papadopulos had anticipated this and in 1990 submitted a pertinent paper to the *Medical Journal of Australia*. This was thrice rejected on the advice of an anonymous, "established expert reviewer" who stated:

> *The author tries to argue that Kaposi's sarcoma cannot be caused by HIV infection, and that therefore AIDS is not due to HIV infection* [Papadopulos made no such claim]. *The arguments put forward by the author are quite unsatisfactory, and are not supported by even a desultory reading of the literature quoted. In addition, the author fails to examine the body of epidemiological, immunological and cellular*

> *literature concerning the pathology, pathogenesis and clinical associations of this fascinating manifestation of HIV infection.*[364]

Yet it was this very "epidemiological, immunological and cellular literature" that eventually led the "established experts" to accept that, "this fascinating manifestation of HIV infection" is *not* due to alleged HIV infection. Obviously the expert reviewer realized that the failure of HIV to explain KS was bad news for the rest of the AIDS theory. At the very least, KS should have ceased being an AIDS indicator disease. This was not to be and KS remains on the list with the other 26 diseases, all supposedly related to the claimed "virus" whose characteristics can apparently change to fit the model.

The suppression of The Perth Group's work has been a crime against the individuals who have been labelled as harboring a "deadly virus". As Jon Rappoport wrote in his 1988 book *AIDS Inc.: scandal of the century*, "there is no way to measure the full effect of telling a person he has AIDS, or has tested positive for the 'AIDS virus'."[365] Furthermore it has been a crime against humanity due to the billions of dollars that the AIDS industry consumes, with funding only going to those doctors and scientists who subscribe to the virus model. The pharmaceutical industry has also benefitted greatly of course with its "antiviral" chemicals. Their various drug concoctions have been involved in the deaths of thousands of people, particularly in the 1980s and 1990s as outlined in chapter 3 of *Virus Mania*, "AIDS: From Spare Tire to Multibillion-Dollar Business".[366]

However, The Perth Group's efforts over the last four decades have not been in vain. An inadvertent effect of the COVID-19 fraud has been an explosion of interest in their devastating and unrefuted critiques of HIV/ AIDS as well as the broader implications for virology itself.

Chapter 6 - All Pandemics Lead To Vaccines

"Even if objective evidence, in reaction, sickness and death, were lacking (which it is not), that vaccines and sera can cause disease, no very profound depth of intelligence is needed to envisage the ingenuousness of injecting the filthy products of disease into a healthy person to keep him well."

— Dr Ulric Williams.[367]

"Most people in Global Health were trained in institutions, work on projects, or work in foundations funded or owned by these same few individuals. Global public health has become a private club of a small number of very wealthy people."

— Dr David Bell, former WHO medical officer.[368]

What are Vaccines Doing?

This book has outlined many aspects of how the illusion is maintained of "germs" being a constant threat to humanity. Despite access to some of the highest standards of living the world has ever seen, we are supposed to be believe that "infectious diseases" that all but disappeared in the 20th century are now worse than ever. In fact, they are alleged to be so bad that the only way forward is stay-at-home orders, invasive human tracking, face masks, and mandated mass inoculations with experimental injections. Even on their own scientifically unestablished premise that contagion between humans takes place, how is it that the previous management strategies have been so quickly thrown out the window? By the late 1900s, these so called infectious diseases were essentially said to be conquered by modern medicine. The outlier was the "new" disease in the 1980s called 'AIDS' with the equally newly invented "human immunodeficiency virus" (HIV) said to be its cause.

Despite overwhelming evidence showing that the incidence and severity of almost all of these historical "childhood" diseases had fallen into comparative insignificance by the 1980s, something very odd happened subsequently. In 1986, the CDC rubber stamped the childhood vaccine schedule to administer a total of 12 shots for 8 diseases.[369] By 2019, the recommended schedule consisted of a total of 54 shots for 16 diseases[370] and it has continued to climb. For decades, parents have been duped into believing that the reason we are not seeing deadly diseases ravaging populations anymore is due to this myriad of injections (some vaccines are given orally) going into the youngest members of our community. Nothing could be further from the truth. As Dr Sam Bailey reported in 2021, such a claim has never been backed by real life data:

> *We frequently hear that vaccines are one of the most effective public health interventions of the 20th century. Apparently among U.S. children born between 1995 and 2013, vaccination is estimated to have prevented 322 million illnesses, 21 million hospitalizations and 732,000 premature deaths, with overall cost savings of $1.38 trillion. It certainly sounds fantastic but can we find actual trials or sound data to back this up? These claims can be found in a profile article from the CDC which fails to provide any particular data, and a sketchy modeling paper* ["Benefits from Immunization During the Vaccines for Children Program Era - United States, 1994–2013"[371]] *that essentially claims higher vaccination rates in themselves must equal great benefits at minimal costs. This was established through estimations though and sweeping assumptions.*[372]

Unfortunately, when it comes to vaccines the majority of the planet is naive to reality and has been highly conditioned by means of folklore and the repetitive and relentless narratives engineered by the pharmaceutical industry and their enablers. Virtually all of us are born into an environment where even questioning the use of vaccines is considered *verboten*. However, while claims such as, "it is indisputable that vaccination has made an enormous contribution to human and animal health, especially in the developing world,"[373] may appear in the scientific journals, those that have looked at the data quickly realize that this is nothing short of blatant propaganda amounting to an outright lie.

In *Dissolving Illusions*, Humphries and Bystrianyk completely dismantle the notion that vaccines had much, if anything to do with the great reductions in morbidity and mortality that were seen in common diseases last century.[374] Their data have been collated directly from official sources and many of the charts have been made freely available to the public, such as the ones featured in this book. Despite such information being easily accessible, public health institutions around the world continue to recommend the wholesale deployment of almost every vaccine that comes to market. In addition, the *Virus Mania* authors have spent years requesting to see the evidence that many of these health institutions claim they rely upon, but to date not one has been able to produce evidence that vaccine recipients have better health outcomes.[375]

Tragically, childhood diseases have increased markedly since the 1980s and they have nothing to do with the type of diseases seen prior to the increased standards of living which are generally enjoyed in developed countries since last century. Poor dietary practices and obesity are certainly taking their toll on the young today, with a new epidemic of metabolic problems. However, the prevalence of asthma, allergic and inflammatory conditions has also risen dramatically and this is now affecting developing

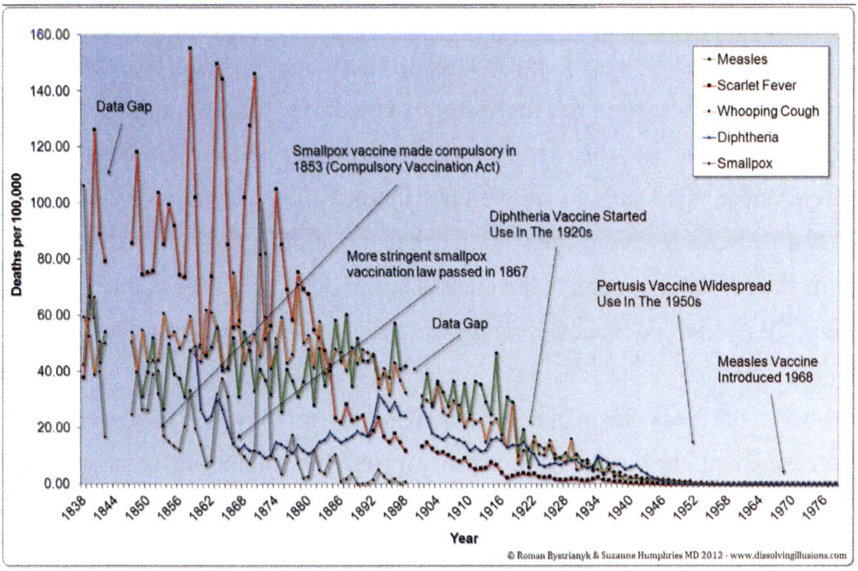

The "enormous" contribution to health that has been attributed to some common vaccines has been shown to be evidently unfounded and highly misleading. Source: https://dissolvingillusions.com/graphs-images/

countries as well. In 2011, the World Allergy Organization (WAO) notably reported that:

> *The prevalence of allergic diseases worldwide is rising dramatically in both developed and developing countries. These diseases include asthma; rhinitis; anaphylaxis; drug, food, and insect allergy; eczema; and urticaria (hives) and angioedema. This increase is especially problematic in children, who are bearing the greatest burden of the rising trend which has occurred over the last two decades.*[376]

In its 2013 'White Book' update the WAO stated that even if there are allergy-related issues with childhood vaccines, "vaccination programs are essential and avoiding or denying vaccinations will cause immense human suffering, which would be much more problematic than the allergy epidemic itself."[377] However, the report does not provide the evidential data that would be required to make this conclusion. In fact, unlike most of the statements in the report, that particular claim is completely unreferenced. The authors were either mindlessly repeating vaccine dogma or had decided to avoid questioning their use in case it attracted derision from their establishment colleagues. They would certainly want to avoid being "Wakefielded" (see epilogue).

All sorts of ideas have been put forward as to why we have seen this increase in allergic and inflammatory problems, including some authors who proposed in their title, "Is the Global Rise of Asthma an Early Impact of Anthropogenic Climate Change?"[378] Conspicuous by its absence in almost every analysis is the correlation of these inflammatory problems with the massive increase in childhood vaccinations. Such is the resistance to the idea that vaccines are causing a health crisis, it is essentially ignored by those in the medical industry and their funders.

A large part of the reason it is ignored is no doubt the consequences for those within the system who point out that they have identified problems with vaccines. In 2020, U.S. physician Dr Paul Thomas published the comparative health outcomes for 3324 pediatric patients over a period of 10 years.[379] The unvaccinated kids had far less visits to the medical center, particularly with inflammatory and allergic conditions. Compared to unvaccinated children, the most vaccinated children had relative risks of office visits of 16.0 for asthma, 20.6 for allergic rhinitis, 11.3 for sinusitis, and 6.5 for breathing issues. If the authorities were genuinely interested in health outcomes then they should have thanked Dr Thomas for his data and commenced an urgent investigation into the matter. Instead they suspended his medical license and said that his young patients needed to follow the CDC vaccination schedule. As stated on his website:

After publishing the most significant real-world, peer-reviewed study showing data, over time, that children receiving fewer vaccines were healthier than those following the CDC vaccine schedule, the Oregon Medical Board (OMB), emergently and without filing charges, took his license. This emergency suspension resulted in Dr. Paul losing not only his license but all health plan contracts, hospital privileges, board certifications, and his ability to practice medicine and make a living for this last year. His two-week trial with the OMB, scheduled for January 2022, is estimated to cost over $250,000 in legal fees and fines just to get through the trial, which will undoubtedly require appeals that can take years.[380]

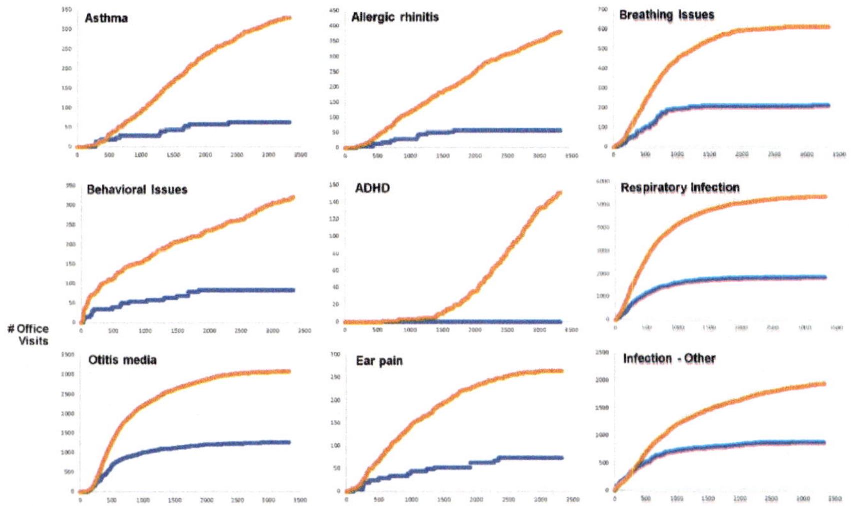

Cumulative office visits in the vaccinated (upper lines/orange) vs. unvaccinated (lower lines/blue) patients born into Dr Paul Thomas's practice. The number of office visits for the unvaccinated is adjusted by a sample size multiplier factor (4.9) to the expected value as if the number of unvaccinated in the study was the same as the number of vaccinated. Source: https://www.mdpi.com/1660-4601/17/22/8674/htm

The Bill Gates Factor

In April 2020, in the early days of the COVID-19 "pandemic," Microsoft founder Bill Gates appeared on *The Ellen Show* to advise the United States and the world that, "if the whole country does a better job of shutting down and we get prioritization of the testing that's going on, what policies should we have? Because until we get almost everybody vaccinated globally, we still won't be fully back to normal."[381] As has typically been the case, Gates was not required to provide any evidence for his fantastic claims and predictions involving health and medicine. Indeed, the following month investigative journalist James Corbett reported on the meteoric rise of the billionaire Gates to become the world's foremost medical "advisor":

> *Bill Gates is no public health expert. He is not a doctor, an epidemiologist or an infectious disease researcher. Yet somehow he has become a central figure in the lives of billions of people, presuming to dictate the medical actions that will be required for the world to go "back to normal." The transformation of Bill Gates from computer kingpin to global health czar is as remarkable as it is instructive, and it tells us a great deal about where we are heading as the world plunges into a crisis the likes of which we have not seen before.*[382]

A document from the the 2018 annual meeting of the World Health Assembly revealed that the Bill & Melinda Gates Foundation (BMGF) contributed almost US$322 million to the WHO's General and Fiduciary Funds in 2017, making it the second-largest donor overall for that year.[383] Only the United States at US$401 million had contributed more. Enormous yearly donations have been a regular feature from Gates and have not slowed down. In 2021, the Foundation contributed over US$375 million to the WHO to remain the second-largest donor overall, on that occasion only the nation of France contributed more.[384] That kind of money can certainly buy a great deal of influence over the organization that purports to conduct global health policy. However, the pull of Gates does not end with direct funding to the WHO. In 2021, 'GAVI, the Vaccine Alliance' gave over US$244 million to the WHO.[385] And GAVI in turn was funded to the tune of US$1.6 billion by the Bill & Melinda Gates Foundation between the years 2016 and 2020.[386] Once again, the Gates Foundation was the second largest donor to GAVI with only the unitary-state of the United Kingdom contributing more.

GAVI, which was formed in 2000, describes itself as, "a global Vaccine Alliance, bringing together public and private sectors with the shared goal of saving lives and protecting people's health by increasing equitable and sustainable use of vaccines."[387] However, as author Jacob Levich wrote in 2018, an investigation into its practices more accurately identifies GAVI as, "a consortium connecting major international institutions (WHO, UNICEF, the World Bank) with the big powers of the pharmaceutical industry (Janssen, GSK, Merck, Sanofi Pasteur, Pfizer, et al.) – all mediated and steered by the Gates Foundation."[388]

As if these arrangements were not already incestuous enough, April 2020 saw GAVI, along with the Coalition for Epidemic Preparedness Innovations (CEPI), the WHO, and UNICEF launch COVAX.[389] COVAX was another group ostensibly formed to ensure that there was "equitable access" to vaccines, a euphemistic term meaning an even bigger market for the pharmaceutical industry. And it was certainly a boon for the vaccine-manufacturing corporations, with COVAX reporting that it had "secured" almost 18 billion COVID-19 vaccines by the start of November 2022.[390] The role of acquiring coordinator for the COVAX program was granted to UNICEF. And to complete the merry-go-round of funding, UNICEF received US$101 million from the Gates-backed GAVI in 2021 alone.[391]

GAVI - The Vaccine Alliance is an unholy alliance of some of the most corrupt organizations in the world. One of its roles is to extract huge amounts of money from "donor country" citizens for transfer to "vaccine manufacturers" such as Pfizer. There are many other public and private participants who also benefit from this arrangement regardless of whether they are aware of the overall agenda. Source: GAVI Annual Progress Report 2018.

The Oslo, Norway headquartered CEPI was launched at the World Economic Forum's conference in Davos in 2017. Its major funders were Japan (US$125 million), Norway (US$120 million), and Germany (US$10.6 million in 2017 alone which later became US$90 million), the Wellcome Trust (US$100 million), along with GlaxoSmithKline, and the Gates Foundation (US$100 million).[392] As well as this vast funding, CEPI (along with GAVI) is a beneficiary of the 'International Finance Facility for Immunisation', a financial instrument backed by multiple countries that leverages investments to provide billions of dollars more for the vaccine industry.[393]

In January 2022, the Wellcome Trust and the Bill & Melinda Gates Foundation pledged to inject an additional US$300 million into CEPI.[394] At this announcement it was reported that:

> *The Bill & Melinda Gates Foundation and Wellcome will each provide US$150 million to push forward CEPI's efforts. These critical pledges come as CEPI moves towards its pioneering Global Pandemic Preparedness Summit, to be hosted in March 2022 by the UK Government. The Summit will bring together leading figures from governments, industry, philanthropy, and civil society to unite behind this revolutionary aim in global health security and back the $3.5 billion investment needed to end pandemics.*

It should not need to be pointed out that there is no sign that these "pandemics" are coming to an end. All the evidence points to increasing numbers of alleged and orchestrated pandemics, fraudulently created and promulgated by the very institutions that claim to prevent and control them. However, do not expect to see anything but overall praise in the corporate media for the Gates Foundation's various "health" related operations. In November 2021 it was revealed by *MintPress News* that the Foundation had given more than US$319 million to media outlets who then publish favorable stories about their endeavors:

> *While other billionaires' media empires are relatively well known, the extent to which Gates's cash underwrites the modern media landscape is not...Recipients of this cash include many of America's most important news outlets, including CNN, NBC, NPR, PBS and The Atlantic...Added*

> *together, these Gates-sponsored media projects come to a total of $319.4 million. However, there are clear shortcomings with this non-exhaustive list, meaning the true figure is undoubtedly far higher.*[395]

The web of influence did not end there. Gates money is also directed towards other outlets such as academic journals that produce material of interest that is then channelled directly through the paid for play media. As the *MintPress News* article elaborated:

> *Also not included are grants aimed at producing articles for academic journals. While these articles are not meant for mass consumption, they regularly form the basis for stories in the mainstream press and help shape narratives around key issues. The Gates Foundation has given far and wide to academic sources, with at least $13.6 million going toward creating content for the prestigious medical journal The Lancet. And, of course, even money given to universities for purely research projects eventually ends up in academic journals, and ultimately, downstream into mass media.*[396]

The control that the Gates Foundation exerts on "pandemic' narratives cannot be underestimated. In addition to the above-mentioned, hundreds of millions of dollars of Gates funding had also poured into many other highly influential channels such as:

1. The Imperial College London, where promoted "experts" such as the notoriously inaccurate Professor Neil Ferguson produced modeling of the alleged pandemic that formed the excuse for lockdowns and restrictions on civil rights.
2. Johns Hopkins University, which provided COVID-19 "resources" including the misleading data and statistics promoted by the media.

3. The National Institute of Allergy and Infectious Diseases, presided over by Dr Anthony Fauci, the chief medical advisor to the US government.
4. The CDC, responsible for advising the US government on medical policy and vaccines.
5. The University of Oxford, involved in vaccine research and development.
6. The research of Professor Chris Whitty, the Chief Medical Officer for England and advisor for various policy responses.[397]

Speaking from the World Economic Forum in Davos in January 2019, Bill Gates made the ambiguous statement that his foundation's donations of more than US$10 billion to organizations including GAVI had been responsible for a "20-to-1 return" in economic benefit.[398] It was unclear how these perceived "benefits" were calculated and who they ended up going to. What is unambiguously clear however, is that all of these organizations are intricately linked and under the pervasive influence of the BMGF. It is also clear that the billions of dollars in revenue passing through these organizations ultimately ends up in the hands of the pharmaceutical industry and other vested interests. For example, in 2021 Pfizer's gross profit was US$50.5 billion, a 52% increase from 2020 and the majority of this was due to its COVID-19 vaccine.[399] By 2022, Pfizer's profits had increased another 45% to US$65.4 billion.[400]

Most of this was derived from tax payers whose governments not only give their money to middleman organizations such as GAVI and CEPI but also directly to Big Pharma. For example, Public Services and Procurement Canada made arrangements to procure up to 236 million doses of the Pfizer COVID-19 injection alone, more than 6 doses for every man, woman and child in Canada.[401] Pfizer would be more than happy to oblige, particularly when this transfer of wealth from the Canadian citizenry to the corporation comes with protective indemnity. A leaked, "Manufacturing and supply agreement between Pfizer and the Albania Ministry of Health," exposed the fact that countries giving their money to Pfizer were being asked to, "indemnify, defend and hold harmless Pfizer...from and against any and all suits, claims, actions, demands, losses, damages, liabilities, settlements, penalties, fines, costs and expenses...arising out of, relating to, or resulting from the Vaccine."[402] Presumably Pfizer entered into similar arrangements with other governments around the world.

With regard to the COVID-19 vaccines, Big Pharma's sales were increased by government policies that punished those not accepting the pointless and unsafe injections. For example, in New Zealand the injections were mandatory for those working in the health and education sectors, police, defense force, food and drink services, and gyms.[403] For these workers it was presented as a case of take the jab or lose your job. And those New Zealanders who elected not to accept the injections were denied service from restaurants, gyms, some health care facilities, and hairdressers, as well as being prohibited from air travel. Those without "vaccine passes" were also prevented from visiting family members residing in care facilities. In October 2021, when a reporter stated to Jacinda Ardern that it created, "two different classes of people if you're vaccinated or unvaccinated, you have all these rights if you are vaccinated," the then Prime Minister casually replied with a smile on her face, "that is what it is, so yep."[404]

In essence, what has been established is another great transfer scheme to take money from the public and punish those not going along with it. A scheme that has been refined and grown over the decades. It started with the mostly voluntary childhood vaccination schedules and yearly influenza shots. The COVID-19 era brought in a new phase of coerced mass worldwide vaccination said to be necessary because of an alleged new health crisis. However, there are plans to increase the scope and number of vaccines even further as we will discuss in the next section.

Big Pharma Invents Demand

In 2007, PricewaterhouseCoopers (PWC), one of the "Big Four" corporations in international accounting published a report entitled, "Pharma 2020: The vision: Which path will you take?"[405] They advised the pharmaceutical industry that:

> *The population is growing and aging; new areas of medical need are emerging; and the diseases from which people in developing countries suffer are increasingly like those that trouble people living in the developed world. These changes will generate some huge opportunities for Pharma...Older people typically consume more medicines than younger people; four in five of those aged over 75 take at least one prescription product, while 36% take four or more. So the grey factor will boost the need for medicines dramatically.*

Clearly, there was no reflection on the actual causes of disease or the best way to manage health problems. Apparently, in the PWC model of "health," the increasing "need" for drugs may be indexed to the advanced development of a nation possessing an older population. This is music to the ears of Big Pharma of course. The PWC report suggested there were all sorts of opportunities for pharmaceutical manufacturers to ply their products and interestingly devoted a significant amount of coverage to greatly expanding the employment of vaccines:

> *Fears about bio-terrorism and a flu pandemic have also kick-started a new wave of public investment in vaccines, while philanthropic institutions like the Bill & Melinda Gates Foundation are funding research into vaccines for malaria and other tropical diseases...Moreover, the range of indications they are researching is surprisingly varied. It*

> *includes vaccines for cocaine addiction, diabetes, hypertension, Alzheimer's disease, psoriasis, food allergies, rheumatoid arthritis and nicotine withdrawal.*[406]

Earlier chapters in this book have outlined the fact that such contagious pandemics and "bio-terrorism" claims are fraudulent narratives that have no basis in biological reality. What is even more concerning is that vaccines, which as a class of pharmaceutical have never been shown to lead to better health outcomes in the population, are now being disturbingly proposed for use far beyond their original "infectious disease" paradigm.

Germ theory has no sound scientific basis and yet for well over a century the world has been assaulted with an increasing array of products that stem from its claims. Are we about to witness a further swindle as these agents that do not work in even their alleged traditional role are unleashed upon the unsuspecting population under another guise? Further, we now witness the "approval" of barely tested experimental products, unleashed on a preconditioned populace in a manner that has abandoned any pretense of scientific caution and established ethics.

To continue to achieve and expand these outcomes we are likely to see further public relations campaigns portraying Big Pharma as a benevolent force for all of humanity rather than a clutch of corporate entities cashing in on "public-private partnerships". The irony of Pfizer's heroic portrayal in the mainstream media did not escape the Health Freedom Defense Fund. In an article titled, "The Story of Pfizer Inc. - A Case Study in Pharmaceutical Empire and Corporate Corruption" they reported that:

> *Few companies in the history of medicine have received as much attention as Pfizer Inc. has received these last three years of the Corona Crisis. Through the course of relentless*

media coverage and amidst all the sound and fury, Pfizer has managed to avoid scrutiny of its previous criminal conduct and is universally portrayed in the mainstream media as a benevolent enterprise whose mission is to nobly service humanity...In total, since 2000 Pfizer has accumulated $10,945,838,549 in penalties and incurred 96 violations covering a wide range of offenses. Pfizer's portfolio of corporate crimes rivals that of the most corrupt companies in history. But that did not stop Pfizer from becoming a corporate celebrity with its COVID-19 vaccine. Indeed, the company has benefited handsomely from that product, whose $36.8 billion in 2021 sales made it the highest-selling pharmaceutical product in history.[407]

While the majority of people were made worse off during the COVID era due to fear propaganda, lockdowns, and economic suppression, the great vaccine swindle was handsomely filling the coffers of Big Pharma. Dr David Bell, former medical officer and scientist at the WHO, exposed that the involuntary transfer of wealth from the public to the vaccine industry and its associated beneficiaries is planned to continue. In a 2023 interview he explained that, "this will be funded by billions of dollars of tax payers' money. They are estimating ten and a half billion in additional money per year and the big winners will be those that make the vaccines."[408]

The vaccine manufacturers have sewn things up so that they are paid based on pre-orders of the products, rather than what is actually used. In December 2023 it was revealed that European tax payers had lost at least €4 billion through dumped COVID-19 vaccines. *Politico* reported that, "since the first coronavirus vaccines were approved in late 2020, EU countries have collectively taken delivery of 1.5 billion doses (more than three for every person in Europe). Many of these now lie in landfills across the Continent."[409] While we would applaud the dumping of all vaccines, it

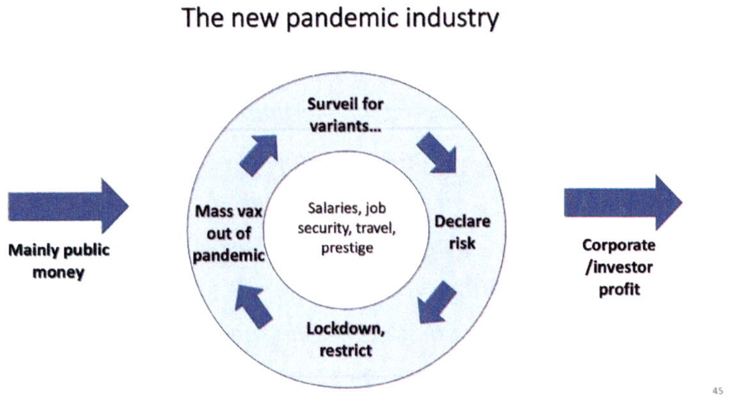

Dr David Bell has identified the various beneficiaries of the "pandemic industry" and produced this infographic summary. The public pay the price in both monetary terms as well as the measures that are employed against them. Source: https://www.ukcolumn.org/video/david-bell-why-policymakers-should-reject-whos-pandemic-proposals

nevertheless illustrated the brazen daylight robbery that took place in Europe alone. Big Pharma was not finished yet though and it was also reported that, "the jabs will keep coming, with the revised contract with Pfizer locking European countries into buying vaccines until at least 2027."[410]

Case Study: 'HPH' & Her Licence to Lie

According to major media outlets in New Zealand, one of the experts during the alleged COVID-19 pandemic was 'vaccinologist' Helen Petousis-Harris. The associate professor at the University of Auckland has been involved in vaccine promotion for the past three decades but none of the fawning media outlets have informed the public of her various conflicts of interest or questioned her often highly inaccurate or baseless claims.

Our interest in Petousis-Harris was raised when she was named as an "expert" assisting the Medical Council of New Zealand in their farcical prosecution attempts of Dr Sam Bailey from 2020 through to 2023.[411] We did not participate in the process or attend their *ultra vires*[412] proceedings. Nevertheless, the so-called vaccinologist has not been shy in promulgating a series of misrepresentations and outright lies that can be seen by all in the public record.

As early as February 2020, Petousis-Harris was being interviewed by state-funded broadcaster *Radio New Zealand* to announce that vaccines were the likely solution to COVID-19. When asked about the development of these vaccines, her response was not yet the "safe and effective" mantra that would subsequently be broadcast and repeated *ad infinitum* to the New Zealand public on a 24/7 basis. She stated, "some people will be saying, oh, make sure it's safe, oh, and make sure it works [laughs]…and you can't license a vaccine that is, ah, not been proven to be acceptably safe and also has gotta work…under these conditions there are ways to fast track. And when you've got a situation like this you can probably, ah, roll your vaccine out in a way that is almost in trial conditions."[413] The interview was mixed in with sound bites from the "Decade of Vaccines" frontman Bill Gates[414] and while discussing social media she went on to explain that one of the major "concerns" of the largely Gates-funded World Health Organization was, "the misinfodemic and the misinformation that's flying around." Unsurprisingly, she has been a persistent advocate for internet censorship to allow the organizations she works for an unchallenged pro-vaccine podium.

On the 8th of May, 2021, when two New Zealand deaths temporally associated with the Pfizer/BioNTech injections were under investigation, Petousis-Harris admitted to not having all the details but proclaimed, "I know enough to know they are not in any way related to the vaccine."[415] Going even further out on a limb, the next day while being interviewed on the government-run TVNZ *1 News* show, she made a preposterous and unfounded claim that the experimental injections had not killed *any* of the millions of recipients stating, verbatim, "so the reports of deaths of course because we're vaccinating hundreds of millions of people, and of course we see deaths afterwards. And but so far even after all those doses there's no suggestion that this vaccine actually causes people to die."[416]

The ludicrous claims from Petousis-Harris continued in her September 2021 article "Covid whoppers: 10 of the biggest vaccine myths debunked," when she made the blanket declaration, "no, vaccines can't harm children," and also proclaimed, "there is a lot more risk from the disease than there is from the vaccine."[417] Petousis-Harris was the actual myth promoter. Aside from the fact that she was no more equipped to provide evidence of the "novel disease" than her sponsors, she was certainly unable to point to any vaccine monitoring data beyond a few months. But she had no hesitation in advising wholesale injections for everyone, including children.

In February 2022, when a New Zealand High Court ruled against vaccine mandates for Defense force and police staff, Petousis-Harris expressed her "disappointment" to a state-sponsored media platform.[418] Despite legislation protecting health consumers' rights, which explicitly guarantee, "the right to be provided with services that take into account the needs, values, and beliefs of different cultural, religious, social, and ethnic groups,"[419] Petousis-Harris bizarrely claimed, "the decision legally and morally undermines the mandates." Her inability to comment on legal matters and moral philosophy was certainly demonstrated, but so too was her chronic inability to provide "expert" commentary on vaccines, her advertised specialty.

An example of the deception Petousis-Harris is immersed in was exemplified in a 2021 *NZ Research Review* publication titled, "Countering Vaccine Misinformation" in which the "expert" comments attributed to her read as follows:

In the more than twenty years that I have been engaged in addressing disinformation and misinformation the themes have remained unchanged. However, the tools used to spread it have taken on a new form and the sophistication in packaging fallacies has metamorphosised into a very new set of challenges. Public health was not prepared for the rise in social media platforms as weapons of mass destruction. Still now it remains impotent against the tsunami of well-funded, well-orchestrated programmes of disinformation.[420]

There is certainly a tsunami of well-funded, well-orchestrated programmes of disinformation. During the COVID-19 fraud much of it stemmed from the pharmaceutical industry and their paid promoters such as Petousis-Harris. The last paragraph of the "independent medical publisher" review reads, "this publication has been created with an unrestricted educational grant from GSK [GlaxoSmithKline], Pfizer and Seqirus." These three corporations control assets worth around US$292 billion,[421] making her claim regarding who is well-funded look as vacuous as any of her other COVID claims. After all, it is Petousis-Harris who is supported by some of the most powerful organizations in the world.

The New Zealand media predictably failed to inform the public that Petousis-Harris was not an "independent expert" in these matters, but essentially a vaccine salesperson. Amongst other associations, she was the Chair of the WHO Global Advisory Committee on Vaccine Safety until August 2020,[422] and a member of the Bill & Melinda Gates Foundation and Big Pharma-sponsored, "International Society for Vaccines". Additionally, Petousis-Harris is a former member of the International Brighton Collaboration Science Board.[423] The Brighton Collaboration claims to be, "a community aiming to promote and improve vaccine safety," but its true agenda has been exposed by Vera Sharav:

> *This "authoritative" consortium exerts extraordinary influence on vaccination policies worldwide and ensures that vaccine safety assessments enhance vaccine utilization goals. Vaccine stakeholders effectively control the science, the research, and the reports that get published in medical and public health journals. The broad range of the Brighton Collaboration's international projects, initiatives, and tools for vaccine safety assessments reflect the bias of its partners, all of who are stakeholders in the business of vaccines; their interest is in ensuring high utilization of vaccines...Thus, grants are awarded only to those whose research proposals are designed to validate the safety of vaccines. A second goal is to prevent research that could document safety hazards that would undermine vaccination policies.*[424]

Petousis-Harris was interviewed on New Zealand radio on the 6th of December, 2023, in the wake of the COVID-19 vaccination status and death rate dataset leak by whistleblower, Barry Young. She continued to brandish her license to lie and to add to her long list of easily falsifiable claims suggested that a mere ten people in the entire nation had been significantly injured by the vaccines. NZDSOS responded to her overt "litany of lies" the following week:

> *In dismissing adverse events following immunisation, she fully reveals herself as an actual dis-info agent or incompetent. Petousis-Harris plucked the number ten out of the sky as her guesstimate of the number of people living with long-term consequences. ACC* [the Accident Compensation Corporation] *has accepted well over a thousand claims. The government planned for 1.1% chronic disability even before the batches began arriving. One look at the most recent Medsafe Safety Report (from Nov 2022) documents that over a year ago there*

were 3,688 reports of serious injury. However, we are not convinced that is the true number, as an OIA [Official Information Act request] *from April 2023 asked about the number of serious adverse events and the response provided a chart on page 2 detailing over 13,000 serious reports.*[425]

The Cause of the Rise in Vaccine "Misinformation"

Just before the start of the COVID-19 era the European Commission and the World Health Organization co-hosted an event they called the Global Vaccination Summit. The event took place on the 12th of September, 2019, in Brussels, Belgium with the goal to, "propel global action against vaccine preventable diseases and against the spread of vaccine misinformation."[426] It was notable that they mentioned the word "misinformation" that became a buzzword from 2020 onwards and used to label any information that went against government and corporate media narratives. As well as the usual line-up of "political leaders, high-level representatives from the UN and other international organizations, health ministries, leading academics, scientists and health professionals," it was also interesting to note that some "social media influencers" were invited to the event but none of their names were disclosed. In "Roundtable 1 - In Vaccines we trust" it was stated that:

Europe and other parts of the globe are witnessing a steady decline in the uptake of key vaccines, in particular childhood vaccines...This worrying trend may be explained by vaccine hesitancy, including complacency, lack of confidence, and other practical and logistical factors that could hamper access to vaccination. This situation has also been fuelled by spreading of misinformation about the benefits and risks of vaccines. Concerns about a specific vaccine in one country can influence perceptions in a neighbouring country, or spill

> *over to other vaccines, putting the public health achievements of past decades at risk. The WHO has declared vaccine hesitancy to be one of the ten threats to global health in 2019.*[427]

In typical fashion no information was provided about the nature of the "misinformation" and no information was provided about the alleged "benefits" of childhood vaccines. The document went on to note that, "on questions related to vaccination, people trust health professionals, in particular doctors, more than all other sources of information, on questions related to vaccination." Once again a remarkable coincidence that within a year, doctors that questioned the need for the soon to be released COVID-19 vaccines became arguably the most heavily persecuted group in the "pandemic" theater, a group that also included both authors.

At the Global Vaccination Summit "Roundtable 2 - The magic of science: boosting vaccine research, development and innovation" the "problem" of vaccine development and costs were raised. They reassured participants that, "a number of partnerships and models have been created to enable more effective types of cooperation and create incentives for industry investment in vaccine development."[428]

In "Roundtable 3 - Vaccines protecting everyone, everywhere: galvanizing a global response to ensure health, security and prosperity through immunisation" the theme was back to claims about "misinformation" stating, "ownership of immunisation programmes will need to increasingly rest with families and communities who are resistant to misinformation and who understand the health, security and prosperity benefits of vaccines."[429]

GAVI, "the vaccine alliance" also mentioned the word 'misinformation' in its 2018 Annual progress report that was published in September 2019, just a few months before the alleged COVID pandemic. In a section titled "Strategic focus area," it stated:

> *Globally, vaccine hesitancy is a major concern and has been reported in more than 90% of countries. Frontline workers are key to building parental confidence as conflicting advice can be especially damaging. Hesitant parents are more likely to seek out information on vaccines on the Internet and from other sources where misinformation and rumours can spread rapidly. WHO recently named vaccine hesitancy as a top ten risk to global health.*[430]

It was noteworthy that in GAVI's five previous Annual progress reports (2013-2017), each up to 100 pages in length, the word 'misinformation' did not appear once.[431]

By 2020, the establishment publications mentioning 'misinformation' went in to overdrive. For example, the Sabin-Aspen Vaccine Science & Policy Group published a 173-page document in May 2020 titled "Meeting the Challenge of Vaccination Hesitancy".[432] One would have to suspect that it was being prepared prior to the declaration of the COVID-19 "pandemic" just a few months earlier. The word 'misinformation' was peppered throughout the document and it even featured an entire section dedicated to, "online misinformation about vaccines". The introduction section had nothing to do with health and everything to do with getting more shots into arms, as though "vaccine acceptance" and the maximal number of injections given had become virtues in themselves:

> *Although vaccination remains a well-accepted social norm worldwide, a combination of factors—including misinformation spread on social media; decreased trust in institutions including government, science, and industry; and weaknesses within health systems—has emerged to diminish*

> *confidence among some populations...This body of work clarifies many of the reasons for vaccine hesitancy, including the tempting retreat to the perceived safety of inaction; considers how social movements emerge and succeed and how to build such a movement to broaden vaccine acceptance; and examines the value of activities that foster behavior change to drive vaccine use...Along with our dedicated members, we are especially grateful to our funder, the Bill & Melinda Gates Foundation, which understood the urgency of combatting vaccine hesitancy and gave us the support so essential to doing so.*

As outlined earlier in this chapter, none of these organizations can be considered remotely independent from one another and the conflicts of interest are enormous. The publications reviewed here are just a small selection of the many that all began promoting the concept of vaccine and health "misinformation" in late 2019 and early 2020. This of course is highly unlikely to have happened by chance.

Pushback to the COVID-19 narrative and injections was anticipated and so the label of 'misinformation' was already established in advance for anything at odds with the fostered beliefs. Hence the rise in vaccine misinformation in recent years has stemmed from the industry itself, as it attempts to gaslight the public into believing it comes from those pointing out factual scientific inconsistencies.

In producing their paper, the Sabin-Aspen Group stated they had, "vigorous discussions, informed by background research papers and expert presentations."[433] The reality was that discussions were with themselves and they did not present or consider any of the scientific arguments against their organization's proclamations. Naturally, such opposing arguments can be automatically dismissed in advance as "misinformation".

Indeed, distracting the public from what constitutes so-called misinformation and then turning vaccine rollouts into mere marketing exercises is the new favored approach. In October 2017, the Johns Hopkins Center for Health Security published a 76-page document entitled "SPARS Pandemic 2025-2028: A Futuristic Scenario for Public Health Risk Communications".[434] Their project team described it as:

> *...a hypothetical scenario designed to illustrate the public health risk* ***communication challenges*** *that could potentially emerge during a naturally occurring infectious disease outbreak requiring development and distribution of novel and/ or investigational drugs, vaccines, therapeutics, or other medical countermeasures.* [authors' emphasis]

The fictional scenario included the introduction of the "Corovax" vaccine and the anticipated responses from the public. In essence the document focussed on the public marketing and behavioral aspects of the pandemic along with the expected resistance from some quarters.

Of note was the frequent mention of 'ZapQ', a new social media platform that emerged during the imaginary SPARS pandemic. It featured on 14 pages of the document, including in the following examples:

- "...governmental organizations were not able to effectively access all social media platforms. ZapQ groups, for example, had closed memberships and typically could only be accessed via invitations from group members." (P20)
- "...Republican ZapQ groups..." (P34)
- "The anti-vaccination movement migrated to ZapQ upon its emergence in 2022..." (P43)

Obviously it continued the theme of "communication challenges" and their concerns about how to centralize and regulate the spread of information. Just as striking though is the remarkable coincidence that the SPARS scenario was published on the 31st of October, 2017, and the entity 'QAnon' began posting on the 4chan website on the 28th of October, 2017.[435] We are not claiming to have established a connection between the two but believe it warrants at least a degree of suspicion.

Chapter 13 of the SPARS document, titled "Lovers and Haters," presented those against the vaccine as "activists" and "mistaken" or involved with groups that utilized "select quotes" under the undue influence of social media sites. The government responses along with the pharmaceutical and vaccine roll outs were portrayed as benevolent while those against such measures were said to lack sophistication with nothing more to offer than catch phrases and short tweets. Comically they imagined in their scenario that, "the response was particularly vitriolic from the burgeoning natural medicine movement." Having been part of the natural health community for several years our experience is that the advocates are peaceful and voluntarist in nature. As so many have come to recognize, it is the standard operating practice of delegitimization to demonize, isolate and ignore opponents. The time of robust, considered intellectual argument has long since been supplanted by mindless auto-triggering.

Clearly it has been the pushers of allopathic medicine who have employed the greatest vitriol. Government diktats and threats enforced by state thugs at gunpoint became the *status quo* at the dawn of the COVID era as the public was gulled and coerced into "accepting" vaccines as the only way out. The apparent solution was promoted by legacy media and Big Tech while they also relentlessly suppressed factual material and censored dissident voices. The tyrants lost on scientific grounds long ago and their actions indicated then as they do now, that they know it will become increasingly difficult to market the well-known generic vaccines, let alone "novel" vaccines in the future, unless they have complete control of the narrative. In the authors' estimation such a dystopian outcome is unlikely to be achieved and cannot be maintained…

Sic semper tyrannis*[436] *("Thus always to tyrants")...*

History is replete with examples of totalitarian strategies bringing about their own inevitable downfall. As Dr Mark Bailey and Dr John Bevan-Smith wrote about the COVID-19 fraud in 2021:

> *Tyrannies come and go. This one, in its ascendancy, is already choking on the chicken bone of its own hubris. The scientific and ideological facades that this scam relies on will bring about its own fall and with its collapse a new dawning for us all to inherit. Closet tyrants, when they eventually emerge, are always naked, empty vessels full of other people's ideas, waging war on the innocent to hide from what they lack. They have not yet learned that control is a dead-end street, or that, that which sets the human spirit soaring is nothing more than acceptance.*[437]

The number of people that became aware of the fraud of virology and germ theory increased immensely during the COVID era. The number of people that started to question vaccines was even greater and that number continues to grow by the day. The weaponization of medical "science," indeed, the medicalization of tyranny, in the recent period has been a unique form of tyranny, but tyranny all the same with its roots in fear, deception, coercion and violence. In concluding the final chapter of this book, we hope we have exposed it for what it is and suggest the antidote is there for the taking.

Summary

We hope in reading this far, that the reader has been able to appreciate and learn that apparent "pandemics" do not at first glance require, "everyone to be in on it." In fact, it is quite the opposite. All it takes is one person at the WHO to declare a 'global pandemic'. At that point the so-called leaders of member states declare states of emergency in their respective nations, while a complicit and paid for media broadcasts a doomsday message around the clock. Information refuting a developing narrative is strictly censored across Big Tech platforms. For the majority of the population it all points to a worldwide medical emergency, even if nothing is happening in their own vicinity.

The case numbers used to justify the responses are meaningless as the case definitions have been reduced to the result of a molecular detection reaction as we highlighted previously in the unfit-for-purpose RAT and PCR tests. The appearance of a spreading pandemic is simply the illusory result of these *new tests* spreading around rather than any new disease. One might argue it is part of the co-opted medical system's march along an anti-humanity line with an anti-scientific reductionistic testing and 'case' model that is quite disconnected from actual living biology and health.

The alarming claims that new "infectious" diseases are coming for humanity, particularly via 'germs' being harbored by animals, lacks as much scientific evidence as it does common sense. Animals are just one of the scapegoats for human disease and tragically this sort of misplaced belief is used as the outrageous justification to slaughter and destroy healthy livestock in the millions.

Those who question or do not go along with the government's actions are ridiculed and demonized as they point out the overt flip-flopping nature of the official story. Doctors and other health practitioners do not have to be "in on it" either. The majority will stay silent in order to maintain incomes and professional status. It has been made abundantly apparent to them that those who speak out will face censure, prosecution attempts and possible unemployment. In private interactions, some of our former colleagues have exhibited nothing less than intellectual and ethical laziness with their claims that we can defer to the proclamations of the ordained wizards.

However, it is clear that the biggest reason that fake pandemics "take" is that the majority of people still feel *some* threat from microbes, whether they be real biological entities such as bacteria or imagined ones such as viruses. Conversely, when one can see that this model of 'pathogens' is invalid, the entire possibility of a contagious pandemic is bankrupt and finished. There is no point debating "downstream" arguments such as whether vaccines could be beneficial because they are based on a faulty premise and are thus never indicated. This is not just the case for COVID-19 vaccines. It is the case for all vaccines.

This is the reason we have focused our attention on the "upstream" arguments and contributed to the refutations of the virus model and germ theory more widely. The end of the belief in these erroneous concepts is the end of the belief in all pandemics and the myriad of damaging health and socioeconomic effects that result from the political and medico-pharmaceutical interventions carried out in the name of "the science". The demise of such belief would precipitate the spectacular collapse of the multi-billion dollar pandemic industry (and its governmental cousin, unfettered political control) so one cannot anticipate that the vested interests will stop promoting the prevailing model. The most powerful thing we can do as individuals is to walk away and say "no thanks - no way" to their products and interventions.

Perhaps a tipping point will be reached whereby if a WHO Director-General makes an announcement such as, "we have never before seen a pandemic sparked by a coronavirus,"[438] more people will agree and even add that, "nor will we ever see one." It cannot be emphasized enough that everything coming out of the pandemic industry rests to some degree of a belief in the scientifically unfounded concept of microbes causing contagious diseases.

One of the biggest challenges in writing the chapters for this book was what *not* to include. As stated in the introduction we did not seek to produce another reference tome or write a treatise focussing specifically on one aspect such as virology. The goal was to provide an overview of how alleged pandemics are actually manufactured crises by exposing the shaky "science" underlying some well known examples. These are certainly not the exceptions. Indeed, our research over the years has revealed it is the prevailing theme.

Those looking for more in-depth coverage of particular "infectious" diseases and their historical aspects can consult *Virus Mania*, as well as websites such as theperthgroup.com (HIV/AIDS) and Mike Stone's comprehensive ViroLIEgy.com. Finally, our website drsambailey.com has new content added every week and covers everything from the original mistaken claims concerning the Tobacco Mosaic "Virus" in the 1800s,[439] through to present-era mRNA technology in vaccines.[440] We also analyze real epidemics such as cancer, and even investigate the problems with products such as sunscreen in the 21st century.[441]

Epilogue

When we were trained as doctors we did not learn about health, we learnt about disease. We memorized thousands of terms related to pathology and then almost as many "treatment" protocols in the form of pharmaceuticals and surgical procedures (see also note 37). We were part of the world of allopathic medicine that has been elevated to the status of high reverence amongst the public. It is an undeserved status. While there are certainly occasions of acute limb and life saving interventions, these episodes are in the tiny minority of interactions with the medical system.

Calling it a "health" system is also a deceptive misnomer. As a friend in Switzerland once remarked to us, "yes, we also have one of those but it should be called the sick system." Indeed, it is a system that can barely cure anyone. It might surprise those outside the system that the word 'cure' is often discouraged from use for doctors in training. Hence, the mindset of the new doctor is corrupted from the start: instead of seeing the body as something that has been created in perfection, they see it as something that is prone to breakdowns. From "bad genes" to "bad luck" or "age-related" problems, the doctor is there to make a diagnosis and patch things up. The public have been trained to accept these 'diagnoses' as legitimate and for many it brings a sense of relief. Unfortunately, such labels all too often feed straight into the allopathic business model of long-term drugs or surgery.

Although neither of the authors felt particularly at home during our time in the medical system, we are now nothing less than disgusted by it. The average doctor does not improve the health of their patients because they work from a paradigm that typically neglects real causes and often leads to harm. One may ask, "but how can they all be in on it?" We reply that most practitioners within the medico-pharma juggernaut know not what they do. On the whole, they genuinely believe they are helping their patients and the community. While one of their prescriptions may make a patient feel a bit better, ease some pain, or "clear up" a rash, the supposed treatments almost invariably interfere with the healing attempts of the body. The temporary suppression or masking of symptoms fails to address the underlying causes and sets the patient up for even worse trouble in the future. It is a grave mistake to treat symptoms as if they are the source of the problems.

One does not have to look further than vaccines to see how entrenched in dogma the typical medical practitioner has become. When a doctor proclaims that the vaccines they advocate are evidenced-based, you are witnessing one of the most disturbing frauds in history. As we have said previously, doctors are among the worst people in the world to comment on vaccines.[442] They usually recommend them even though they have not studied the nature of the disease, the historical data including when the vaccine was introduced, and what is actually in the vials. When an adverse event occurs there is typically a cognitive dissonance for the vaccine promoter who does their bit to maintain the "safe and effective" mantra, not realizing that it is a marketing slogan invented by the pharmaceutical industry.[443] However, neither should we underestimate their fear of being ostracized from the medical community. Almost every doctor is told about the "fall" of Dr Andrew Wakefield, including the loss of his practicing license and income. Only a minority of us looked at what Dr Wakefield actually said and were all the better for it.

We have gone even further upstream in our analysis of vaccines and have contributed to the refutations of the very existence of viruses and germ theory. There is no need to enter into arguments about which vaccines might be beneficial or the possibility of developing such a vaccine in the future – it is all a scientific dead end. For us and increasing numbers of people around the world, germ theory and the virus model are finished and hence all vaccines as well. We live perfectly well without any fear of germs and ignore the unnecessary interventions directed towards them.

We are often asked whether it was hard to give up two decades of our lives dedicated to training and working in the medical world and some have even suggested we have "thrown away" established medical careers. However, that would only be the case if we prized being part of that system. The truth is that the only thing we have thrown away are scientifically bankrupt models and harmful beliefs. We kept a few nuggets but cast aside the majority of the practices we were taught. Overall we gained so much more in health and well-being for our family as well as the joy of being able to share our material with others around the world.

We would like to finish this book with a message of hope. When the cracks in the facade of virology, germ theory, or the medical system are first seen there can appear to be a void and a sense that something needs to replace it. However, as so much of it is an artificial construct there should really be a feeling of relief because *nothing* is required to replace such nonsense. The reductionist chemistry set models and their purported 'solutions' can be safely ignored as their purpose is to serve the medico-pharmaceutical industry, not us. The body is always trying to return towards its natural state, which is perfection, as in the image of God. The intricacies of how our biology works is a true wonder and only nature can heal.

As Dr Ulric Williams discovered almost 100 years ago, real health is achieved through right thinking and right living.[444] It may initially sound simplistic but everything we do can be measured up to this powerful maxim. As a family it has, and continues to provide guidance in how to improve ourselves and our environment. We invite you to continue on this journey with us with the knowledge that life is for living, not living in fear.

"Let there be light," and there was light.

About the Authors

Dr Samantha Bailey trained and worked as a conventional doctor over two decades before a new understanding of health compelled her to leave the medical system. In 2020 she started what was to become New Zealand's largest Youtube health channel with her videos gaining millions of views and an international following. She is a co-author of *Virus Mania: How the Medical Industry Continually Invents Epidemics, Making Billion-Dollar Profits at Our Expense*. With her husband, Dr Mark Bailey, the couple have made their extensive collection of medical and health information freely available through their website www.drsambailey.com

Dr Mark Bailey won an undergraduate scholarship to the University of Canterbury in 1994 and then completed his medical training at the University of Otago in 1999. He worked in many specialties as a resident doctor and was also a clinical trials research physician for several years. In 2016 he left clinical practice due to dissatisfaction with the allopathic medical system. Since early 2020 he has been the duo's chief researcher with a focus on microbiology, the existence of viruses, as well as historical and epistemological issues within medical science. Mark is the author of *A Farewell To Virology (Expert Edition)* and co-author of *The COVID-19 Fraud & War on Humanity*.

References & Notes

[1] Kennedy, R.F., "Day of Affirmation Address at Cape Town University," Jameson Hall, Cape Town, South Africa, 6 Jun 1966: https://www.americanrhetoric.com/speeches/rfkcapetown.htm

[2] "Catastrophic Contagion," 23 Oct 2022: https://catastrophiccontagion.centerforhealthsecurity.org/

[3] Bailey, M., *A Farewell to Virology (Expert Edition)*, 15 Sep 2022: https://drsambailey.com/a-farewell-to-virology-expert-edition/

[4] Engelbrecht, T., et al., *Virus Mania*, 3rd English Edition, Books on Demand, 2021: https://drsambailey.com/shop-2/

[5] Williams, U., Bailey, S., *Terrain Therapy*, Dr Samantha Bailey, 2022: https://drsambailey.com/terrain-therapy/

[6] Bailey, S., "What is Making People Sick?," *drsambailey.com*, 2 Feb 2022: https://drsambailey.com/resources/videos/viruses-unplugged/what-is-makingpeople-sick/

[7] Lanka, S., "The Virus Misconception," *Wissenschafftplus*, Jan 2020: http://wissenschafftplus.de/uploads/article/wissenschafftplus-the-virus-misconception-part-1.pdf

[8] Cowan, T., et al., "The 'Settling The Virus Debate' Statement," 14 Jul 2022: https://drsambailey.com/resources/settling-the-virus-debate/

[9] Bailey, S., "Germ Theory vs Terrain Theory," *drsambailey.com,* 26 May 2021: https://drsambailey.com/resources/videos/germ-theory/germ-theory-vs-terrain-theory/

[10] Ibid.

[11] https://dissolvingillusions.com/graphs-images/#Charts

[12] Hudson, N., "COVID origins, the timeline of bullshit and pre-meditation," *Doc Malik*, 1 Jan 2024: https://rumble.com/v3wxjzm-covid-origins-the-timeline-of-bullshit-and-pre-meditation.html

[13] McGrail, S., "Roche Acquires TIB Molbiol to Boost Molecular Diagnostics Profile," *PharmaNewsIntelligence*, 15 Sep 2021: https://pharmanewsintel.com/news/roche-acquires-tib-molbiol-to-boost-molecular-diagnostics-profile (archived)

[14] Nicola, S., "A Berlin Biotech Company Got a Head Start on Coronavirus Tests," *Bloomberg*, 12 Mar 2020: https://www.bloomberg.com/news/articles/2020-03-12/a-berlin-biotech-company-got-a-head-start-on-coronavirus-tests (archived)

[15] Hollingsworth, J., "A coronavirus test can be developed in 24 hours. So why are some countries still struggling to diagnose?," *CNN*, 25 Mar 2020: https://edition.cnn.com/2020/03/24/asia/testing-coronavirus-science-intl-hnk/index.html (archived)

[16] Enserink, M., "Dispute simmers over who first shared SARS-CoV-2's genome," *Science*, 29 Mar 2023: https://www.science.org/content/article/dispute-simmers-over-who-first-shared-sars-cov-2-s-genome (archived)

[17] *Authors' note: we have the PCR protocol appearing on the WHO website on the 13th of January, 2020. The one day discrepancy may be due to time zone differences.

[18] Corman, V., et al., "Detection of 2019 novel coronavirus (2019-nCoV) by real-time RT-PCR," *Eurosurveillance*, 23 Jan 2020: https://www.eurosurveillance.org/content/10.2807/1560-7917.ES.2020.25.3.2000045#metrics_content

[19] Huang, C., et al., "Clinical features of patients infected with 2019 novel coronavirus in Wuhan, China," *Lancet*, 24 Jan 2020: https://www.thelancet.com/journals/lancet/article/PIIS0140-6736(20)30183-5/fulltext

[20] Rothe, C., et al., "Transmission of 2019-nCoV Infection from an Asymptomatic Contact in Germany," *N Engl J Med*, 30 Jan 2020: https://www.nejm.org/doi/pdf/10.1056/nejmc2001468

[21] Kennedy, R.F., "Day of Affirmation Address at Cape Town University," Jameson Hall, Cape Town, South Africa, 6 Jun 1966: https://www.americanrhetoric.com/speeches/rfkcapetown.htm

[22] *"the theory that certain diseases are caused by the invasion of the body by microorganisms, organisms too small to be seen except through a microscope.": https://www.britannica.com/science/germ-theory (archived)

[23] "Prof. Tim Noakes – We Will Win," *drsambailey.com*, 12 Oct 2021: https://drsambailey.com/resources/videos/interviews/prof-tim-noakes-we-will-win/

[24] Cowan, T., et al., "The 'Settling The Virus Debate' Statement," 14 Jul 2022: https://drsambailey.com/resources/settling-the-virus-debate/

[25] Bailey, M., *A Farewell to Virology (Expert Edition)*, 15 Sep 2022: https://drsambailey.com/a-farewell-to-virology-expert-edition/

[26] Bailey, M. & Bevan-Smith, J., *The COVID-19 Fraud & War on Humanity*, 11 Nov 2021: https://drsambailey.com/the-covid-19-fraud-war-on-humanity/

[27] Titus, J., "Larry & Carstens' Excellent Pandemic," *BestEvidence*, 14 Aug 2021: https://www.youtube.com/watch?v=VYOEvurCVuk

[28] *In this book, 'contagion' is taken to mean the transmission of disease via microbes specifically. Interestingly, the word originated in the 1400s and prior to the rise of the belief in germ theory (around the end of the 19th century) it was defined as, "'a touching, contact', often in a bad sense": https://www.etymonline.com/word/contagion While the now accepted definition relies on the fallacious concept of pathogenic 'germs', the original definition would remain consistent with illness following contact with biological and environmental toxins. Given that it also meant, "a harmful or corrupting influence," we could even extend this to toxic psychological influences, including fear, manifesting as illness.

[29] Williams, U., Bailey, S., *Terrain Therapy*, Dr Samantha Bailey, 2022: https://drsambailey.com/terrain-therapy/

[30] Trebing, W., *Good-bye Germ Theory. Ending A Century Of Medical Fraud And How To Protect Your Family*. Xlibris Corporation United States of America, MD Publishing House, CT, 2006

[31] Bailey, M., *A Farewell to Virology (Expert Edition)*, 15 Sep 2022: https://drsambailey.com/a-farewell-to-virology-expert-edition/

[32] "Allopathic medicine," *Wikipedia*: https://en.wikipedia.org/wiki/Allopathic_medicine (accessed 13 Aug 2023)

[33] "Allopathy," *Miriam-Webster Dictionary*, Internet Archive (17 May 2022): https://web.archive.org/web/20220517090832/https://www.merriam-webster.com/medical/allopathy

[34] "Allopathy," *Miriam-Webster Dictionary*: https://www.merriam-webster.com/dictionary/allopathy (accessed 4 Nov 2022)

[35] Weller, I., "The gay bowel," *Gut*, 26 (9), 1985: https://gut.bmj.com/content/gutjnl/26/9/869.full.pdf

[36] Scarce, M., *Smearing the Queer: Medical Bias in the Health Care of Gay Men,* Routledge, 1999

[37] *The fantastical notion that tens of thousands of specific diseases exist (as listed on the MalaCards database) did not escape the attention of Jon Rappoport. See "How many diseases are there? - Welcome to the absurdity of modern medicine," 2 Feb 2024: https://jonrappoport.substack.com/p/how-many-diseases-are-there

[38] Illich, I., *Medical Nemesis*, London: Calder & Boyars, 1975

[39] Fauci, A., "Dr. Anthony Fauci on 'Face the Nation', *CBS News*, 28 Nov 2021: https://www.cbsnews.com/news/transcript-dr-anthony-fauci-on-face-the-nation-november-28-2021/

[40] Gallagher, G., "Fauci: 'No doubt' Trump will face surprise infectious disease outbreak," healio, 11 Jan 2017: https://www.healio.com/news/infectious-disease/20170111/fauci-no-doubt-trump-will-face-surprise-infectious-disease-outbreak

[41] Agence France-Presse, "A man lies dead in the street: the image that captures the Wuhan coronavirus crisis," *The Guardian*, 31 Jan 2020: https://www.theguardian.com/world/2020/jan/31/a-man-lies-dead-in-the-street-the-image-that-captures-the-wuhan-coronavirus-crisis

[42] John Ioannidis, "Infection fatality rate of COVID-19 inferred from seroprevalence data," *Bull World Health Organ*, submitted 13 May 2020: https://apps.who.int/iris/bitstream/handle/10665/340124/PMC7947934.pdf (archived)

[43] Bailey, S., "What is Making People Sick?," *drsambailey.com*, 2 Feb 2022: https://drsambailey.com/resources/videos/viruses-unplugged/what-is-making-people-sick/

[44] Bailey, S., "Unscientific Human Experiments," *drsambailey.com*, 2 Nov 2021: https://drsambailey.com/resources/videos/covid-19/unscientific-human-experiments/

[45] "SARS," *Wikipedia*: https://en.wikipedia.org/wiki/SARS (accessed 14 Jun 2023)

[46] Williams, U., Bailey, S., *Terrain Therapy*, Dr Samantha Bailey, 2022: https://drsambailey.com/terrain-therapy/

[47] "Sampling for Severe Acute Respiratory Syndrome (SARS) diagnostic tests," World Health Organisation, 23 Apr 2003: https://web.archive.org/web/20220426225801/https://www.who.int/publications/m/item/sampling-for-severe-acute-respiratory-syndrome-(sars)-diagnostic-tests

[48] "WHO COVID-19: Case Definitions," World Health Organization, 7 Aug 2020: https://web.archive.org/web/20200902130408/https://www.who.int/publications/i/item/WHO-2019-nCoV-Surveillance_Case_Definition-2020.1

[49] "Section 5: The Epidemiologic Approach," in Lesson 1: Introduction to Epidemiology, Centers for Disease Control and Prevention: https://www.cdc.gov/csels/dsepd/ss1978/lesson1/section5.html

[50] "Case Definition," *Britannica*: https://www.britannica.com/science/case-definition

[51] Corman, V., et al., "Detection of 2019 novel coronavirus (2019-nCoV) by real-time RT-PCR," *Eurosurveillance*, 23 Jan 2020: https://www.eurosurveillance.org/content/10.2807/1560-7917.ES.2020.25.3.2000045#metrics_content

[52] "Laboratory testing for 2019 novel coronavirus (2019-nCoV) in suspected human cases," WHO, 19 Mar 2020: https://www.who.int/publications/i/item/10665-331501 (archived)

[53] Corman, V., et al., "Diagnostic detection of 2019-nCoV by real-time RT-PCR," WHO, 17 Jan 2020: https://www.who.int/docs/default-source/coronaviruse/protocol-v2-1.pdf?sfvrsn=a9ef618c_2

[54] Ghebreyesus, T., "WHO Director-General's opening remarks at the media briefing on COVID-19 - 11 March 2020," 11 Mar 2020: https://www.who.int/director-general/speeches/detail/who-director-general-s-opening-remarks-at-the-media-briefing-on-covid-19---11-march-2020 (archived)

[55] "Who is 'patient zero' in the coronavirus outbreak?," *BBC Platform*, 24 Feb 2020: https://www.bbc.com/future/article/20200221-coronavirus-the-harmful-hunt-for-covid-19s-patient-zero (archived)

[56] Ibid.

[57] "Gaëtan Dugas," *Wikipedia*: https://en.wikipedia.org/wiki/Ga%C3%ABtan_Dugas (accessed 27 Jul 2023)

[58] Auerbach, D., et al., "Cluster of Cases of the Acquired Immune Deficiency Syndrome Patients Linked by Sexual Contact," *The American Journal of Medicine*, Mar 1984: https://www.amjmed.com/article/0002-9343(84)90668-5/pdf

[59] Shilts, R., *And the Band Played On*, St. Martin's Press, 1987

[60] "The Columbus of AIDS," *National Review*, 6 Nov 1987

[61] "1854 Broad Street cholera outbreak," *Wikipedia*: https://en.wikipedia.org/wiki/1854_Broad_Street_cholera_outbreak (accessed 4 Aug 2023)

[62] Engelbrecht, T., et al., *Virus Mania*, 3rd English Edition, Books on Demand, 2021: https://drsambailey.com/shop-2/

[63] Yong, S., et al. "Connecting clusters of COVID-19: an epidemiological and serological investigation," *The Lancet, Infectious diseases*, 21 Apr 2020: https://www.thelancet.com/journals/laninf/article/PIIS1473-3099(20)30273-5/fulltext

[64] Bailey, S., "Covid 19: 'Asymptomatic Transmission'," *drsambailey.com*, 4 May 2021: https://drsambailey.com/resources/videos/covid-19/covid-19-asymptomatic-transmission/

[65] "Mary Mallon," *Wikipedia*: https://en.wikipedia.org/wiki/Mary_Mallon (accessed 10 Aug 2023)

[66] Soper, G., "The Curious Career of Typhoid Mary," *Bulletin of the New York Academy of Medicine*, Oct 1939: https://www.ncbi.nlm.nih.gov/pmc/articles/PMC1911442/pdf/bullnyacadmed00595-0063.pdf

[67] Waddington, C., et al., "An outpatient, ambulant-design, controlled human infection model using escalating doses of Salmonella Typhi challenge delivered in sodium bicarbonate solution," *Clinical infectious diseases,* 1 May 2014: https://doi.org/10.1093/cid/ciu078

[68] "Typhoid," *Merriam-Webster Dictionary*: https://web.archive.org/web/20130702140640/http://www.merriam-webster.com/dictionary/typhoid

[69] *From the Latin, *dosis sola facit venenum*. Even ingesting large volumes of water can result in severe symptoms and death.

[70] Waddington, C., et al., "An outpatient, ambulant-design, controlled human infection model using escalating doses of Salmonella Typhi challenge delivered in sodium bicarbonate solution," *Clinical infectious diseases,* 1 May 2014: https://doi.org/10.1093/cid/ciu078

[71] "Nocebo effect," *Merriam-Webster dictionary*: https://www.merriam-webster.com/dictionary/nocebo%20effect (accessed 16 Aug 2023)

[72] https://viroliegy.com/category/germ-theory/

[73] Stone, M., "Uncovering the Corona Fraud Part 19," *ViroLIEgy.com*, 27 Jan 2024: https://mikestone.substack.com/p/uncovering-the-corona-fraud-part-7e7

[74] "Carlo Urbani," *Wikipedia*: https://en.wikipedia.org/wiki/Carlo_Urbani (accessed 30 Nov 2023)

[75] Engelbrecht, T., et al., *Virus Mania*, 3rd English Edition, Books on Demand, 2021: https://drsambailey.com/shop-2/

[76] "Coronavirus whistleblower doctor Li Wenliang dies from infection in Wuhan, local hospital says," *ABC News*, 7 Feb 2020: https://www.abc.net.au/news/2020-02-07/doctor-who-warned-of-coronavirus-dies-in-china/11941948

[77] Ioannidis, J., "Infection fatality rate of COVID-19 inferred from seroprevalence data," *Bull World Health Organ*, Oct 2021: https://www.ncbi.nlm.nih.gov/pmc/articles/PMC7947934/pdf/BLT.20.265892.pdf/

[78] https://twitter.com/PDChina/status/1225513842807099394

[79] "Virus 'whistleblower' doctor under emergency treatment: hospital," *Global Times*, 7 Feb 2023: https://www.globaltimes.cn//content/1178816.shtml

[80] Zhang, H., "Grief and Wariness at a Vigil for Li Wenliang, the Doctor Who Tried to Warn China About the Coronavirus," *The New Yorker*, 11 Feb 2020: https://www.newyorker.com/news/news-desk/grief-and-wariness-at-a-vigil-for-li-wenliang-the-doctor-who-tried-to-warn-china-about-the-coronavirus

[81] "Outbreak (film)," *Wikipedia* :https://en.wikipedia.org/wiki/Outbreak_(film)

[82] "disease communicated to humans by animals," *Online Etymology Dictionary*: https://www.etymonline.com/word/zoonosis

[83] *The massive increase in the use of the word 'zoonotic' since the year 1995 when the film *Outbreak* was released can be seen here: https://books.google.com/ngrams/graph?content=zoonotic&year_start=1800&year_end=2019&corpus=en-2019&smoothing=1

[84] Humphries, S. & Bystrianyk, R., *Dissolving Illusions: Disease, Vaccines, and The Forgotten History*, 2013: https://dissolvingillusions.com/

[85] *Professor Virginia Berridge described how the UK Public Health Laboratory Service (the progenitor of today's UK Health Security Agency) would have been shut down by Prime Minister Margaret Thatcher if it had not been for HIV/AIDS. See *AIDS in the UK: The Making of Policy, 1981–1994*, Oxford University Press, 1996.

[86] Diaz, A., "Mysterious pneumonia kills 3, infects 9 in Argentina: 'Similar to COVID'," *New York Post*, 1 Sep 2022: https://nypost.com/2022/09/01/mysterious-pneumonia-kills-three-people-in-argentina/

[87] Cilloniz, C., et al., "Microbial Etiology of Pneumonia: Epidemiology, Diagnosis and Resistance Patterns," *Int. J. Mol. Sci.*, 17(12), 2120, 16 Dec 2016

[88] "WHO COVID-19 Case definitions: Updated in Public health surveillance for COVID-19 | COVID-19: Surveillance, case investigation and epidemiological protocol," 16 Dec 2020: https://www.who.int/publications/i/item/WHO-2019-nCoV-Surveillance_Case_Definition-2020.2 (archived)

[89] Diaz, A., "Mysterious pneumonia kills 3, infects 9 in Argentina: 'Similar to COVID'," *New York Post*, 1 Sep 2022: https://nypost.com/2022/09/01/mysterious-pneumonia-kills-three-people-in-argentina/

[90] Bailey, M. & Bailey, S., "Monkeypox Mythology," *drsambailey.com*, 23 May 2022: https://drsambailey.com/monkeypox-mythology/

[91] "Zoonotic Diseases," *Centers for Disease Control and Prevention*, https://www.cdc.gov/onehealth/basics/zoonotic-diseases.html (accessed 3 Sep 2022)

92 "Outbreak (film)," *Wikipedia* :https://en.wikipedia.org/wiki/Outbreak_(film)

93 "Zoonotic Diseases," *Centers for Disease Control and Prevention*, https://www.cdc.gov/onehealth/basics/zoonotic-diseases.html (accessed 3 Sep 2022)

94 Kessler, R., "Disease X: The Next Pandemic," *EcoHealth Alliance*: https://www.ecohealthalliance.org/2018/03/disease-x (accessed 3 Sep 2022)

95 "About Us," *Global Virome Project*: https://www.globalviromeproject.org/who-we-are (accessed 3 Sep 2022)

96 Zaugg, J., "The virus hunters who search bat caves to predict the next pandemic," *CNN*, 26 Apr 2020: https://edition.cnn.com/2020/04/26/health/virus-hunters-bat-cave-coronavirus-hnk-intl/index.html

97 "Coronavirus" articles and videos at www.drsambailey.com

98 Bailey, M., *A Farewell to Virology (Expert Edition)*, 15 Sep 2022: https://drsambailey.com/a-farewell-to-virology-expert-edition/

99 Thomson, B., "Revolting footage shows Chinese woman eating a whole bat at a fancy restaurant as scientists link the deadly coronavirus to the flying mammals," *Daily Mail Australia*, 24 Jan 2020: https://www.dailymail.co.uk/news/article-7920573/Revolting-footage-shows-Chinese-woman-eating-bat-scientists-link-coronavirus-animal.html

100 "SARS," *Wikipedia*: https://en.wikipedia.org/wiki/SARS (accessed 30 Nov 2023)

101 Wang, N., "Serological Evidence of Bat SARS-Related Coronavirus Infection in Humans, China," *Virological Sinica*, 8 Jan 2018: https://link.springer.com/article/10.1007/s12250-018-0012-7

102 "2 February 2022: Biosecurity, Borders and Trade Programme accounting officer assessment," *www.gov.uk*: https://www.gov.uk/government/publications/defra-accounting-officer-assessments/2-february-2022-biosecurity-borders-and-trade-programme-accounting-officer-assessment

103 "New pilot requirement for tree suppliers announced to strengthen UK biosecurity," *www.gov.uk*: https://www.gov.uk/government/news/new-pilot-requirement-for-tree-suppliers-announced-to-strengthen-uk-biosecurity

[104] Engelbrecht, T., et al., *Virus Mania*, 3rd English Edition, Books on Demand, 2021: https://drsambailey.com/shop-2/

[105] Bolotnikova, M., "US bird flu outbreak: millions of birds culled in 'most inhumane way available'," *The Guardian*, 6 Jun 2022: https://www.theguardian.com/environment/2022/jun/06/us-bird-flu-outbreak-millions-of-birds-culled-in-most-inhumane-way-available

[106] "Certificate of Analysis VetMAXTM-Gold AIV Detection Kit," *ThermoFisher Scientific*, 24 Aug 2022

[107] Bolotnikova, M., "US bird flu outbreak: millions of birds culled in 'most inhumane way available'," *The Guardian*, 6 Jun 2022: https://www.theguardian.com/environment/2022/jun/06/us-bird-flu-outbreak-millions-of-birds-culled-in-most-inhumane-way-available

[108] "Neil Ferguson (epidemiologist)," *Wikipedia*: https://en.wikipedia.org/wiki/Neil_Ferguson_(epidemiologist) (accessed 16 Dec 2023)

[109] "Insight: Slaughtered on Suspicion," *UK Column*, 4 Aug 2015: https://www.ukcolumn.org/video/insight-slaughtered-on-suspicion

[110] Stenfeldt C. & Arzt J., "The Carrier Conundrum; A Review of Recent Advances and Persistent Gaps Regarding the Carrier State of Foot-and-Mouth Disease Virus," *Pathogens*, 28 Feb 2020: https://www.ncbi.nlm.nih.gov/pmc/articles/PMC7157498/

[111] Brown, T., "Italian greyhound belonging to gay couple in Paris catches monkeypox after sharing bed with its infected owners, scientists reveal," *Daily Mail Australia*, 15 Aug 2022: https://www.dailymail.co.uk/news/article-11110645/Italian-greyhound-belonging-gay-couple-Paris-catches-monkey-pox.html

[112] Ibid.

[113] Bailey, M. & Bailey, S., "Monkeypox Mythology," *drsambailey.com*, 23 May 2022: https://drsambailey.com/monkeypox-mythology/

[114] Diaz, A., "Mysterious pneumonia kills 3, infects 9 in Argentina: 'Similar to COVID'," *New York Post*, 1 Sep 2022: https://nypost.com/2022/09/01/mysterious-pneumonia-kills-three-people-in-argentina/

[115] Cambridge, E., "COVID CRISIS Shocking photos inside Wuhan lab show broken seal on unit storing 1,500 virus strains including bat coronavirus," *The Sun*, 19 Apr 2020: https://www.thesun.co.uk/news/11429828/photo-wuhan-lab-broken-seal-unit-virus-store-leak/ (archived)

[116] Ibid.

[117] "United States Senate today announced: 'Corona is a lie'! The media is covering up the truth," *thepeoplesvoice.org*, 12 Jun 2021: http://www.thepeoplesvoice.org/TPV3/Videos.php/2021/06/12/united-states-senate-today-announced

[118] Owen, G., "WHO chief 'believes Covid DID leak from Wuhan lab' after a 'catastrophic accident' in 2019 despite publicly maintaining 'all hypotheses remain on the table'," *The Mail*, 18 Jun 2022: https://www.dailymail.co.uk/news/article-10930501/WHO-chief-believes-Covid-DID-leak-Wuhan-lab-catastrophic-accident-2019.html

[119] Mercola, J., "Fauci's Team Involved in Research to Create Deadly Version of Spanish Flu Virus," *The Defender*, 8 Sep 2022: https://childrenshealthdefense.org/defender/fauci-deadly-spanish-flu-virus-cola/

[120] Engelbrecht, T., et al., *Virus Mania*, 3rd English Edition, Books on Demand, 2021: https://drsambailey.com/shop-2/

[121] Chan, M., et al., "Pandemic 1918 Influenza Virus Does Not Cause Lethal Infection in Rhesus or Cynomolgus Macaques," *Journal of Virology*, 4 Aug 2022: https://doi.org/10.1128/jvi.00728-22

[122] Pound, P. & Bracken, M., "Is animal research sufficiently evidence based to be a cornerstone of biomedical research?," *BMJ*, 30 May 2014: https://doi.org/10.1136/bmj.g3387

[123] Taylor, K., et al., "Estimates for Worldwide Laboratory Animal Use in 2005," *ATLA*, 1 Jul 2008: https://doi.org/10.1177/026119290803600310

[124] Varma, J., "As a Doctor: Why are so many viruses popping up again?," *The Washington Post*, 19 Sep 2022: https://www.washingtonpost.com/wellness/2022/09/19/virus-outbreaks-ebola-monkeypox-coming-back/

[125] Morand, S. & Lajaunie, C., "Outbreaks of Vector-Borne and Zoonotic Diseases Are Associated With Changes in Forest Cover and Oil Palm Expansion at Global Scale," *Frontiers in Veterinary Science*, 24 Mar 2021: https://doi.org/10.3389/fvets.2021.661063

[126] https://www.weforum.org/agenda/2019/10/future-predictions-what-if-get-things-right-visions-for-2030/ (archived)

[127] Allwood, J., et al., "Absolute Zero," University of Cambridge, 29 Nov 2019: https://web.archive.org/web/20210812151339/https://www.ukfires.org/wp-content/uploads/2019/11/Absolute-Zero-online.pdf

[128] Magness, P., "The Failure of Imperial College Modeling Is Far Worse than We Knew," *American Institute for Economic Research*, 22 Apr 2021: https://www.aier.org/article/the-failure-of-imperial-college-modeling-is-far-worse-than-we-knew/

[129] 'In the very act of committing a misdeed - Red-handed': https://www.merriam-webster.com/dictionary/in%20flagrante%20delicto

[130] Bracchi, P., "Naked hypocrisy: How Professor Lockdown's mistress was telling the public to stay at home two weeks before the Government only to be caught in secret trysts with her lover," *The Daily Mail*, 7 May 2020: https://www.dailymail.co.uk/news/article-8294315/Naked-hypocrisy-Professor-Lockdowns-mistress-telling-public-stay-home.html (archived)

[131] "Ebola," *Wikipedia*: https://en.wikipedia.org/wiki/Ebola (accessed 28 Sep 2022)

[132] Ibid.

[133] "Ebola (Ebola Virus Disease) - Diagnosis," *The Centers for Disease Control and Prevention*: https://www.cdc.gov/vhf/ebola/diagnosis/index.html (archived)

[134] Bowen, E., et al., "Viral Haemorrhagic Fever in Southern Sudan and Northern Zaire," *The Lancet*, 12 Mar 1977: https://doi.org/10.1016/s0140-6736(77)92001-3

[135] Prokupecz, S. & Shoichet, C., "New York doctor now Ebola free, will be released from hospital," *CNN*, 10 Nov 2014: https://edition.cnn.com/2014/11/10/health/new-york-doctor-craig-spencer-ebola-free/

[136] "What the New York City Ebola Patient Was Doing Before He Was Hospitalized," *New York Times*, 24 Oct 2014: https://www.nytimes.com/interactive/2014/10/23/nyregion/new-york-city-ebola-patient-timeline-map.html

137 Santora, M., "Doctor in New York City Is Sick With Ebola," *New York Times*, 23 Oct 2012: https://www.nytimes.com/2014/10/24/nyregion/craig-spencer-is-tested-for-ebola-virus-at-bellevue-hospital-in-new-york-city.html

138 "List of Ebola outbreaks," *Wikipedia*: https://en.wikipedia.org/wiki/List_of_Ebola_outbreaks (accessed 28 Sep 2022)

139 Warrick, J., "Ebola crisis rekindles concerns about secret research in Russian military labs," *Washington Post*, 24 Oct 2014: https://www.washingtonpost.com/national/health-science/2014/10/23/ce409716-5945-11e4-b812-38518ae74c67_story.html

140 Stone, R., "Russian Scientist Dies After Ebola Lab Accident," *Science*, 28 May 2004: https://doi.org/10.1126/science.304.5675.1225b

141 "Ebola virus disease in the United Kingdom," *Wikipedia*: https://en.wikipedia.org/wiki/Ebola_virus_disease_in_the_United_Kingdom (accessed 30 Sep 2022)

142 Bailey, S., "Bioweapons BS," *drsambailey.com*, 1 Oct 2022: https://drsambailey.com/resources/videos/viruses-unplugged/bioweapons-bs/

143 "Public health aspects of the new insecticides," *The American journal of digestive diseases*, 1 Nov 1953: https://doi.org/10.1007/BF02883493

144 Rosenau, M., "Experiments to determine mode of spread of influenza," *JAMA*, 2 Aug 1919: https://jamanetwork.com/journals/jama/article-abstract/221687

145 Ibid.

146 Stone, M., "Challenging Influenza," *ViroLIEgy*, 16 Apr 2023: https://viroliegy.com/2023/04/16/challenging-influenza/

147 Roytas, D., "What Really Causes Influenza? Part 1," *Humanley*, 5 Mar 2022: https://www.humanley.com/blog/what-really-causes-influenza-part-1

148 Webster, R., et al. editors, *Textbook of Influenza - 2nd Edition*, Wiley Blackwell, 2013

149 Editorials, "Milton Joseph Rosenau," *American Journal of Public Health*, May 1946: https://www.ncbi.nlm.nih.gov/pmc/articles/PMC1625820/

[150] "Milton J. Rosenau," *Wikipedia*: https://en.wikipedia.org/wiki/Milton_J._Rosenau (accessed 21 Sep 2022)

[151] Rosenau, M., "Experiments to determine mode of spread of influenza," *JAMA*, 2 Aug 1919: https://jamanetwork.com/journals/jama/article-abstract/221687

[152] Zuger, A., "'You'll Catch Your Death!' An Old Wives' Tale? Well...," *New York Times*, 4 Mar 2003: https://www.nytimes.com/2003/03/04/science/you-ll-catch-your-death-an-old-wives-tale-well.html

[153] "Common cold," *Wikipedia*: https://en.wikipedia.org/wiki/Common_cold

[154] *See also note 28.

[155] "cold (adj.)," *Online Etymology Dictionary:* https://www.etymonline.com/word/cold

[156] Greenhough, B., "Where species meet and mingle: The Common Cold Unit 1946-1990," Dept. of Geography, Queen Mary, University of London, Jul 2008: https://www.academia.edu/1322109/Where_species_meet_and_mingle_The_Common_Cold_Unit

[157] Ibid.

[158] "Why thousands went on holiday to the Common Cold Unit," *BBC*, 13 Jul 2019: https://www.bbc.com/news/av/stories-48923865

[159] Jackson, G., "The Medical Research Council Common Cold Unit, Harvard Hospital, Salisbury, Wilts, England," *Clinical Infectious Diseases*, 1 Nov 1989: https://doi.org/10.1093/clinids/11.6.1020

[160] Greenhough, B., "Where species meet and mingle: The Common Cold Unit 1946-1990," Dept. of Geography, Queen Mary, University of London, Jul 2008: https://www.academia.edu/1322109/Where_species_meet_and_mingle_The_Common_Cold_Unit

[161] Ibid.

[162] Mahase, E., "Covid-19: First coronavirus was described in The BMJ in 1965," *British Medical Journal*, 16 Apr 2020: https://doi.org/10.1136/bmj.m1547

[163] Ibid.

[164] Almeida, J. & Tyrrell, D., "The Morphology of Three Previously Uncharacterized Human Respiratory Viruses that Grow in Organ Culture," *Journal of General Virology*, 1 Apr 1967: https://www.microbiologyresearch.org/docserver/fulltext/jgv/1/2/JV0010020175.pdf

[165] "Virology: Coronaviruses," *Nature*, 16 Nov 1968: https://www.nature.com/articles/220650b0.pdf

[166] Kendall, E., et al., "Virus Isolations From Common Colds Occurring in a Residential School," *British Medical Journal*, 14 Jul 1962: https://www.ncbi.nlm.nih.gov/pmc/articles/PMC1925312/pdf/brmedj02979-0032.pdf

[167] Ibid.

[168] Tyrrell, D., et al., "Cultivation of "difficult" viruses from patients with common colds," *British Medical Journal*, 9 Mar 1968: https://www.ncbi.nlm.nih.gov/pmc/articles/PMC1985339/pdf/brmedj02074-0036.pdf

[169] Ibid.

[170] "Common cold," *Wikipedia*: https://en.wikipedia.org/wiki/Common_cold

[171] Tyrrell, D., "The origins of the Common Cold Unit," *Journal of the Royal College of Physicians of London*, Apr 1990: https://www.ncbi.nlm.nih.gov/pmc/articles/PMC5387570/pdf/jrcollphyslond90348-0069.pdf

[172] Ibid.

[173] Richmond, C., "David Tyrrell," *British Medical Journal*, 18 Jun 2005: https://www.ncbi.nlm.nih.gov/pmc/articles/PMC558394/

[174] Fendrick, A., et al., "The Economic Burden of Non–Influenza-Related Viral Respiratory Tract Infection in the United States," *JAMA*, 24 Feb 2003: https://jamanetwork.com/journals/jamainternalmedicine/fullarticle/215118

[175] Roytas, D., *Can You Catch A Cold?: Untold History and Human Experiments*, 2024: https://www.humanley.com/books

[176] *The 'magic bullet' was mentioned by German Nobel laureate Paul Ehrlich in 1907. He proposed that an allopathic drug can treat a disease by killing specific microbes without harming the body. In the year 2024, *Wikipedia* continued to state that it is a "scientific concept": https://en.wikipedia.org/wiki/Magic_bullet_(medicine) (archived)

[177] Engelbrecht, T., et al., *Virus Mania*, 3rd English Edition, Books on Demand, 2021: https://drsambailey.com/shop-2/

[178] "TCM history - the Sui & Tang Dynasties," *shen-nong.com*

[179] "Takaki Kanehiro," *Wikipedia*: https://en.wikipedia.org/wiki/Takaki_Kanehiro

[180] Glogner, M., "Position of Beri-Beri among Infectious Diseases," *The Indian Medical Gazette*, 1 Jan 1894: https://europepmc.org/article/PMC/5197223

[181] *Ibid. In reporting on his "successful" results with quinine, Glogner ironically stated, "I have not been deceived in this, and I now give briefly the results of the quinine treatment of Beri-Beri patients in order to support the assertion that Beri-Beri is a disease caused by an amoeba."

[182] *Like Glogner "treating" a microbe imagined to be the cause of beriberi, we observed a similar phenomenon in the COVID-era with physicians claiming that they were successfully treating an imagined SARS-CoV-2 "viral infection" with their various pharmaceutical protocols.

[183] Hegyi, J. & Schwartz, R., "Pellagra: Dermatitis, dementia, and diarrhea," *International Journal of Dermatology*, 24 Dec 2003: https://doi.org/10.1111/j.1365-4632.2004.01959.x

[184] Sambon, L., "Remarks On The Possibility Of The Acclimatisation Of Europeans In Tropical Regions," *BMJ*, 9 Jan 1897: https://doi.org/10.1136/bmj.1.1880.61

[185] Gentilcore, D., "Louis Sambon and the Clash of Pellagra Etiologies in Italy and the United States, 1905–14," *Journal of the History of Medicine and Allied Sciences*, 4 Mar 2015: https://doi.org/10.1093/jhmas/jrv002

[186] Ibid.

[187] Ibid.

188 Leslie, C., "'Fighting an Unseen Enemy': The Infectious Paradigm in the Conquest of Pellagra," *Journal of Medical Humanities*, Dec 2002: https://doi.org/10.1023/A:1016842301517

189 Wood, E., *A treatise on pellagra, for the general practitioner,* D. Appleton and company, New York and London, 1912: https://archive.org/details/atreatiseonpell00woodgoog/

190 Leslie, C., "'Fighting an Unseen Enemy': The Infectious Paradigm in the Conquest of Pellagra," *Journal of Medical Humanities*, Dec 2002: https://doi.org/10.1023/A:1016842301517

191 "Pellagra," *Wikipedia*: https://en.wikipedia.org/wiki/Pellagra (accessed 22 Sep 2022)

192 Casal, G., "Historia natural, y medica de el Principado de Asturias," 1762 (published posthumously): https://babel.hathitrust.org/cgi/pt?id=uc1.31378008344825&seq=1

193 "What is Polio?," *Centers for Disease Control and Prevention*: https://www.cdc.gov/polio/what-is-polio/index.htm (accessed 22 Sep 2022)

194 Mueller, S., et al., "Poliovirus and poliomyelitis: A tale of guts, brains, and an accidental event," *Virus Research*, Aug 2005: https://doi.org/10.1016/j.virusres.2005.04.008

195 "Polio," *Wikipedia*: https://en.wikipedia.org/wiki/Polio (accessed 24 Sep 2022)

196 Engelbrecht, T., et al., *Virus Mania*, 3rd English Edition, Books on Demand, 2021: https://drsambailey.com/shop-2/

197 "Polio," *Wikipedia*: https://en.wikipedia.org/wiki/Polio (accessed 24 Sep 2022)

198 Engdahl, F., "Toxicology vs Virology - Rockefeller Institute and the Criminal Polio Fraud," *www.williamengdahl.com*, 12 Jul 2022: http://www.williamengdahl.com/englishNEO12July2022.php (Video version: https://drsambailey.com/resources/videos/corruption-and-medicine/toxicology-vs-virology-rockefeller-institute-and-the-criminal-polio-fraud/

199 Ma, X., et al., Rabies surveillance in the United States during 2019," *Journal of the American Veterinary Medical Association,* 1 Jun 2021: https://doi.org/10.2460/javma.258.11.1205

200 "Rabies vaccine," *Wikipedia*: https://en.wikipedia.org/wiki/Rabies_vaccine (accessed 25 Sep 2022)

201 Geison, G., *The Private Science of Louis Pasteur*, Princeton University Press, 1995.

202 Ibid.

203 Leverson, M., "English city of Leicester as example of benefits of abolition of vaccination," *Bridgeport Evening Farmer*, 21 Aug 1909.

204 Geison, G., "Pasteur's Work on Rabies: Reexamining the Ethical Issues," *The Hastings Center Report*, Apr 1978: https://doi.org/10.2307/3560403

205 Bailey, S., "What About Rabies?," *drsambailey.com*, 5 Aug 2022: https://drsambailey.com/resources/videos/viruses-unplugged/what-about-rabies/

206 Mihalovic, D., "Measles Vaccine? Biologist Proves Measles Virus DOESN'T EXIST!," *The Liberty Beacon*, 1 Feb, 2017: https://www.thelibertybeacon.com/measles-vaccine-biologist-proves-measles-virus-doesnt-exist/

207 Ravensburg District Court ruling, 12 Mar 2015: https://wissenschafftplus.de/uploads/article/Protokoll_13_4_20150001.pdf

208 State jurisdiction of Baden-Württemberg ruling, 16 Feb 2016: http://lrbw.juris.de/cgi-bin/laender_rechtsprechung/document.py?Gericht=bw&GerichtAuswahl=Oberlandesgerichte&Art=en&sid=46bf3db2df690aba6e4874acafaf45b6&nr=20705&pos=0&anz=1 (archived)

209 "Anti-Vaxxer Biologist Stefan Lanka Bets Over $100K Measles Isn't A Virus; He Wins In German Federal Supreme Court," *anonhq.com*, 21 Jan 2017: https://anonhq.com/anti-vaxxer-biologist-stefan-lanka-bets-100k-measles-isnt-virus-wins-german-federal-supreme-court/

210 Enders, J., & Peebles, T., "Propagation in tissue cultures of cytopathogenic agents from patients with measles," *Proc Soc Exp Biol Med*, June 1954: https://pubmed.ncbi.nlm.nih.gov/13177653/

211 Bech, V., "Studies on measles virus in monkey kidney tissue cultures. 2. Development of cytopathic changes and identification of the cultivated agents by complement fixation tests," *Acta Pathol Microbiol Scand*, 1958: https://pubmed.ncbi.nlm.nih.gov/13508251

[212] Nakai, M. & Imagawa, D., "Electron Microscopy of Measles Virus Replication," *J. Virol*, Feb 1969: https://www.ncbi.nlm.nih.gov/pmc/articles/PMC375751/

[213] Lund et al., "The molecular length of measles virus RNA and the structural organization of measles nucleocapsids," *The Journal of General Virology*, 1 Sep 1984: https://europepmc.org/article/MED/6540797

[214] Horikami, S., & Moyer, S., "Structure, Transcription, and Replication of Measles Virus," in *Current Topics in Microbiology and Immunology*, 1995: https://link.springer.com/chapter/10.1007/978-3-642-78621-1_3

[215] Daikoku, et al., "Analysis of Morphology and Infectivity of Measles Virus Particles," *Bulletin of the Osaka Medical College*, 2007: https://www.osaka-med.ac.jp/deps/b-omc/articles/532/532daikoku.pdf (archived)

[216] State jurisdiction of Baden-Württemberg ruling, 16 Feb 2016: http://lrbw.juris.de/cgi-bin/laender_rechtsprechung/document.py?Gericht=bw&GerichtAuswahl=Oberlandesgerichte&Art=en&sid=46bf3db2df690aba6e4874acafaf45b6&nr=20705&pos=0&anz=1 (archived)

[217] Lanka, S., "The Virus Misconception," *Wissenschafftplus*, Jan 2020: http://wissenschafftplus.de/uploads/article/wissenschafftplus-the-virus-misconception-part-1.pdf

[218] "Anti-Vaxxer Biologist Stefan Lanka Bets Over $100K Measles Isn't A Virus; He Wins In German Federal Supreme Court," *anonhq.com*, 21 Jan 2017: https://anonhq.com/anti-vaxxer-biologist-stefan-lanka-bets-100k-measles-isnt-virus-wins-german-federal-supreme-court/

[219] Ibid.

[220] "Germany: New Act Makes Measles Vaccinations Mandatory," Library of Congress, 11 Mar 2020: https://www.loc.gov/item/global-legal-monitor/2020-03-11/germany-new-act-makes-measles-vaccinations-mandatory/

[221] https://wissenschafftplus.de/uploads/article/goVIRUSgogogo.pdf

[222] https://truthseeker.se/wp-content/uploads/2021/10/goVIRUSgo.pdf

223 "Global Pharmaceuticals Market Report 2021: Market is Expected to Grow from $1228.45 Billion in 2020 to $1250.24 Billion in 2021 - Long-term Forecast to 2025 & 2030," *GlobeNewswire*, 31 Mar 2021: https://www.globenewswire.com/en/news-release/2021/03/31/2202135/28124/en/Global-Pharmaceuticals-Market-Report-2021-Market-is-Expected-to-Grow-from-1228-45-Billion-in-2020-to-1250-24-Billion-in-2021-Long-term-Forecast-to-2025-2030.html

224 "Pfizer reports 92% operational growth in full-year 2021 revenues," *Pharmaceutical Technology*, 9 Feb 2022: https://www.pharmaceutical-technology.com/news/pfizer-full-year-2021-revenues/

225 Gøtzsche, P., *Deadly Medicines and Organised Crime*, Radcliffe Publishing Ltd, London, 2013.

226 *Our well being is also assaulted in new and ever changing ways we have yet to fully understand or even recognize, for example the unending industrially scaled evolution of environmental and electromagnetic pollutants.

227 Williams, U., Bailey, S., *Terrain Therapy*, Dr Samantha Bailey, 2022: https://drsambailey.com/terrain-therapy/

228 "Therapeutic Drug Use," *CDC: National Center for Health Statistics*: https://www.cdc.gov/nchs/fastats/drug-use-therapeutic.htm (accessed 21 Oct 2022)

229 Kogan, M., et al., "Over-the-counter Medication Use Among US Preschool-age Children," *JAMA*, 5 Oct 1994: https://pubmed.ncbi.nlm.nih.gov/8089884/

230 "Understanding Over-the-Counter Medicines," *fda.govt*: https://www.fda.gov/drugs/buying-using-medicine-safely/understanding-over-counter-medicines (accessed 22 Oct 2022)

231 Gøtzsche, P., *Deadly Medicines and Organised Crime*, Radcliffe Publishing Ltd, London, 2013.

232 Farber, C., "Words the Front - Interview Kary Mullis," *Spin*, Jul 1994

233 Kutter, S., "Virologe Drosten im Gespräch 2014 - Der Körper wird ständig von Viren angegriffen," 16 May 2014: https://www.wiwo.de/technologie/forschung/virologe-drosten-im-gespraech-2014-die-who-kann-nur-empfehlungen-aussprechen/9903228-2.html

[234] Stone, M., "Uncovering the Corona Fraud Part 17," *ViroLIEgy News*, 2 Dec 2023: https://mikestone.substack.com/p/uncovering-the-corona-fraud-part-f14

[235] Kolata, G., "Faith in Quick Test Leads to Epidemic That Wasn't," *New York Times*, 22 Jan 2007, https://web.archive.org/web/20210504212859/https://www.nytimes.com/2007/01/22/health/22whoop.html

[236] "Lessons from 'the pertussis epidemic that wasn't'," *Relias Media*, 1 Apr 2007: https://www.reliasmedia.com/articles/102179-lessons-from-the-pertussis-epidemic-that-wasn-t

[237] Kolata, G., "Faith in Quick Test Leads to Epidemic That Wasn't," *New York Times*, 22 Jan 2007: https://web.archive.org/web/20210504212859/https://www.nytimes.com/2007/01/22/health/22whoop.html

[238] Ibid.

[239] "Pertussis," New Zealand Ministry of Health, https://www.health.govt.nz/our-work/diseases-and-conditions/communicable-disease-control-manual/pertussis#casedef (archived)

[240] Butler, H., "Pertussis : MOH Changes the Diagnosis Criteria - 31 May, 2012," *Beyond Conformity*, 19 Jun 2012: https://www.beyondconformity.org.nz/hilary-s-desk/pertussis_moh_changes_the_diagnosis_criteria-31_may-2012

[241] "Lessons from 'the pertussis epidemic that wasn't'," *Relias Media*, 1 Apr 2007: https://www.reliasmedia.com/articles/102179-lessons-from-the-pertussis-epidemic-that-wasn-t

[242] Gøtzsche, P., "Expert Report - Effect of DTP Vaccines on Mortality in Children in Low-Income Countries," 19 Jun 2019: https://vaccinescience.org/wp-content/uploads/2019/07/Expert-Report-Effect-of-DTP-Vaccines-on-Mortality-in-Children-in-Low-Income-Countries.pdf

[243] "Tdap (Tetanus, Diphtheria, Pertussis) VIS," Centers for Disease Control and Prevention, 6 Aug 2021: https://www.cdc.gov/vaccines/hcp/vis/vis-statements/tdap.html

[244] Ibid.

245 "Best Practices for Healthcare Professionals on the Use of Polymerase Chain Reaction (PCR) for Diagnosing Pertussis," Centers for Disease Control and Prevention: https://www.cdc.gov/pertussis/clinical/diagnostic-testing/diagnosis-pcr-bestpractices.html (accessed 21 Nov 2021)

246 "PCR Troubleshooting Guide," ThermoFisher Scientific: https://www.thermofisher.com/au/en/home/life-science/cloning/cloning-learning-center/invitrogen-school-of-molecular-biology/pcr-education/pcr-reagents-enzymes/pcr-troubleshooting.html (accessed 21 Nov 2021)

247 "Whooping cough," *Wikipedia*: https://en.wikipedia.org/wiki/Whooping_cough (accessed 29 Jul 2021)

248 "Pertussis (Whooping Cough)," Centers for Disease Control and Prevention: http://www.cdc.gov/pertussis/about/causes-transmission.html (archived)

249 Bisgard, K., et al., "Infant Pertussis Who Was the Source?," *The Pediatric Infectious Disease Journal*, Nov 2004: https://journals.lww.com/pidj/Fulltext/2004/11000/Infant_Pertussis__Who_Was_the_Source_.2.aspx

250 Wendelboe, A., et al., "Transmission of Bordetella pertussis to Young Infants," The Pediatric Infectious Disease Journal, Apr 2007: https://journals.lww.com/pidj/Fulltext/2007/04000/Transmission_of_Bordetella_pertussis_to_Young.5.aspx

251 Humphries, S. & Bystrianyk, R., *Dissolving Illusions: Disease, Vaccines, and The Forgotten History*, 2013: https://dissolvingillusions.com/

252 Letter from Victoria Romanus, MD, PhD, Department of Epidemiology Swedish Institute of Infectious Disease Control, Stockholm Sweden, August 25, 1995

253 Humphries, S. & Bystrianyk, R., *Dissolving Illusions: Disease, Vaccines, and The Forgotten History*, 2013: https://dissolvingillusions.com/

254 Still, G., *The history of paediatrics : the progress of the study of diseases of children up to the end of the XVIIIth century*, London: H. Milford, Oxford University Press, 1931

255 Hatfield, M., *The acute contagious diseases of childhood*, Chicago: G. P. Engelhard & company, 1901

[256] Guilfoile, P., *Whooping Cough*, Chelsea House, 2010

[257] Warfel, J., et al., "Nonhuman Primate Model of Pertussis," *Infection and Immunity*, 16 Mar 2012: https://journals.asm.org/doi/10.1128/iai.06310-11

[258] Ibid.

[259] Warfel, J., et al., "Acellular pertussis vaccines protect against disease but fail to prevent infection and transmission in a nonhuman primate model," *Proceedings of the National Academy of Sciences of the United States of America*, 14 Jan 2014: https://www.pnas.org/content/111/2/787#sec-8

[260] "Pertussis (Whooping Cough)," Centers for Disease Control and Prevention: http://www.cdc.gov/pertussis/about/causes-transmission.html (archived)

[261] Liu, C., et al., "Staphylococcus aureus and the ecology of the nasal microbiome," *Science Advances*, 5 Jun 2015: https://hsrc.himmelfarb.gwu.edu/sphhs_enviro_facpubs/132

[262] Craig, R., et al., "Asymptomatic Infection and Transmission of Pertussis in Households: A Systematic Review," *Clinical Infectious Diseases*, 1 Jan 2020: https://academic.oup.com/cid/article/70/1/152/5525423

[263] Althouse, B. & Scarpino, S., "Asymptomatic transmission and the resurgence of Bordetella pertussis," *BMC Medicine*, 24 Jun 2015: https://bmcmedicine.biomedcentral.com/articles/10.1186/s12916-015-0382-8

[264] Mooi, F, et al., "Pertussis resurgence: waning immunity and pathogen adaptation – two sides of the same coin," *Epidemiology & Infection*, 13 Feb 2013: https://www.cambridge.org/core/journals/epidemiology-and-infection/article/pertussis-resurgence-waning-immunity-and-pathogen-adaptation-two-sides-of-the-same-coin/2C4624385819C751F0C4E9448D4ABF04

[265] *In 1936, Japanese doctors reported, "among 81 cases with which vitamin C therapy was tried, in 34 cases a clear improvement of the symptoms or perfect healing was obtained, in 32 cases improvement of the symptoms, while in 15 cases effects were indeterminate," but there was little subsequent interest from the 'germ' and drug focused medical world: https://drsuzanne.net/wp-content/uploads/2011/12/Japanese-vit-C-whooping-cough.pdf (archived)

[266] Wensley, A, et al., "Risk factors for pertussis in adults and teenagers in England," *Epidemiology & Infection*, 5 Apr 2017: https://www.cambridge.org/core/journals/epidemiology-and-infection/article/risk-factors-for-pertussis-in-adults-and-teenagers-in-england/E73FEBECFB46E5B0AC6BA1F2790F079E

[267] "Pertussis (Whooping Cough) - Pertussis in Other Countries," Centers for Disease Control and Prevention, 12 May 2013: https://web.archive.org/web/20130512041451/http:/www.cdc.gov/pertussis/countries.html

[268] Winter, K., et al., "Risk Factors Associated With Infant Deaths From Pertussis: A Case-Control Study," *Clinical Infectious Diseases*, 1 Oct 2015: https://academic.oup.com/cid/article/61/7/1099/289804

[269] Altunaiji, S., et al., "Antibiotics for whooping cough (pertussis)," *Cochrane Database of Systematic Reviews 2007*, Issue 3

[270] Aryal, S., "Gene Cloning- Requirements, Principle, Steps, Applications," Microbe Notes, 6 Sep 2018: https://microbenotes.com/gene-cloning-requirements-principle-steps-applications/

[271] "Thermus aquaticus," *Wikipedia*: https://en.wikipedia.org/wiki/Thermus_aquaticus

[272] "History of the Polymerase Chain Reaction Video history Collection," Smithsonian Institution Archives, 1992-1993: https://siarchives.si.edu/collections/siris_arc_217745

[273] Cox, M., et. Al., *Molecular Biology - Principles and Practice*, W. H. Freeman and Company, 2012

[274] Engelbrecht, T. & Demeter, K., "COVID19 PCR Tests are Scientifically Meaningless," *off-Guardian*, 27 Jun 2020: https://off-guardian.org/2020/06/27/covid19-pcr-tests-are-scientifically-meaningless/

[275] Henningsen, P., "New Zealand: A One Horse Race in the Zero COVID Sweepstakes," *21st Century Wire,* 20 Aug 2021: https://21stcenturywire.com/2021/08/20/new-zealand-a-one-horse-race-in-the-zero-covid-sweepstakes/

[276] Fisayo-Bambi, J., "Tanzania: goat, paw paw, jackfruit test positive for coronavirus," *africanews*, 6 May 2020: https://www.africanews.com/2020/05/06/tanzania-how-can-goat-papaya-pawpaw-test-positive-to-corona-morning-call/

[277] "John Magufuli," *Wikipedia*: https://en.wikipedia.org/wiki/John_Magufuli (accessed 8 Nov 2022)

[278] "the study of genetic material recovered directly from environmental or clinical samples by a method called sequencing.": https://en.wikipedia.org/wiki/Metagenomics

[279] James, D., "PCR Inventor: 'It doesn't tell you that you are sick'," *off-Guardian*, 5 Oct 2020: https://off-guardian.org/2020/10/05/pcr-inventor-it-doesnt-tell-you-that-you-are-sick/

[280] Farber, C., "Was the COVID-19 Test Meant to Detect a Virus?," *Uncoverdc*, 7 Apr 2020: https://uncoverdc.com/2020/04/07/was-the-covid-19-test-meant-to-detect-a-virus/

[281] "Global status report on road safety 2018," World Health Organization, 17 Jun 2018: https://www.who.int/publications/i/item/9789241565684

[282] Seladi-Schulman, J., "COVID-19 vs. SARS: How Do They Differ?," *Healthline*, 2 Apr 2020: https://www.healthline.com/health/coronavirus-vs-sars#bottom-line

[283] "PCR Pandemic: Interview with Virus Mania's Dr Claus Köhnlein," Dr Sam Bailey, 27 Oct 2020: https://odysee.com/@drsambailey:c/pcr-pandemic-interview-with-virus-mania:9

[284] Sender, R., et al., "Are We Really Vastly Outnumbered? Revisiting the Ratio of Bacterial to Host Cells in Humans," *Cell*, 28 Jan 2016: https://doi.org/10.1016/j.cell.2016.01.013

[285] Bailey, M., "Rapid Antigen Tests – Making "Viruses" Real Again," *drsambailey.com*, 24 Mar 2022: https://drsambailey.com/rapid-antigen-tests-making-viruses-real-again/

[286] Ibid.

[287] Harcourt, J., et al., "Severe Acute Respiratory Syndrome Coronavirus 2 from Patient with Coronavirus Disease, United States," *Emerging Infectious Diseases*, 26 Jun 2020: https://wwwnc.cdc.gov/eid/article/26/6/20-0516_article

[288] Holshue, M., et al., "First Case of 2019 Novel Coronavirus in the United States," *N Engl J Med*, 5 Mar 2020: https://pubmed.ncbi.nlm.nih.gov/32004427/

[289] Public Health England, "Cell Line Profile - Vero," Oct 2016: https://www.phe-culturecollections.org.uk/media/122249/vero-cell-line-profile.pdf

[290] Khamsi, R., "Scientists May Be Using the Wrong Cells to Study Covid-19," 6 Aug 2020: https://www.wired.com/story/scientists-may-be-using-the-wrong-cells-to-study-covid-19/

[291] European Collection of Authenticated Cell Cultures, "Fundamental Techniques in Cell Culture - 4th Edition," Merck, 2018: https://www.phe-culturecollections.org.uk/media/161749/ecacc-lab-handbook-fourth-edition.pdf (archived)

[292] Jochems, C., et al., "The use of fetal bovine serum: ethical or scientific problem?," *Altern Lab Anim*, Mar-Apr 2002: https://pubmed.ncbi.nlm.nih.gov/11971757/

[293] "What is fetal bovine serum collection?" RSPCA Australia: https://kb.rspca.org.au/knowledge-base/what-is-fetal-bovine-serum-collection/

[294] Johnson, M., "Fetal Bovine Serum," *Labome.com*: https://www.labome.com/method/Fetal-Bovine-Serum.html

[295] ATCC Technical document, "Passage Number Effects In Cell Lines," 2021: https://www.atcc.org/resources/technical-documents/passage-number-effects-in-cell-lines

[296] Neumann, E., et al., "Cell culture and passaging alters gene expression pattern and proliferation rate in rheumatoid arthritis synovial fibroblasts," *Arthritis Research & Therapy*, 12 May 2010: https://arthritis-research.biomedcentral.com/articles/10.1186/ar3010

[297] ATCC Tech Bulletin, "Reference Strains: How many passages are too many?," 2021: https://www.atcc.org/resources/technical-documents/reference-strains-how-many-passages-are-too-many

[298] McClintock, B., "The Significance of Responses of The Genome to Challenge," Nobel speech, 8 Dec 1983

[299] Fan Wu, et al., "A new coronavirus associated with human respiratory disease in China," *Nature*, 3 Feb 2020: https://www.ncbi.nlm.nih.gov/pmc/articles/PMC7094943/

[300] Spencer, G., "New Genome Comparison Finds Chimps, Humans Very Similar at the DNA Level," *NIH News*, 31 Aug 2005: https://www.genome.gov/15515096/2005-release-new-genome-comparison-finds-chimps-humans-very-similar-at-dna-level

[301] Chen, Y., et. al., "Emerging coronaviruses: Genome structure, replication, and pathogenesis," *J Med Virol*, 7 Feb 2020: https://www.ncbi.nlm.nih.gov/pmc/articles/PMC7167049/

[302] "Great Discussion on the Origin, Authority, and Tendency of the Bible," J B Yerrington & Son, 1854

[303] "The CDC's Claim on SARS-CoV-2" in Bailey, M., *A Farewell to Virology (Expert Edition)*, 15 Sep 2022: https://drsambailey.com/a-farewell-to-virology-expert-edition/

[304] *However, this would still not constitute direct evidence for the virus hypothesis because these cell culture experiments are an artificial proxy environment (*in vitro*) with abnormal cell types. The virologists could only assume that the same phenomenon occurs in a living organism (*in vivo*).

[305] Cowan, T., et al., "The 'Settling The Virus Debate' Statement," 14 Jul 2022: https://drsambailey.com/resources/settling-the-virus-debate/

[306] Harcourt, J., et al., "Severe Acute Respiratory Syndrome Coronavirus 2 from Patient with Coronavirus Disease, United States," *Emerging Infectious Diseases*, 26 Jun 2020: https://wwwnc.cdc.gov/eid/article/26/6/20-0516_article

[307] Webb, D., *The Great Taking*, David Rogers Webb, 2023: https://thegreattaking.com/

[308] Rappoport, J., "New Study: Death Following COVID Vaccination," *Substack*, 21 Nov 2023: https://jonrappoport.substack.com/p/new-study-death-following-covid-vaccination

[309] "antivax," dictionary.com: https://web.archive.org/web/20230306071514/https://www.dictionary.com/browse/antivax

[310] Engelbrecht, T., et al., *Virus Mania*, 3rd English Edition, Books on Demand, 2021: https://drsambailey.com/shop-2/

[311] Ghebreyesus, T., "WHO Director-General's opening remarks at the media briefing on COVID-19 - 11 March 2020," 11 Mar 2020: https://www.who.int/director-general/speeches/detail/who-director-general-s-opening-remarks-at-the-media-briefing-on-covid-19---11-march-2020 (archived)

[312] Ibid.

[313] *The United Nations General Assembly also cheerleads these plans and designated December the 27th as the International Day of Epidemic Preparedness in its Resolution on December the 7th, 2020: https://documents.un.org/doc/undoc/gen/n20/345/68/pdf/n2034568.pdf?token=pYxmR91eOzMhrtb8Gh&fe=true

[314] "Official Information Act request relating to COVID-19 Advertising Costs - Ref: OIA-2021/22-1116," 14 Apr 2022: https://fyi.org.nz/request/18889/response/72390/attach/4/DPMCOIA%20REPLY%20Bristow.pdf

[315] "Public Interest Journalism Fund," Ministry for Culture & Heritage: https://mch.govt.nz/media-sector-support/journalism-fund (accessed 3 Dec 2023)

[316] "Deputy Prime Minister Winston Peters attacks state-funded media independence," *Radio New Zealand*, 27 Nov 2023: https://www.rnz.co.nz/news/political/503394/deputy-prime-minister-winston-peters-attacks-state-funded-media-independence (archived)

[317] "COVID-19 updates," The official website of the New Zealand Government: https://www.beehive.govt.nz/feature/covid-19-updates

[318] Haynes, M., "FLASHBACK: New Zealand PM told public 'we are your single source of truth'," *LifeSite News*, 16 Jul 2021: https://www.lifesitenews.com/news/flashback-new-zealand-pm-told-public-we-are-your-single-source-of-truth/

[319] New Zealand Government Press Conference, 13 Aug 2020: https://www.beehive.govt.nz/sites/default/files/2020-08/130820%20Pm%20and%20DG%201pm%20press%20conference.pdf

[320] "New Zealand PM Admits COVID Fear Is Propaganda," *Banned.video*, 13 Mar 2021: https://banned.video/watch?id=604c15428dc93040dd576a16

[321] Ibid.

[322] https://twitter.com/tomhanks/status/1237909897020207104

[323] Gunia, A., "Tom Hanks and Rita Wilson Test Positive for COVID-19," *TIME*, 11 Mar 2020: https://time.com/5801534/tom-hanks-rita-wilson-coronavirus/ (archived)

[324] "Tom Hanks says he has the 'blahs' but no fever in isolation," *Associated Press*, 17 Mar 2020: https://www.apnews.com/73393dbfaf7f1c1eed1ef29e45433314d

[325] Staff, "Newspaper headlines: PM's intensive care move dominates front pages," *BBC*, 7 Apr 2020: https://www.bbc.co.uk/news/blogs-the-papers-52193331 (archived)

[326] "Coronavirus: Boris Johnson moved to intensive care as symptoms worsen," *BBC*, 7 Apr 2020: https://www.bbc.com/news/uk-52192604 (archived)

[327] White, D., "'HULK-LIKE STRENGTH' Does Boris Johnson have underlying health conditions?," *The Sun*, 7 Apr 2020: https://www.thesun.co.uk/news/11343727/boris-johnson-underlying-health-conditions/ (archived)

[328] Brand, P., "Exclusive: Prime Minister Boris Johnson pictured drinking at Downing Street party during lockdown," ITV News, 23 May 2022: https://www.itv.com/news/2022-05-23/exclusive-pm-pictured-drinking-at-downing-street-party-during-lockdown (archived)

[329] "Roundtable 1: In Vaccines we trust," from the Global Vaccination Summit, 19 Sep 2019

[330] Colton, E., "Here are Fauci's biggest flip-flops and backtracks amid the coronavirus pandemic," *Washington Examiner*, 1 Dec 2020: https://www.washingtonexaminer.com/news/here-are-faucis-biggest-flip-flops-and-backtracks-amid-the-coronavirus-pandemic

[331] Dang, S., "Twitter partners with AP, Reuters to battle misinformation on its site," *Reuters*, 3 Aug 2021: https://www.reuters.com/technology/twitter-partners-with-ap-reuters-battle-misinformation-its-site-2021-08-02/

[332] Redshaw, M., "Conflict of Interest: Reuters 'Fact Checks' COVID-Related Social Media Posts, But Fails to Disclose Ties to Pfizer, World Economic Forum," *The Defender*, 11 Aug 2021: https://childrenshealthdefense.org/defender/reuters-fact-check-covid-social-media-pfizer-world-economic-forum/

[333] Bailey, S., "How To Spot Covid-19 Misinformation," *drsambailey.com*, 19 Oct 2021: https://drsambailey.com/resources/videos/censorship/how-to-spot-covid-19-misinformation/

[334] "CARES Act," *Wikipedia*: https://en.wikipedia.org/wiki/CARES_Act (archived)

[335] Goodrich, K., "How the CARES Act Supports America's Healthcare System in the Fight Against COVID-19," *Jackson Walker*, 30 Mar 2020: https://www.jw.com/news/insights-cares-act-healthcare-provisions-covid19/ (archived)

[336] Ibid.

[337] *'Hypernormalisation' was coined by Russian professor of anthropology Alexei Yurchak: "…everyone in the Soviet Union knew the system was failing, but no one could imagine an alternative to the status quo, and politicians and citizens alike were resigned to maintaining the pretense of a functioning society.": https://en.wikipedia.org/wiki/HyperNormalisation

[338] Vilet, E. & Shultz, A., "Biden's Bounty on Your Life: Hospitals' Incentive Payments for COVID-19," *Association of American Physicians and Surgeons*, 17 Nov 2021: https://aapsonline.org/bidens-bounty-on-your-life-hospitals-incentive-payments-for-covid-19/

[339] *See "The Death of Magician Roy Horn—and the Dubious Approval of Remdesivir by Dr. "Baron of Lies" Anthony Fauci," in *Virus Mania*, 3rd English Edition.

[340] Vilet, E. & Shultz, A., "Biden's Bounty on Your Life: Hospitals' Incentive Payments for COVID-19," *Association of American Physicians and Surgeons*, 17 Nov 2021: https://aapsonline.org/bidens-bounty-on-your-life-hospitals-incentive-payments-for-covid-19/

[341] Azar, A., "Declaration Under the Public Readiness and Emergency Preparedness Act for Medical Countermeasures Against COVID-19," Office of the Secretary, US Department of Health and Human Services, 17 Mar 2020: https://www.govinfo.gov/content/pkg/FR-2020-03-17/pdf/2020-05484.pdf

[342] "Public Readiness and Emergency Preparedness Act," *Wikipedia*: https://en.wikipedia.org/wiki/Public_Readiness_and_Emergency_Preparedness_Act (accessed 4 Jan 2024)

343 Azar, A., "Declaration Under the Public Readiness and Emergency Preparedness Act for Medical Countermeasures Against COVID-19," Office of the Secretary, US Department of Health and Human Services, 17 Mar 2020: https://www.govinfo.gov/content/pkg/FR-2020-03-17/pdf/2020-05484.pdf

344 "Pandemic funding, liability shield clear Congress," *CIDRAP News*, 29 Dec 2005: https://www.cidrap.umn.edu/avian-influenza-bird-flu/pandemic-funding-liability-shield-clear-congress

345 "Public Readiness and Emergency Preparedness Act," *Wikipedia*: https://en.wikipedia.org/wiki/Public_Readiness_and_Emergency_Preparedness_Act (accessed 4 Jan 2024)

346 https://drsambailey.com/wp-content/uploads/2024/02/Receipt-and-Dispatch-Data-OIA-21339-CRM0401037-Pfizer-Comirnaty.pdf

347 "Aneurin Bevan," *Wikiquote*: https://en.wikiquote.org/wiki/Aneurin_Bevan

348 "Guidance statement COVID-19 vaccine and your professional responsibility," Dental & Medical Councils of New Zealand, 28 Apr 2021: https://www.mcnz.org.nz/assets/standards/Guidelines/Guidance-statement-COVID-19-vaccine-and-your-professional-responsibility.pdf (archived)

349 "COVID-19: Vaccines," New Zealand Ministry of Health: https://web.archive.org/web/20210502053233/https://www.health.govt.nz/our-work/diseases-and-conditions/covid-19-novel-coronavirus/covid-19-vaccines

350 Bailey, S., "Will I Be Struck Off?," *drsambailey.com*, 5 Aug 2023: https://drsambailey.com/resources/videos/corruption-and-medicine/will-i-be-struck-off/

351 "MCNZ Served Legal Papers by NZDSOS," *NZDSOS*, 19 Aug 2023: https://nzdsos.com/2023/08/19/mcnz-served-legal-papers-by-nzdsos/

352 "Expectations for COVID-19 vaccination released for doctors and dentists," Medical Council of New Zealand: https://www.mcnz.org.nz/about-us/news-and-updates/expectations-for-covid-19-vaccination-released-for-doctors-and-dentists/ (accessed 22 Nov 2023)

353 "MCNZ Served Legal Papers by NZDSOS," *NZDSOS*, 19 Aug 2023: https://nzdsos.com/2023/08/19/mcnz-served-legal-papers-by-nzdsos/

354 Dawes, M., et al., "Sicily statement on evidence-based practice," *BMC Medical Education*, 5 Jan 2005: https://www.ncbi.nlm.nih.gov/pmc/articles/PMC544887/

355 Engdahl, F., "Toxicology vs Virology - Rockefeller Institute and the Criminal Polio Fraud," *www.williamengdahl.com*, 12 Jul 2022: http://www.williamengdahl.com/englishNEO12July2022.php

356 "What the Perth Group has argued," *The Perth Group*: https://www.theperthgroup.com/whatargued.html

357 Papadopulos-Eleopulos, E., et al., *HIV – A virus like no other*, posted at the Perth Group website 12 Jul 2017: https://www.theperthgroup.com/HIV/TPGVirusLikeNoOther.pdf

358 "Appendix A - AIDS-Defining Conditions," *Morbidity and Mortality Weekly Report*, CDC, 5 Dec 2008: https://www.cdc.gov/mmwr/preview/mmwrhtml/rr5710a2.htm

359 "The Evidence That HIV Causes AIDS," United States NIAID: https://web.archive.org/web/20090117143001/http://www.niaid.nih.gov/factsheets/evidhiv.htm

360 "NIH / ANTIBODIES," *The Perth Group*, Jul 2000: https://www.theperthgroup.com/OTHER/nihantibodiesshort.html

361 "Papers and letters published in scientific journals," *The Perth Group*: https://www.theperthgroup.com/paperspublished.html

362 "Papers and letters rejected by editors of scientific journals," *The Perth Group*: https://www.theperthgroup.com/rejected.html

363 A critical appraisal of the evidence for the existence of HIV," *The Perth Group*: https://www.theperthgroup.com/REJECTED/RACSRPH.doc

364 Turner, V. & McIntyre, A., "The Yin & Yang of HIV - Part 1 of 3," *Nexus Magazine*, Jun-Jul 1999: https://cruinthe.tripod.com/nexus/articles/hivnotaids1.html

365 Rappoport, J., *AIDS Inc.: scandal of the century*, Human Energy Press, 1988: https://www.amazon.com/AIDS-Inc-Jon-Rappoport/dp/0954659015

366 Engelbrecht, T., et al., *Virus Mania*, 3rd English Edition, Books on Demand, 2021: https://drsambailey.com/shop-2/

[367] Williams, U., Bailey, S., *Terrain Therapy*, Dr Samantha Bailey, 2022: https://drsambailey.com/terrain-therapy/

[368] https://worldcouncilforhealth.org/multimedia/global-health-dr-david-bell/

[369] "CDC Recommended Childhood Vaccine Schedule: 1986 vs 2019," *Children's Health Defense*: https://childrenshealthdefense.org/wp-content/uploads/CDC-Recommended-Childhood-Vaccine-Schedule-1986-vs-2019.pdf

[370] Ibid.

[371] Whitney, C., "Benefits from immunization during the vaccines for children program era - United States, 1994-2013," *MMWR*, 25 Apr 2014: https://www.cdc.gov/mmwr/preview/mmwrhtml/mm6316a4.htm

[372] Bailey, S., "Immune System & Vaccines Part 2," *drsambailey.com*, 6 Apr 2021: https://drsambailey.com/resources/videos/vaccines/immune-system-vaccines-part-2/

[373] Greenwood, B., "The contribution of vaccination to global health: past, present and future," *Philos Trans R Soc Lond B Biol Sci.*, 369(1645), 19 Jun 2014

[374] Humphries, S. & Bystrianyk, R., *Dissolving Illusions: Disease, Vaccines, and The Forgotten History*, 2013: https://dissolvingillusions.com/

[375] Engelbrecht, T., et al., *Virus Mania*, 3rd English Edition, Books on Demand, 2021: https://drsambailey.com/shop-2/

[376] Pawankar, R., et al., editors, "White Book on Allergy," World Allergy Organization, 2011: https://www.worldallergy.org/UserFiles/file/WAO-White-Book-on-Allergy_web.pdf

[377] Pawankar, R., et al., editors, "White Book on Allergy: Update 2013," World Allergy Organization, 2013: https://www.worldallergy.org/UserFiles/file/WhiteBook2-2013-v8.pdf

[378] Beggs, P. & Bambrick, H., "Is the Global Rise of Asthma an Early Impact of Anthropogenic Climate Change?," *Environmental Health Perspectives*, 1 Aug 2005: https://doi.org/10.1289/ehp.7724

379 Lyons-Weiler, J. & Thomas, P., "Relative Incidence of Office Visits and Cumulative Rates of Billed Diagnoses Along the Axis of Vaccination," Nov 2020: http://dx.doi.org/10.3390/ijerph17228674

380 "Dr. Paul's Fight for Medical Freedom!": https://www.drpaulsfight.com/ (accessed 1 Nov 2022)

381 "Bill Gates on Finding a Vaccine for COVID-19, the Economy, and Returning to 'Normal Life'," *The Ellen Show*, 13 Apr 2020: https://www.youtube.com/watch?v=5oEcxMfwJnw

382 Corbett, J., "Who Is Bill Gates? - Part One: How Bill Gates Monopolized Global Health," 1 May 2020: https://www.corbettreport.com/gates/

383 "WHO - Voluntary contributions by fund and by contributor, 2017," *World Health Assembly*, 19 Apr 2018: https://apps.who.int/gb/ebwha/pdf_files/WHA71/A71_INF2Corr1-en.pdf

384 "WHO - Voluntary contributions by fund and by contributor, 2021," World Health Assembly, 25 Apr 2022: https://apps.who.int/gb/ebwha/pdf_files/WHA75/A75_INF5-en.pdf

385 Ibid.

386 "Annual Contributions and Proceeds," GAVI, The Vaccine Alliance: https://www.gavi.org/news-resources/document-library/annual-contributions-and-proceeds

387 https://www.gavi.org/our-alliance (accessed 2 Nov 2022)

388 Levich, J., "Disrupting global health," from *Routledge Handbook on the Politics of Global Health*, Routledge, London, 2018: https://doi.org/10.4324/9781315297255

389 "COVAX," *Wikipedia*: https://en.wikipedia.org/wiki/COVAX (accessed 2 Nov 2022)

390 "COVID-19 Market Dashboard," *UNICEF*: https://www.unicef.org/supply/covid-19-market-dashboard (accessed 2 Nov 2022)

391 "Funding Compendium 2021," *UNICEF*: https://www.unicef.org/media/124541/file/Funding%20compendium%202021.pdf

392 "Coalition for Epidemic Preparedness Innovations," *Wikipedia*: https://en.wikipedia.org/wiki/Coalition_for_Epidemic_Preparedness_Innovations (accessed 3 Nov 2022)

393 "International Finance Facility," *Wikipedia*: https://en.wikipedia.org/wiki/International_Finance_Facility#International_Finance_Facility_for_Immunisation (accessed 3 Nov 2022)

394 "Bill & Melinda Gates Foundation and Wellcome pledge $300 million to CEPI to fight COVID-19 and combat threat of future pandemics," CEPI, 19 Jan 2022: https://cepi.net/news_cepi/bill-melinda-gates-foundation-and-wellcome-pledge-300-million-to-cepi-to-fight-covid-19-and-combat-threat-of-future-pandemics/

395 MacLeod, A., "Revealed: Documents show Bill Gates has given $319 million to Media Outlets," *mintpressnews*, 15 Nov 2021: https://www.mintpressnews.com/documents-show-bill-gates-has-given-319-million-to-media-outlets/278943/

396 Ibid.

397 "Committed grants," Bill & Melinda Gates Foundation: https://www.gatesfoundation.org/about/committed-grants

398 Belvedere, M., "Bill Gates: My 'best investment' turned $10 billion into $200 billion worth of economic benefit," CNBC, 23 Jan 2019: https://www.cnbc.com/2019/01/23/bill-gates-turns-10-billion-into-200-billion-worth-of-economic-benefit.html (archived)

399 "Pfizer Gross Profit 2010-2022 | PFE," *macrotrends*: https://www.macrotrends.net/stocks/charts/PFE/pfizer/gross-profit

400 Ibid.

401 "Procuring vaccines for COVID-19," Government of Canada: https://web.archive.org/web/20221024004314/https://www.canada.ca/en/public-services-procurement/services/procuring-vaccines-covid19.html

402 "Manufacturing and supply agreement between Pfizer and Albania Ministry of Health," (Pfizer draft 6 Jan 2021): https://americasfrontlinedoctors.org/2/files/manufacturing-and-supply-agreement-between-pfizer-and-albania-ministry-of-health/

403 "Unite against COVID-19 - Vaccinations and work," New Zealand government, Dec 2021: https://web.archive.org/web/20211220095718/https://covid19.govt.nz/covid-19-vaccines/vaccinations-and-work/

404 "PM Ardern on how NZ will look under the 'traffic light' system," *NZ Herald Youtube*, 23 Oct 2021: https://www.youtube.com/watch?v=ZdMSRolWCyQ

405 "Pharma 2020: The vision, Which path will you take?," *PricewaterhouseCoopers*, 2007: https://www.pwc.com/gx/en/industries/pharmaceuticals-life-sciences/publications/pharma-2020/pharma-2020-vision-path.html

406 Ibid.

407 "The Story of Pfizer Inc. – A Case Study in Pharmaceutical Empire and Corporate Corruption," *Health Freedom Defense Fund*, 19 Jun 2023: https://healthfreedomdefense.org/the-story-of-pfizer-inc-a-case-study-in-pharmaceutical-empire-and-corporate-corruption/

408 Bell, D., "Why policymakers should reject WHO's pandemic proposals," *UK Column*, 21 May 2023: https://www.ukcolumn.org/video/david-bell-why-policymakers-should-reject-whos-pandemic-proposals

409 Martuscelli, C. & Cokelaere, H., "EU countries destroy €4B worth of COVID vaccines," *Politico*, 18 Dec 2023: https://www.politico.eu/article/europe-bonfire-covid-vaccines-coronavirus-waste-europe-analysis/ (archived)

410 Ibid.

411 Bailey, S., "Will I Be Struck Off?," *drsambailey.com,* 5 Aug 2023: https://drsambailey.com/resources/videos/corruption-and-medicine/will-i-be-struck-off/

412 "beyond the legal or constitutional power of a court, etc.": https://www.etymonline.com/word/ultra%20vires

413 Brettkelly, S., "Coronavirus - floods of information in a misinfodemic," The Detail, *Radio NZ*, 27 Feb 2020

414 Corbett, J., "Bill Gates' Decade of Vaccines," *HoweStreet.com*, 9 May 2020: https://www.howestreet.com/2020/05/bill-gates-decade-of-vaccines/

415 "Covid 19 coronavirus: Vaccine safety committee investigating two deaths in NZ," *NZ Herald*, 8 May 2021

416 "Deaths of people who had Covid vaccination 'no cause for concern' – vaccinologist," *1News*, 9 May 2021: https://www.youtube.com/watch?v=pKuSGbGizC4

417 Petousis-Harris, H., "Covid whoppers: 10 of the biggest vaccine myths debunked," *Otago Daily Times*, 24 Sep 2021

418 Manson, B., "High Court mandate decision 'disappointing' - expert," *stuff*, 25 Feb 2022: https://web.archive.org/web/20220225072952/https://www.stuff.co.nz/national/300527056/high-court-mandate-decision-disappointing--expert

419 New Zealand Legislation, "Health and Disability Commissioner (Code of Health and Disability Services Consumers' Rights) Regulations 1996"

420 Petousis-Harris, H. & Chan, A., "Countering Vaccine Misinformation," *NZ Research Review*, 22 Nov 2021: https://www.researchreview.co.nz/nz/Clinical-Area/Internal-Medicine/Cardiology/Educational-Series-Countering-Vaccine-Misinformat.aspx

421 2020/2021 Annual reports, GSK: https://www.gsk.com/media/7377/fy-2021-results-announcement.pdf, Pfizer: https://s21.q4cdn.com/317678438/files/doc_financials/2020/ar/PFE-2020-Form-10K-FINAL.pdf, CSL/Seqirus: https://investors.csl.com/site/PDF/1ae5bb7e-85a8-4b8a-b7c6-88af598de069/CSLAnnualReport

422 https://cdn.who.int/media/docs/default-source/pvg/global-vaccine-safety/former-membersaugust-2020.pdf?sfvrsn=a6e8b7af_9

423 Brighton Collaboration, "Our Team": https://brightoncollaboration.us/team/

424 Sharav, V., "The Vaccine Program: Betrayal of Public Trust & Institutional Corruption—Part 3 of 7," 25 Jan 2018: https://childrenshealthdefense.org/news/vaccine-program-betrayal-public-trust-institutional-corruption-part-3-7/

425 "Deconstructing Helen Petousis-Harris' Litany of Lies on The Platform," NZDSOS, 12 Dec 2023: https://nzdsos.com/2023/12/12/petousis-harris-excess-death-the-platform/

[426] "Global Vaccination Summit," World Health Organisation, 19 Sep 2019: https://web.archive.org/web/20191021042111/https://www.who.int/news-room/events/detail/2019/09/12/default-calendar/global-vaccination-summit

[427] "Roundtable 1: In Vaccines we trust," from the Global Vaccination Summit, 19 Sep 2019

[428] "Roundtable 2 - The magic of science: boosting vaccine research, development and innovation," from the Global Vaccination Summit, 19 Sep 2019

[429] "Roundtable 3: Vaccines Protecting Everyone, Everywhere," from the Global Vaccination Summit, 19 Sep 2019

[430] GAVI Annual Progress Report 2018, Sep 2019: https://www.gavi.org/sites/default/files/publications/progress-reports/Gavi-Progress-Report-2018.pdf

[431] GAVI Annual Progress Reports: https://www.gavi.org/progress-report

[432] "Meeting the Challenge of Vaccine Hesitancy," The Sabin-Aspen Vaccine Science & Policy Group: https://www.sabin.org/app/uploads/2022/04/Sabin-Aspen-report-2020_Meeting-the-Challenge-of-Vaccine-Hesitancy.pdf

[433] Ibid.

[434] "SPARS Pandemic 2025-2028: A Futuristic Scenario for Public Health Risk Communications," Johns Hopkins Center for Health Security, 31 Oct 2017: https://archive.org/details/spars-pandemic-scenario_202104

[435] Martineau, P., "The Storm Is the New Pizzagate — Only Worse," 19 Dec 2017: https://nymag.com/intelligencer/2017/12/qanon-4chan-the-storm-conspiracy-explained.html (archived)

[436] *Quote inspired by W.D. James, *Philosopher's Holler*, 28 Dec 2023: https://wdjames.substack.com/p/sorelian-myth-dangerous-ideas-part

[437] Bailey, M. & Bevan-Smith, J., *The COVID-19 Fraud & War on Humanity*, 11 Nov 2021: https://drsambailey.com/the-covid-19-fraud-war-on-humanity/

[438] Ghebreyesus, T., "WHO Director-General's opening remarks at the media briefing on COVID-19 - 11 March 2020," 11 Mar 2020: https://www.who.int/director-general/speeches/detail/who-director-general-s-opening-remarks-at-the-media-briefing-on-covid-19---11-march-2020 (archived)

[439] Bailey, S., "Tobacco Mosaic 'Virus' - The beginning & end of virology," *drsambailey.com*, 5 Apr 2022: https://drsambailey.com/resources/videos/viruses-unplugged/tobacco-mosaic-virus-the-beginning-and-end-of-virology/

[440] Bailey, S., "What's Next for mRNA Vaccines?," *drsambailey.com*, 14 Jan 2023: https://drsambailey.com/resources/videos/vaccines/whats-next-for-mrna-vaccines/

[441] Bailey, S., "Does Sunscreen Cause Cancer?," *drsambailey.com*, 23 Sep 2023: https://drsambailey.com/resources/videos/natural-health-remedies/does-sunscreen-cause-cancer/

[442] Bailey, S., "A for Antivaxxer," *drsambailey.com*, 25 Nov 2023: https://drsambailey.com/resources/videos/vaccines/a-for-antivaxxer/

[443] Bailey, S., "Safe and Effective, Then and Now," *drsambailey.com*, 4 Aug 2021: https://drsambailey.com/resources/videos/corruption-and-medicine/safe-and-effective-then-and-now/

[444] Williams, U., Bailey, S., *Terrain Therapy*, Dr Samantha Bailey, 2022: https://drsambailey.com/terrain-therapy/

Printed in Great Britain
by Amazon

39336380R00139